Walking Through Revelation:
With a Common Man

By
LaVere Ray Beug

ACW Press
5501 N. 7th Ave. #502
Phoenix, AZ 85013

Publisher's Cataloging-in-Publication
(Provided by Quality Books, Inc.)

Beug, LaVere Ray.
    Walking through Revelation with a common man /
by LaVere Ray Beug. — 1st ed.
    p. cm.
    Includes bibliographical references
    ISBN 1-892525-06-2

    1. Bible. N.T. Revelation—Commentaries.
    I. Title

BS2825.3.B48 1999   228'.07
                                    QBI98-1542

Printed in the United States of America

To obtain more copies please contact:
LaVere Ray Beug
8316 N. Lombard, Suite 319
Portland, OR 97203
See the order form in the back of this book.

Dedication

I thank the Father, the Son, and the Holy Spirit for guiding my thoughts on this book. I thank my wife, Linda, for putting up with me for the seven years that it took to complete this project. The Bible says a wife of noble character is our crown and has far more value than rubies (Prov. 12:4; 31:10).

Linda encouraged me during the process when no one else did. She influenced many of the topics that I included. She blessed me with her help; I could not have finished without her.

I thank each of these people for each reading selected chapters of this book: Daniel A. Fernandez, Pastor Tyhrus H. Miles, Joyce Bailey, and Kathy Janke.

Contents

Vision 6—Revelation 17–19

Vision 7—Revelation 20–22

Introduction

WHY, PAPA?

One day I was reading a Bible story about Jesus on the cross to Christine, my three-year-old granddaughter. As I read, Christine asked, "Why, Papa?"

I explained that Jesus died on the cross because he loves us.

Christine asked, "Why, Papa?"

I said, "Jesus went to the cross so that we could live with him in Heaven."

Christine asked, "Why, Papa?"

I told her, "Jesus wants us to live with him in Heaven because he loves us."

Christine asked again, "Why, Papa?"

As I thought about the words, "Why, Papa?" I began to understand why I am writing *Walking through Revelation: With a Common Man*. I want to help people understand what the Bible and the Revelation of Jesus Christ, says to each of us today. Jesus Christ spoke often to us from the Bible and his Revelation.

The Book of Revelation reveals a picture of God's unending love, grace, and mercy. Revelation gives us hope in the promises of our Creator and provides us with a glimpse of our risen Savior, the God of Authority. The images in Revelation show us a God of power who controls the universe. It also reveals that nothing will stop his plan for the salvation of his children.

UNDERSTANDING REVELATION

Many modern readers find the Revelation of Jesus Christ obscured in mystery. Some Christians do not understand or read much in the last book of the Bible. These children of the Father feel confused because of all the symbolism and the ongoing imagery, which makes numerous passages in Revelation seem difficult to understand. Perhaps the Lord did not intend for us to grasp it in total.

The Book of Revelation has four major interpretations. They come from different viewpoints of how the book fits in the Bible. Our Almighty God uses each interpretation to reach various types of people. Every understanding of the Book of Revelation has a unique purpose in God's plan of salvation.

THE CODE OF REVELATION

Revelation gives us a different look at the Kingdom of God than the rest of the NT. John wrote the Revelation of Jesus Christ to Christians under persecution. He only wanted the Christian Church to understand the meaning, so he used rich symbolism from the Old and the New Testaments as a type of code. Christians understood the symbolism, but non-Christians did not.

Much of the code in Revelation comes from OT prophets such as: Isaiah, Jeremiah, Ezekiel, Daniel, Joel, and Malachi. Revelation follows the themes from the apocalyptic writing of these prophets. Apocalyptic literature uses abundant symbolism from the OT. If we apply the meanings from OT symbolism and Bible stories, these will help us interpret the Book of Revelation.

AUTHORITY OF SCRIPTURE

The Holy Scripture has remained true in all parts and always will. God breathed his thoughts and words of righteousness into the Bible (2 Tim. 3:16). Prophecy of Scripture never originated from man. All prophecy came from God through the power of the Holy Spirit (2 Pet. 1:19–21). The Bible lives today, and the principles in it come from the Creator.

The Word of God will last forever. Jesus Christ says that his Words will never pass away (Matt. 24:35). I believe the Bible has to interpret itself. Passages in the Bible help us to understand other passages. We cannot form a doctrine on a single passage or section of Scripture.

When we encounter a problem, other passages help us understand the difficult sections. The Holy Spirit gives us insight into puzzling parts of the Bible. The Bible shows us the Truth of God's Word. We finally accept the Bible as God's inspired Word by faith. God gives us faith to believe as a gift (Eph. 2:8).

A SPIRITUAL BOOK

Apocalyptic means to uncover, disclose, or reveal thoughts from God. This type of writing uses imagery and pictures to symbolize coming events.

In the Book of Revelation, the symbolic language displays spiritual realities and events. The people of God can apply the spiritual truths of Revelation to individual churches and Christians.

Revelation is a spiritual book that looks at the Church and the world from a spiritual viewpoint rather than from a physical viewpoint. The apocalyptic images give us spiritual principles from God's Word, and the rich imagery points to spiritual life for some and death for others living on the earth.

The pictures and symbols in Revelation point to spiritual happenings in the Gospel Age. Although much of Revelation has more than one meaning, I will focus on the spiritual meaning of the images. Jesus gives his Revelation for the entire Gospel Age, and those spiritual purposes and principals apply to each of us today.

PARTS SEEM DIFFICULT

Some areas of the Revelation of Jesus Christ and this book may seem difficult to comprehend on the first reading. Parts of *Walking through Revelation* often explain themselves from other sections. The Book of Revelation uses rich symbolism to reveal the thoughts of our Savior. Some may find it useful to read this book more than once, or use it as a reference to clear up cloudy sections of Revelation. Reading the Bible references and praying always help us understand the Lord's Revelation.

Revelation depicts conflict and evil standing beside the Church that Jesus loves. The book portrays the limited power and authority of Satan's kingdom. The Revelation of Jesus Christ reveals our present and future hope of glory. The book discloses that, even in times of suffering and tribulation, the children of God win.

Revelation illustrates that God will proclaim his Gospel to the entire world. In the end, the Christians, or "saints of God," triumph over evil with the Lord's help. The Sovereign Unchanging God declares victory in the battle for the spiritual life of his children.

The Almighty God sits on his Throne in Heaven and rules his creation. In this vision, our Savior gives us these messages: he control's the universe, he control's the world, he control's our country, and he control's our city.

SEVEN SEPARATE VISIONS

If we divide the Revelation of Jesus Christ into seven visions, the book seems to make sense. Each of the seven separate visions covers a similar time span between the first and the Second Coming of Christ. Each vision looks at the Christian Church and the Gospel Age from a different perspective.

Most of us have looked at homes either to rent or to buy. Sometimes when we cannot enter a house, we need to look at it from the outside. The view through each window appears different from the views through the other windows. If we walk around the house and look in all the windows, we interpret how the house looks on the inside. Likewise, in the Revelation, each vision gives us a different interpretation of the Gospel.

OUTLINE FOR THE SEVEN VISIONS

Vision one—chapters 1–3.
Christ working in the churches.
Vision two—chapters 4–7.
God's Throne. The slain Lamb. The seals. The sealing of the Church.
Vision three—chapters 8–11.
The trumpets. God protects the Church.
Vision four—chapters 12–14.
Satan attacks the Church. The satanic trinity.
Vision five—chapters 15–16.
The bowls of wrath.
Vision six—chapters 17–19.
The fall of Babylon. The Lamb's wedding supper.
Vision seven—chapters 20–22.
The 1,000 years. Judgment of Satan. The eternal victory of Christ.

PRAYER AND THE TOOLS OF GOD

We will learn how to use the tools of God in a practical way. The Bible shows us different prayers for our use. Prayers help the children of God live a victorious Christian life. In this book, I will show the wisdom and the prayers that the Bible and the Holy Spirit have given me in the last twenty years.

I based all the anecdotes on true events, but I have changed some of the names to protect the innocent and the guilty.

I use references (KJV for the King James Version, and NIV for the New International Version) for the Bible verses quoted. On Bible verses that I refer to, I only show the reference without KJV or NIV.

I quote parts of the verse above, from Revelation, in italics and with an ellipse. Such as … *from the Revelation of Jesus Christ.*

I use Greek words for reference in italic and with parentheses. *Christ* (*Christos*), meaning "the anointed one or the Messiah." Each Greek word has an endnote using the Strong's numbering system for the Greek and Hebrew words. The meaning for each word comes from a Greek or a Hebrew Lexicon.

GOD'S VIEW OF THE CHURCH

Walking through Revelation helps us look at the universal Christian Church from the Creator's spiritual viewpoint. Jesus shows us, through John's vision, how the Father, the Son, and the Holy Spirit see the Church.

The Godhead watches the Church oppressed by dark spiritual forces, and yet the Church walks in victory. They see the members of the Church stained by sin, and yet purified by the blood of Jesus Christ. They watch the present and future Church harassed by world values, and yet blessed and redeemed for God's purpose.

The Church of Jesus Christ will persevere by the power of the Holy Spirit. Our timeless and Sovereign God will fulfill his Word and his promises to his children. The Revelation of Jesus Christ gives God's people hope and blessings throughout the Gospel Age.

The Book of Revelation helps us give praise and worship the Almighty God. It abundantly provides us a picture of the grandeur and majesty of the Lord on his Throne. We see a God who's timeless and never changes. We see a Savior who loves each of us beyond our understanding. We see a God who gives us the gift of life that will last forever.

CHAPTER 1

Son of Man—Almighty God

THE LOVE OF GOD

Who can measure the love of God? His faithful love reaches to the remote ends of the earth. God's love surrounds all people from the lowest valley to the highest mountain. The precious love of God never fails. It always satisfies with kindness, peace, and joy.

I sometimes think about God and wonder, "How big is God?" The Bible says that God knows every detail about us. The Father knows what we need even before we know that we need it (Matt. 6:8).

The next time you drive through your city or neighborhood, pick a street and think of each separate house. In each house lives a person or a family made up of individual people. Every man, woman, and child has desires and dreams in life. These dreams differ for every person in every house. The Creator knows each person's thoughts and desires, and he knows every detail of their life. When we multiply the millions of details in each person's life by the billions of people around the world, we can truly ask, "How big is God?"

> ⁴He determines the number of the stars and calls them each by name. ⁵Great is our Lord and mighty in power; his understanding has no limit. ¹¹the LORD delights in those who fear him, who put their hope in his unfailing love. (Ps. 147:4, 5, 11, NIV)

However, God's not so big that he sits back and watches the world wind down. He reaches out to touch each person on his or her level. Jesus walks with each of us through the deserts and the gardens of our lives. His love for each of his children always extends toward them. Jesus Christ yearns for a unity with each of us. The Lord delights in his children's love, and he understands our cries for his peace.

WHAT IS TRUTH

The Revelation of Jesus Christ contains the truth of God. We should ask, "What is truth?" Only Jesus Christ knows the full Truth of his Revelation. Our Lord reveals his wisdom to each of us as he wills (Isa. 48:17; Matt. 16:17).

As a child of God, I may understand the truth of the Revelation of Jesus Christ in a different way than other children of God. The Creator uses the many distinct understandings of his Revelation to reach various types of people. We serve an Awesome God who uses Truth to touch our minds, bodies, and spirits.

> ¹**The revelation of Jesus Christ, which God gave him to show his servants what must soon take place. He made it known by sending his angel to his servant John, ²who testifies to everything he saw— that is, the word of God and the testimony of Jesus Christ. ³Blessed is the one who reads the words of this prophecy, and blessed are those who hear it and take to heart what is written in it, because the time is near (Rev. 1:1–3, NIV).**

The Lord sent the Revelation of Jesus Christ to us through his disciple John. An angel testified to John about the Word of Christ. The Revelation of Jesus Christ reveals the wisdom and the Love of God to his children. The Revelation also conceals the true meaning to others. The Holy Spirit, the Spirit of Truth, reveals the Word of God to each of us.

In the Revelation of Jesus Christ, we see Jesus as our Redeemer, our Hope of Glory, and our Faithful and True God. We see a God of Love who longs to know each of us in a special way. The Prince of Peace offers us his peace and his grace that's beyond our understanding.

Revelation reveals a Majestic Eternal God who offers more than we understand. No one on earth knows all about our Lord, and yet he desires our intimate friendship. We stand before our Savior, who opens his arms for each of us.

THE BLESSINGS OF GOD

The Almighty says…*Blessed is the one who reads the words of this prophecy.* We ask, "What does the blessing of God mean?" The word *blessed* (*makanios*) means "happiness and well off."[1] God gives us happiness when we read and follow the Revelation of Jesus Christ.

John said the blessings and happiness come...*because the time is near.* All of my life, I have heard that Jesus is coming soon. If we have recognized the imminent return of Jesus Christ, this will give us joy and happiness as we prepare for his return.

HAPPINESS (PS. 112)

Happy is the person who fears God.
Blessed is he who delights in Christ.
Mighty children shall satisfy him.
Wealth and prosperity come to him.
The glory of dawn floods darkness.
His righteousness endures forever.
He has no fear: his heart trusts God.
Nothing shall move him from Truth.

[4]John to the seven churches which are in Asia: Grace be unto you, and peace, from him which is, and which was, and which is to come; [5a]And from Jesus Christ, *who is* the faithful witness, *and* the first begotten of the dead, and the prince of the kings of the earth (Rev. 1:4, 5a, KJV).

The number seven often symbolizes completeness and perfection in the Bible. This indicates that the seven churches represent all Christian Churches. Jesus speaks to the seven churches in Asia, and he also speaks to each Christian throughout the Gospel Age.

...this was a sacred number often used to symbolize the whole or the completeness of something. Thus the interpretation of these seven standing for all of the congregations of Christ throughout the world would appear to be correct.[2]

Our Lord offers grace and peace to the churches. The Greek word for *grace* (*charis*) gives pleasure, favor, and joy.[3] Grace also implies mercy and kindness from God as he draws us to Christ. God's peace gives us quiet rest, harmony, security, and a sense of assured salvation. Our Savior offers us his peace that's different from the world's peace. The peace of Christ keeps our hearts free from fear and turmoil (John 14:27).

THE HOLY TRINITY

John greets the seven churches in Asia from the three persons of the Godhead. The greetings come from...*him which is, and which was, and* *which is to come*; this points to the Father. The...*seven Spirits* before the Throne point to the Holy Spirit. Then the Son names himself the Faithful Witness and the resurrected Christ. Perhaps John the apostle thinks of the words that he wrote in his Gospel.

> [1]In the beginning was the Word, and the Word was with God, and the Word was God. [2]The same was in the beginning with God. [3]All things were made by him; and without him was not any thing made that was made. [14]And the Word was made flesh, and dwelt among us, (and we beheld his glory, the glory as of the only begotten of the Father,) full of grace and truth (John 1:1–3, 14, KJV).

In these verses, John used the phrase "the Word" in exchange for Jesus Christ. The Word of God created all thrones, all powers, all rulers, and all authorities here on earth and in Heaven. Jesus created the earth and everything in it, even the smallest insects and the specks of dust in the atmosphere.

The Word holds the universe together for all time from the beginning to the end. He's the head of his body the church; he's the firstborn from the dead. Jesus Christ, the King of Glory, controls all things on earth. (Col. 1:15–20).

> [1]In the beginning God created the heaven and the earth. [2]And the earth was without form, and void; and darkness *was* upon the face of the deep. And the Spirit of God moved upon the face of the waters (Gen. 1:1, 2, KJV).

Moses writes about the creation when he starts the Bible with, "In the beginning." John starts his Gospel about Jesus Christ with, "In the beginning." In Genesis 1, we see the Almighty God and the Holy Spirit before the creation of the universe. In John 1, we see Jesus before the creation of the universe.

The Bible does not use the word Trinity, but the Bible contains many references to the Triune God (2 Cor. 13:14). God the Father, Jesus Christ, and the Holy Spirit have always been, and they always will be. With the Lord there's no beginning and no end. The Lord is unchanging: the same throughout eternity (Matt. 28:19).

The three persons of the Trinity are distinct and separate: yet, they are one (Eph. 4:4–6). This gives us the mystery of the Godhead—we wonder how this can be? The Christian Church holds the doctrine of the Trinity as one of their oldest beliefs (1 Pet. 1:2). As we look at the traditional teachings of the Christian Church and study the Bible, we should grow in our understanding and accept the Trinity by faith (Luke 3:21, 22).

ONE GOD—TRINITY IN UNITY

The Father, the Son, the Holy Spirit,
three separate Persons, and yet One.
Divine mystery beyond perception.
We look at One—We look at All.
We pray to One—We pray to All.
We love One—We love All.
One love's us—All love us.
Father–Son–Holy Spirit—One God.

[5b]Unto him that loved us, and washed us from our sins in his own blood, [6]And hath made us kings and priests unto God and his Father; to him *be* glory and dominion for ever and ever. Amen. [7]Behold, he cometh with clouds; and every eye shall see him, and they *also* which pierced him: and all kindreds of the earth shall wail because of him. Even so, Amen. [8]I am Alpha and Omega, the beginning and the ending, saith the Lord, which is, and which was, and which is to come, the Almighty (Rev. 1:5b–8, KJV).

The Almighty Creator walked into the tomb with unlimited energy and raised his Son from the grave. Jesus Christ overcame death by the power of the Resurrection. Our Lord walked that first path from death and the grave to eternal life. Now Jesus sits by the Father in Heaven today and invites each of us to join him at the Throne.

Our Savior...*loved us, and washed us from our sins in his own blood.* The word *washed* (*louo*) meant to bathe or wash a person's body, or to cleanse blood from his wounds.[4] Verse 5 gave us a picture of our Redeemer cleansing sin from people who are dead or wounded in spirit. Our Savior then cleansed their dirty wounds with his blood and gave them life forever (Eph. 1:7; 1 John 1:7).

THE GOLDEN THREAD

One sunny October day, I was walking in a city park near our home in Portland. I saw a gold-colored maple leaf slowly turning in the breeze about five feet above the path. I could not see what held the leaf up and circled it to see why it didn't fall. I finally saw a long thin thread that hung from a spider web in the tree above. The strong thread held the leaf above the walkway.

Thinking about the maple leaf floating in the air, I knew that God holds each of his children by an unseen power. God keeps each of us from falling into the fires of hell by a long slender thread. Our Savior holds us from slipping into the bubbling caldron by the power of his Resurrection. The other end of the invisible thread hooks to the cross of Jesus Christ. As long as we look at Jesus, we will never fall to eternal destruction even when the winds of life buffet us.

"**Father I thank** and praise you for your unending love and mercy. Thanks for the forgiveness of my sins and for eternal life. Lord, I look forward to meeting you at your Throne in Heaven and praising you forever and ever. Amen!"

THE FINAL COMING OF CHRIST

Our Redeemer…*cometh with clouds* when he returns in Glory. Everyone on earth will recognize the final return of our Savior. This will give joy to some and sadness to others. These verses give us an image of Jesus returning in the clouds as he left on Ascension Day (Acts 1:9).

For twenty centuries, Christians have waited for the ascended Christ. Our Lord has many wonders waiting for each of us on that day. We here on earth can only anticipate the tailored gift that awaits each of us.

When the final return of Jesus comes, the Christian church shall be jubilant and happy, because the children of God will see the Messiah in his True Glory. The Church shall recognize that all the promises of God remain true and fulfilled. The men, women, and children of God shall look on his face and declare; "It is finished. Amen!"

> **⁹I John, who also am your brother, and companion in tribulation, and in the kingdom and patience of Jesus Christ, was in the isle that is called Patmos, for the word of God, and for the testimony of Jesus Christ. ¹⁰I was in the Spirit on the Lord's day, and heard behind me a great voice, as of a trumpet, (Rev. 1:9, 10, KJV).**

Early Christian traditions named John, the apostle of Jesus, as the author of Revelation. The Emperor of Rome, Domitian, banished John to the rocky island of Patmos about A.D. 95. The Roman government used the small desolate island for criminals, who were forced to work in the mines on the fifty-square-mile island.

PATMOS—DESOLATION AND GLORY

The cave on Patmos was probably dark, damp, smelly, and a lonely place. We assume that John shared his cave with snakes, rats, and bats.

Because John was a prisoner of Rome, I doubt if his guards gave him a warm feather bed to sleep on. John, at over eighty years of age, was alone with his Savior. Jesus Christ used John's time on Patmos to give us his Revelation.

Imagine the Holy Bible without the Revelation of Jesus Christ. The gift of prophetic insight that Jesus gave to each of us through John completes the Holy Scriptures. Revelation has always played an important part in the understanding of God's Word.

Because of John's obedience and his desire to know God, Jesus Christ gave him this gift. Our Lord also gave this gift to each of us. "Thank you precious Lord for your love gift to us."

John suffered on Patmos because of his witness for Jesus Christ. John followed the early Christian custom and worshiped his God on the first day of the week (Acts 20:17). Our Father raised his Son to life on the first day of the week. The Christian Church then began to worship Jesus on the Resurrection day.

John, the disciple of love, was alone with his Lord in that cold dark cave. As John prayed and communed with his God, he felt the Holy Spirit settle around him. John sensed the Mighty Power and Love of his Savior. John the disciple of love began to listen to his first love.

John looked in his spirit toward Jesus; he began to feel and taste a preview of Heaven. He heard…*a great voice, as of a trumpet.*

> [11]Saying, I am Alpha and Omega, the first and the last: and, What thou seest, write in a book, and send *it* unto the seven churches which are in Asia; unto Ephesus, and unto Smyrna, and unto Pergamos, and unto Thyatira, and unto Sardis, and unto Philadelphia, and unto Laodicea. [12]And I turned to see the voice that spake with me. And being turned, I saw seven golden candlesticks (Rev. 1:11, 12, KJV);

JOHN AND HIS LORD

John knew his Savior. His relationship with Jesus stretched over sixty years. John walked with the Lord on earth as a young disciple. After the death and resurrection of Jesus, John continued to walk with the Lord in intimate friendship.

John's mind and spirit sensed, felt, and saw the awesome presence of our God. John's mind raced as the massive voice identified himself and gave him orders.

The Savior of mankind told John to write the vision in a book and send it to the seven churches in Asia. These seven churches formed a loose circle in the area of Asia Minor. Each church was on a road or in a position to hand the Revelation of Jesus Christ on to other churches in each location.

John turned toward the voice of Majesty and saw...*seven golden candlesticks*. Flames danced at the tips of the candlesticks. Suddenly, the cave flashed to life. John stood in the presence of the Lord God Almighty, who lifted his spirit. John soared with the angels.

> [13]**and among the lampstands was someone "like a son of man," dressed in a robe reaching down to his feet and with a golden sash round his chest. [14]His head and hair were white like wool, as white as snow, and his eyes were like blazing fire. [15]His feet were like bronze glowing in a furnace, and his voice was like the sound of rushing waters. [16]In his right hand he held seven stars, and out of his mouth came a sharp double-edged sword. His face was like the sun shining in all its brilliance (Rev. 1:13–16, NIV).**

John recognizes the One walking in the midst of the candlesticks or lampstands. He beholds the Living Christ and begins to write a description of him. Using familiar passages from the Old and the New testaments, he describes the exalted Holy God. John describes Jesus...*like a Son of Man*, a term used frequently in the Gospels (Matt. 24:30). Jesus' head and hair...*white as snow*, and his feet like...*bronze glowing in a furnace* remind us of Daniel's words.

> [9]"As I looked, "thrones were set in place, and the Ancient of Days took his seat. His clothing was as white as snow; the hair of his head was white like wool. His throne was flaming with fire, and its wheels were all ablaze. [10a]A river of fire was flowing, coming out from before him (Dan. 7:9, 10a, NIV).

Our Lord's hair appeared *white* (*leukos*), indicating "brilliance from whiteness."[5] The Bible uses (*leukos*) to picture the holiness and purity of God and the saints or the angels exalted to a heavenly state. The *eyes* (*ophthalmos*) of Jesus, blazing like fire, symbolize his all-knowing ability to separate good from evil.[6] Jesus sees all the secret things in men's and women's lives, which they want to keep hidden.

The Son of Man holds...*a sharp double-edged sword* in his mouth. The Bible calls God's Word a double-edged sword (Heb. 4:12). The Word penetrates into the thoughts and attitudes of our hearts. The Almighty uses the Word to help us draw near him.

The Lord's voice sounded like ocean waves foaming over the rocks. John then saw the face of Jesus...*like the sun shining in all its brilliance.* Our Glorious Lord called himself the Light of the World and the Bright and Morning Star (John 8:12; Rev. 22:16). Isaiah said that a great light has dawned on the people living in the shadow of death (Isa. 9:2).

SON OF MAN

He stood among the seven candlesticks.
A robe with a golden girdle covered him.
Dazzling whiteness beamed from his head.
He clinched a sharp sword between his teeth.
The Daystar's eyes and feet burned with fire.
Wheels on his Throne sizzled with flames.
A river of fire flowed out from Everlasting.
The Light of the World illuminated the sun.

[17]**And when I saw him, I fell at his feet as dead. And he laid his right hand upon me, saying unto me, Fear not; I am the first and the last:** [18]**I *am* he that liveth, and was dead; and, behold, I am alive for evermore, Amen; and have the keys of hell and of death (Rev. 1:17, 18, KJV).**

John turned and looked with awe at the splendid figure of our Eternal Light, then hit the floor with his face in the dirt! Why did John do this? The saints of God have always reacted in similar ways when they saw the Lord. Saints recognize their own sin when they stand face-to-face with the unlimited power and the pure Holiness of God.

It's difficult for people born into original sin to understand this principal. I could explain the Holiness of God using verses from the Bible, and yet we still would not understand. As mortal men and women, I don't believe anyone on earth fully understands the Holiness of God unless he has experienced it.

Jesus, as he has done throughout the ages, reached down and touched John. God told John...*Fear not.* God has always approached his children with love and compassion saying fear not.

I STILL WAIT FOR MY VISION

In the years that I have known the Lord, he has never chosen to reveal himself to me in this manner. I don't know why the Lord has not shown himself to me like this. I certainly would enjoy the experience! Perhaps the Lord thinks it would go to my head. The Lord in his wisdom always knows what's best for his children.

I remember the year of 1975. For several years, I struggled with the idea of accepting God into my life. In the previous months, it seemed that many people encouraged me to "try" God. My wife, Linda, and the Holy Spirit teamed up against my worldly adventures. I was having plenty of fun in life, and I didn't want God to spoil it.

Finally, I decided to try God. One day I said, "God, if your real, I want to accept you into my life." A peace I had never known before settled around me: From that moment on I knew that God was real!

TRUST IN GOD

I took that small step, and the Lord honored it. By God's grace, my life began to change that day. In the years since 1975, the Holy Spirit has worked through the Bible and the Church to change me. I only worked to help myself before I accepted Jesus Christ as my personal Savior. The Lord changed my attitude, my heart, and my desires. Now I only try to do what the Lord wants me to do.

The Lord has continued to teach me many things about himself through the last twenty plus years. I know that he loves each one of us more then we can comprehend. I know that the Father always reaches out through his Son Jesus to draw his children closer to himself. I understand that he takes care of us and wants us to trust him.

Jesus explained to us that he...*was dead,* but now he lives, and he will continue living forever. Jesus Christ named himself as the one who died on the cross for our sins. He then rose from death to live forever. He identified himself as the Almighty God when he said...*I am the first and the last.*

MARY AT THE EMPTY TOMB

On Sunday morning, Mary Magdalene went to the tomb of Jesus, but she found the tomb empty (John 20). She thought, "Jesus is gone!" Despair overwhelmed Mary as she stood weeping at the empty tomb. Mary thought, "It's terrible that the leaders killed my Lord, but now someone has stolen his body."

Mary remembered how Jesus loved her and forgave her for her past sin (Luke 8:2). She remembered his friendship and his compassion toward her when they traveled from town to town. She remembered the people shouting praises to Jesus the King just a few days before when they had entered Jerusalem (Luke 19:38).

Then her world turned upside down. They took her friend; they beat him, they mocked him, they whipped him, and they crucified him. Mary was alone! Mary turned from the tomb and saw Jesus; he said, "Mary."

Suddenly Mary understood: Jesus lives! Mary looked at Jesus: joy filled her from the top of her head to the tip of her toes. She went away from the empty tomb excited and happy.

Just as Mary recognized Jesus at the empty tomb, each of us needs to acknowledge the risen Lord. When we understand that Jesus lives today, joy will fill our hearts, too.

Jesus told Mary that he was returning to his Father and God, and to our Father and God (John 20:17). Jesus promised us that someday we would leave this world, then he would take us by the hand and lead us to our Father and God.

> ¹⁹**Write the things which thou hast seen, and the things which are, and the things which shall be hereafter; ²⁰The mystery of the seven stars which thou sawest in my right hand, and the seven golden candlesticks. The seven stars are the angels of the seven churches: and the seven candlesticks which thou sawest are the seven churches (Rev. 1:19, 20, KJV).**

Our living God tells John to write what he has...*seen, and the things which are, and the things which shall be hereafter*. In this verse, our Lord gives a preview of his Revelation. Jesus tells John to write about what he has seen, what the Lord shows him in this vision, and what the Lord will show him in coming visions.

CANDLESTICKS GIVE LIGHT

Jesus calls the meaning of the seven stars and seven candlesticks a mystery. The Lord has filled Revelation with many symbols that no one completely understands today. The Revelation of Jesus Christ gives us many pictures and images that point to other parts of Scripture. We shall attempt to understand these symbols from the rest of the Bible.

John describes our Lord walking in the midst of the seven candlesticks in verse 12. Jesus calls the seven candlesticks...*the seven churches*. This points to Jesus as he walks and ministers among his people in the seven churches, which represent the Christian churches throughout the world.

Priests used candlesticks to light the Temple of the OT. (Exod 25:31–40; 27:20, 21). This pointed to Jesus giving us his Light in the NT.

Our Savior wants his followers to let their light shine. Jesus said that we should not hide our light, but put it where all can see it (Matt. 5:14–16). Jesus the Morning Star encourages us to lead our lives in a holy and honest way, and let our light for Christ shine.

THE ANGELS OF THE CHURCHES

Our Lord tells us that...*the seven stars are the angels of the seven churches.* In the NT, *angel (anggelos)* always means a spiritual messenger or angel sent from God.[7] The equivalent Hebrew word *(malakh)* also means an angel or a messenger.[8] The Bible sometimes uses the word *(malakh)* to specify priests as messengers in the OT (Mal. 2:7).

The seven angels that Jesus holds in his hand probably have a dual meaning. Some theologians believe the angels represent the priests or leaders of the congregations. They ask the question, "Why would Jesus address letters to spiritual angels and not to Christian leaders?"

In the NT, angels always refer to spiritual beings. The book of Hebrews says that God sends ministering spirits or angels to minister to people who will inherit salvation (Heb. 1:14). The angels that Jesus holds in his right hand point to the spiritual guardians and messengers sent to the seven churches by our God of mercy. The angels help each church in praise and worship, and they protect the Christians. Jesus sends his angels on missions, and he directs their actions.

From the OT understanding, the angels could also symbolize the priests and leaders of the seven churches. Our Lord paints a picture of his support of the angel of each Christian church.

Whether the angels represent spiritual guardians or physical leaders does not matter. The Almighty God tells each of us that he holds us with his right hand of Power. He reveals his care for us, as he always stays in our midst. Our Lord promises us that he will walk with each of us all the days of our lives. Glory to God.

NOTES

1. Blessed, *makarios*, G3107. Supremely blessed, well off, happy.
2. James Burton, Coffman, *Revelation* (Abilene: A.C.U. Press, 1979), p. 19.
3. Grace, *charis*, G5485. The Divine influence on the heart. Favor and joy.
4. Washed, *louo*, G3068. To wash or cleanse a body.
5. White, *leukos*, G3022. Brilliant light, dazzling.
6. Eyes, *ophthalmos*, G3788. Eyes, ability to penetrate.
7. Angel, *anggelos*, G32. A messenger, angel.
8. Angel, *malakh*, H4397. A messenger, prophet, priest.

CHAPTER 2

Letters to the Churches

GOD LOVES EACH CREATION

I enjoy walking through the city parks of Portland. I love to look at the trees and examine their many different types and sizes. I look at varieties from the tall stately Douglas fir to the small decorative shrubs. Every tree gives beauty in its own way; God created each variety for his own pleasure and purpose.

When God creates his children, he creates them all different. Each person on earth has a different look. Some are dark, some are light, and some have shades in between. Some are large, some are small, and all have unique qualities.

Our Father created all people beautiful in his own image. The Holy God of Love created each for a special purpose. We may not understand why the Lord made each person different; however, the Creator loves each of his creations.

SEVEN TYPES OF CHURCHES

Our Faithful God also makes various types of churches. Each church has specific qualities designed to draw distinct kinds of people. In chapters 2 and 3, our Lord speaks to seven different classes of churches. Jesus gives his Revelation to the seven churches, which represent all the Christian Churches around the world.

But these seven were representative churches and they were strategically located for spreading this message to every part of Asia Minor. The number "7" suggests the idea of completeness; hence the message of this book is for all the churches...[1]

The Revelation of Jesus Christ describes seven different churches located in Asia Minor. The spiritual conditions shown for the churches describe the possible spiritual conditions in all Christian Churches throughout the Gospel Age.

Jesus points out the spiritual problems and successes for each of the seven churches, then gives each church a special remedy to correct the problems. The Lord also reveals ways to stop spiritual poisons that filter into many churches. Christians can apply these universal remedies to their own individual churches.

In his letters to the seven churches, our Lord gave commendations and complaints to individual churches. Then our Faithful God gave each church a promise if they followed his advice.

SEVEN CHURCHES DESCRIBED BY JESUS

CHURCH IN EPHESUS

The city of Ephesus was a primary trading center in Asia Minor. It had a large port that served ships from Greece and Italy. The Romans used the Port of Ephesus to distribute goods and provisions throughout Asia and the East. Rome gave the city much prosperity during the first century when over 250,000 people lived there.

The temple of Diana, one of the Seven Wonders of the World, called Ephesus home. Paul, who ministered in Ephesus for over two years, left the city after a large crowd rioted over Diana. Paul proclaimed the Gospel and led many people away from the worship of Diana. This caused loss of business to the craftsmen who made silver shrines for the gods. The workers stirred up the people and for two hours they shouted, "Great is Diana of the Ephesians" (Acts 19:23–34).

Early Christian tradition claimed that the apostle John moved to Ephesus after his time on Patmos. The early church father Polycrates, bishop of Ephesus in A.D. 190, said John lived to an extreme old age and died a natural death. Church tradition stated that John was carried to church meetings and repeated, "Little children, love one another."

	Commendation	Complaint from Jesus	Counsel from Jesus	Covenant or Promise
Ephesus	Persevered and labored; Tested false apostles	Left your first love	Remember, repent, and return	Will eat from tree of life
Smyrna	Suffered in tribulation and poverty	None	Don't be afraid; Be faithful until death	Crown of life; Not hurt by second death
Pergamum	Remained true to Jesus	They tolerate immorality and other gods	Repent or I will come and fight them	Give Manna; A white stone with a new name
Thyatira	Love, service, faith, and patience	Tolerates Jezebel cult and immorality	Hold on to your faith until I come	Will rule over nations; Receive the morning star
Sardis	A few have clean clothes and are worthy	Seem alive, but are dead	Wake up; Remember, obey, and repent	Will walk with Jesus clothed in white; Name put in Book of Life
Philadelphia	A little strength; Kept the Word; Didn't deny God	None	Hold on so no one takes your crown	Make a pillar in Temple; Write God's name on them
Laodicea	None	Neither hot or cold; only lukewarm; Wretched, poor, blind, and naked	Buy gold refined in fire and white garments	Sit at Christ's Throne

> [1]"To the angel of the church in Ephesus write: These are the
> words of him who holds the seven stars in his right hand and walks
> among the seven golden lampstands: [2]I know your deeds, your
> hard work and your perseverance. I know that you cannot toler-
> ate wicked men, that you have tested those who claim to be apos-
> tles but are not, and have found them false. [3]You have persevered
> and have endured hardships for my name, and have not grown
> weary" (Rev. 2:1–3, NIV).

Jesus who…*holds the seven stars in his right hand* identifies himself as the
Christ. The Greek word for *holds* (*krateo*) reveals that he has power to rule,
to hold faithfully, and not let go.[2] This image describes a God who takes
care of his churches and children.

Jesus encouraged the Ephesian people for their deeds, their hard work,
and their perseverance. The Ephesian Christians *worked* (*kopos*) patiently
through troubles and toil.[3] They persevered through trials and suffering
while they remained loyal to their faith in Christ.

Our Lord painted a picture of the people in the Ephesus Church who
struggled daily to serve their Savior. They did their best to fulfill their individual ministries. Prayer, by these faithful Christians, helped in their daily
troubles.

PRAYER HELPS TO OVERCOME

We zigzag through a battlefield in our Christian lives. As children of
God, we struggle to win victory over the enticement of the Devil in the
Lord's world. The power of God helps push the darkness away when we
walk in the Light of Jesus Christ.

As children of the Father, we need to understand how our enemy works
and what stops his harassment. The Word of God reveals several ways to
protect us. The Bible gives us several different levels of prayers for self-protection. In this book, I shall start with the well-known methods and
progress through the different types of prayer given in Scripture.

SPEAK THE LORD'S PRAYER

The disciples asked Jesus to teach them how to pray: He, knowing its
importance, gave them the Lord's Prayer (Luke 11:1–4). The Christian
Church has used the Lord's Prayer in personal and corporate worship since
the Resurrection of Christ. Jesus gave us the Lord's Prayer to use as a vehi-
cle to lead us to the Throne of our Father. The Lord's Prayer gives us peace,
love, forgiveness, and protection.

In the Lord's Prayer, we give praise to our Father and ask him to send his kingdom to us. We ask that his will be done on earth as in Heaven. We ask our Father to take care of us and to forgive us for the sins that we commit, as we should also forgive others for their sins. We then ask our Father to keep us from temptation and to protect us from evil. Part of the body of Christ then ends the prayer by offering God his kingdom, his power, and his glory forever and ever. Amen! (Matt. 6:9–13).

Speaking the Lord's Prayer gives us protection from the evil one. Every petition in it has a special purpose. A few years ago the Devil was giving me problems, so I began to say the Lord's Prayer at least once every day. It always seemed to help!

We don't understand how God works through all the petitions in the Lord's Prayer, but our Father does. Jesus gave it to his disciples and to us. We should faithfully follow the example of Jesus and say it every day.

> **4"Yet I hold this against you: You have forsaken your first love.
> 5Remember the height from which you have fallen! Repent and do
> the things you did at first. If you do not repent, I will come to you
> and remove your lampstand from its place" (Rev. 2:4, 5, NIV).**

Jesus told the Ephesian Christians they had forsaken their first love. The saints struggled to serve their Savior, and yet something seemed wrong with their relationship to God. Jesus Christ complained that they didn't love him to the fullest.

> 29And Jesus answered him, The first of all the commandments
> is, Hear, O Israel; The Lord our God is one Lord: 30And thou
> shalt love the Lord thy God with all thy heart, and with all thy
> soul, and with all thy mind, and with all thy strength: this is
> the first commandment (Mark 12:29, 30, KJV).

Why do Christians serve God? Do they serve him in order to earn a higher place in Heaven? Do they serve God because they see him as a stern judge who waits for mistakes, or do Christians serve God because they love him and desire to please him?

People fear and love God for many reasons. What does Jesus mean when he speaks of first love? As I understand the Bible, Jesus wants us to live our lives for him. The Lord desires that we include him in all of our actions each day. The small details in our lives reflect our love for him.

The Lord knows our hearts. He knows how we think and what we cherish. He knows the desires we put before him. Jesus loves us with a Love that never stops: he only wants us to love him in return.

OUR FIRST LOVE

Many people have remembered their first love or sweetheart. When we think back to our first love, if some of us can remember that far, we can recall how important that relationship was in our lives. Our whole world revolved around the boy or the girl of our dreams. For most of each day and night, our thoughts focused on our first love. We wanted to spend the rest of our lives with our sweetheart and help fulfill their desires.

It's not unusual for people to have similar experiences with the Lord. Sometimes when a person has a spiritual experience with God, their greatest desire revolves around Jesus Christ. They experience the Lord's intense love and fellowship in many ways.

As the years go by, God's children may stop looking at him with total love and devotion. Many followers of Christ began to take their eyes off Jesus and look to the world for partial fulfillment.

Our Faithful God hovers around his children and tries to draw them back to that intimate relationship. Every situation's different. Some righteous saints never leave their first love. Other saints of God travel in and out of a deep love for the Lord (John 10:9). When people walk away from our God of Grace, he still loves them.

JESUS DEMANDED THEIR FIRST LOVE

A generation had passed in Ephesus since Paul led them to Christ. The Ephesian Christians did not have their initial consuming zeal and fervent love. After their original love faded, the Ephesians continued to work as they had from the beginning. Their attitude changed from love to duty. They may have grown negative in their thoughts and actions.

The Hope of Glory told the Ephesians to...*Remember the height from which you have fallen.* He longed for then to repent and return to their first love for him. The Ephesian Christians needed to make a conscious decision to love God.

Our Eternal Light told the Church of Ephesus that he would remove their lampstand if they did not repent. The lampstand burned with a special light that shined on the people around it. The lampstand made the church visible and the Light from the Gospel drew people to the church.

Churches have declined when Jesus takes away his Gospel Light. This happened many times in the history of the Christian Church.

⁶But this thou hast, that thou hatest the deeds of the Nicolaitanes, which I also hate. ⁷He that hath an ear, let him hear what the Spirit saith unto the churches; To him that overcometh will I give

to eat of the tree of life, which is in the midst of the paradise of God (Rev. 2:6, 7, KJV).

The Lord praised the Ephesians because they detested the works of the Nicolaitanes. The Nicolaitanes (*Nikolaites*), or "destruction of people," followed the ways of Balaam.[4] They ate food sacrificed to idols and committed fornication. The Nicolaitane people sounded similar to many people living today.

Finally, Jesus gives the Ephesian people, and those who overcome, their promise. The Savior says that he would permit them to eat from...*the tree of life, which is in the midst of the paradise of God.* The paradise of God indicates a place similar to the Garden of Eden in Genesis 2:8, where life is perfect and no one ever dies.

CHURCH IN SMYRNA

Smyrna, a city rich and prosperous, was located forty miles north of Ephesus. The past city of Smyrna stood under the modern city of Izmir, Turkey. The city had a good harbor and was at the end of a major road in Asia Minor. Smyrna held a strong loyalty to the Romans. The city supported an imperial cult of emperor worship that persecuted Christians.

> **[8]And unto the angel of the church in Smyrna write; These things saith the first and the last, which was dead, and is alive; [9]I know thy works, and tribulation, and poverty, (but thou art rich) and *I know* the blasphemy of them which say they are Jews, and are not, but *are* the synagogue of Satan (Rev. 2:8, 9, KJV).**

Jesus spoke of the Smyrnean Christian's...*works, and tribulation, and poverty.* The *tribulation* (*thlipsis*) meant "an affliction, a trouble, and a pressing by other forces."[5] Because of the persecution by the Romans and the Jews, the Christians in Smyrna lost their material possessions and the ability to support themselves.

> These people were often thrown out of employment as a result of the very fact of their conversion. Besides, they were usually poor in earthly goods to begin with. Becoming a Christian was, from an earthly point of view, a real sacrifice. It meant poverty, hunger, imprisonment, often death by means of the wild beasts or the stake.[6]

The Romans forced the Smyrnean Christians to live in poverty while they slandered and persecuted them. Yet, Jesus spoke of their afflictions, and then said...*but thou art rich.* I find myself intrigued by this statement about their riches. The metaphor for *riches* (*plousios*) meant these saints abounded in Christian purity, honesty, and eternal possessions.[7]

RICHES FROM JESUS CHRIST

Our Father blesses his children through peace, joy, happiness, and a sense of purpose in life. The *riches* (*plousios*) represent all the blessings from God, whether on this earth or the blessings that will come in Heaven. History shows that during times of persecution the Father's love flows over his children. Because of their hope and the Father's love, the Christians endure their torment.

Our Father adopts us into his family when we commit our lives to Christ. He considers us one of his favorite sons or daughters. Because Jesus Christ claims us as his own child, we have an inheritance. God promises us eternal life, and he gives us his unending love as a bonus.

> [10]**Fear none of those things which thou shalt suffer: behold, the devil shall cast *some* of you into prison, that ye may be tried; and ye shall have tribulation ten days: be thou faithful unto death, and I will give thee a crown of life.** [11]**He that hath an ear, let him hear what the Spirit saith unto the churches; He that overcometh shall not be hurt of the second death (Rev. 2:10, 11, KJV).**

GAMES FROM THE DEVIL

The Smyrnean Christians suffered much from the hands of the Devil's followers. Jesus knew and understood their affliction, but he told them not to fear their future suffering. In a sense, he said, "It only hurts for a little while."

The Devil put some of them into prison to *try* (*peirazo*) them. (*Peirazo*) means "to tempt or test one's faith by enticement."[8] Satan lives and loves to tempt Christians. The Devil tempted the Christians of Smyrna by putting them in prison and then offering them freedom. They only had to say, "I don't know Jesus." If the Devil could cause a Christian to reject his faith in public, then he won a round and humiliated that person.

People in the world have never understood why Christians cling to Jesus Christ. Why did Christians go through suffering and physical death? All they had to say was, "Jesus is not Lord." Then the persecution stopped. The speaking of four short words would have stopped all their suffering!

JESUS INCOMPATIBLE TO SATAN

Jesus lives to give life; Satan lives to give death. Jesus comes to heal and comfort us; Satan comes to bring sickness and antagonize us. Jesus reveals himself as the God of truth and love; Satan reveals himself as the god of lies and hate. Jesus gives us joy, peace, and happiness; Satan gives us misery, strife, and sadness.

Satan becomes more real as I draw closer to God. Because God limits Satan's power over people, the Devil must seek God's permission before he can harass a Christian (Luke 22:31, 32). Satan has little power over us because God has put his seal on us (Rev. 7:3). However, the Lord permits him to buffet us. This should cause our faith to increase as we gain the Lord's strength.

> 6In this you greatly rejoice, though now for a little while you may have had to suffer grief in all kinds of trials. 7These have come so that your faith—of greater worth than gold, which perishes even though refined by fire—may be proved genuine and may result in praise, glory and honour when Jesus Christ is revealed (1 Pet. 1:6, 7, NIV).

God gives beautiful promises in the Bible. Jesus tells us to remain...*faithful unto death, and I will give thee a crown of life.* The Lord gives the crown of life to Christians who persevere through temptations and trials (James 1:12).

GOD PROMISES MUCH

The Christians of Smyrna believed God's promises and looked forward to Heaven. When Jesus met them at Heaven's gate, he probably welcomed them and said, "Well done my precious son or daughter" (Matt. 25:23).

Throughout the Gospel Age, enemies of God have persecuted Christians. It's a dreadful injustice when people beat, jail, or kill children of God. Christians who experience these things testify that the Lord ministers to them in special ways. They draw closer to him than at any other time in their lives.

Jesus promises each of us:...*He that overcometh shall not be hurt of the second death.* The *second death* (*thanatos*) indicates a future misery in the darkness of hell.[9] The future eternal separation from God gives anguish that comes from understanding what they missed.

The Lord says...*He that hath an ear, let him hear what the Spirit saith unto the churches.* In his letter to each of the seven churches, Jesus repeats this to them. To have an ear means to understand and know. Jesus implies that we need to *hear* (*akouo*) or to perceive with various senses.[10] He wants us to understand what the Holy Spirit says in his Revelation.

Our Savior says, if we remain faithful and win the victory, we will go to Heaven with him. He also implied that we could loose the victory. We could experience the second death if we said the four words to reject him. Our God of grace will do everything in his power to keep us from the second death.

CHURCH IN PERGAMUM

Many people in Asia Minor considered Pergamum the first city of Asia because of its splendor and majestic buildings. The city, located 20 miles inland from the Aegean Sea, stood at a commanding position on a hill above a large valley. Pergamum had a large library of 200,000 books and scrolls. The people of the city invented the process of making parchment or paper. Many kings and princes used their wealth to add to the city's beauty.

Worship of false gods consumed the people of Pergamum. The city contained a grove filled with statues and altars. They dedicated the first temple in Asia to a Roman Emperor in 29 B.C.

> [12]"**To the angel of the church in Pergamum write: These are the words of him who has the sharp, double-edged sword.** [13]**I know where you live—where Satan has his throne. Yet you remain true to my name. You did not renounce your faith in me, even in the days of Antipas, my faithful witness, who was put to death in your city—where Satan lives" (Rev. 2:12, 13, NIV).**

The Christians at Pergamum lived in the shadow of Satan's persecution. Jesus praised them because they kept their faith in him. Their trials came from the Roman government through lost jobs, lost homes, and lost food supplies. The trials didn't happen because of economic conditions: they happened because they professed the name of Jesus Christ.

CHRISTIANS IRRITATE PEOPLE

Because the Christian religion condemned all idols and cults, this put the Christian people in a difficult position. For several hundred years, the people of Pergamum had worshiped their idols. They were probably happy and content with their type of worship.

Then the Christians came and said that they had the Only True God. All the other gods were false and from the Devil. It's similar to the child who walked up to a live hornet's nest and hit it with a stick. He only did it once.

Christians stirred up the anger of the local people, the Romans, and the Devil. Finally, the Devil's servants killed Antipas, one of the local leaders of the Pergamum Church. Jesus commended them because they remained faithful to his name.

> [14]"**Nevertheless, I have a few things against you: You have people there who hold to the teaching of Balaam, who taught Balak to entice the Israelites to sin by eating food sacrificed to idols and by committing sexual immorality. [15]Likewise you also have those who hold to the teaching of the Nicolaitans. [16]Repent therefore! Otherwise, I will soon come to you and will fight against them with the sword of my mouth"** (Rev. 2:14–16, NIV).

BALAAM SERVED SATAN—USED GOD

Jesus tells the Pergamum Church that some of their members follow Balaam's teaching. The story of Balaam, a Midianite sorcerer, seems strange by today's standards.

Moses led Israel through the wilderness on the way to the Promised Land. God helped the Israelites destroy the Amorite people because they had resisted Israel (Num. 21:21–35). The people of Moab and Midian feared the Israelites, for Israel wiped out most kingdoms that opposed them. Balak, the king of Moab, summoned the sorcerer Balaam to put a curse on the people of Israel (Num. 22).

The people of the area knew the power of witchcraft that Balaam possessed. He also appeared to worship God. Balaam was confused because he thought he could have a relationship with the Holy God and use witchcraft at the same time. After Balak summoned him to curse the Israelites, Balaam asked the Almighty what he should do. God told him not to curse the Israelites and to send them home (Num. 22:12).

The elders of Moab and Midian came back to Balaam later and asked him to curse the Israelites again. Balaam should have sent them away, but because of their money and his foolishness Balaam saddled his donkey and went with them (Num. 22:21–35).

Three times, the angel of the Lord stood in front of Balaam's donkey. The donkey balked each time, and finally it lay down. Because Balaam had beaten her every time, the Lord opened the donkey's mouth. The donkey asked Balaam why he had beaten her. Then the angel of the Lord revealed himself to Balaam. The angel told Balaam that he was on a reckless path that could cause his death.

The angel of the Lord then told Balaam to go with the men, but only to speak God's words. The Lord did this to get his attention, because Balaam was about to tread on God's chosen people.

Three times the elders of Moab and Midian built altars and sacrificed animals to the Lord. Each time Balaam asked God what he should do. Because God had put his blessing on Israel, the Lord told Balaam he could not curse them. Balaam then spoke a blessing on Israel each of the three times (Num. 23 and 24).

ENTICE THE MEN WITH SEX

Balaam didn't use sorcery to curse Israel that day; he went home. God had spoken to Balaam and told him not to hurt his people. Even after that, Balaam told the elders of Moab and Midian to have their women seduce the men of Israel (Num. 31:16).

The women enticed the Israelite men to have sexual relations with them (Num. 25). The women then invited the men to worship their gods. The men followed the women because they burned with lust for them. The Lord then burned with anger toward the men who sacrificed to other gods (Num. 25:3). God then purged the sexual immorality, which caused the death of 24,000 Israelite men.

The Almighty God let Balaam see the angel of the Lord. The Creator had Balaam's donkey talk to him, but he didn't obey God. He just didn't understand the living Word.

Jesus told the people in the Pergamum church to…*Repent therefore!* The Lord wanted his people to live righteous lives. He called for his children to serve and worship him alone.

> ¹⁷**He who has an ear, let him hear what the Spirit says to the churches. To him who overcomes, I will give some of the hidden manna. I will also give him a white stone with a new name written on it, known only to him who receives it (Rev. 2:17, NIV).**

The Bread of Life spoke to each of us and promised us hidden manna. This gave us an illustration of God's care for his people as they wandered in the wilderness for 40 years. God provided bread or manna to them in a supernatural way. Jesus, the true bread from Heaven, has always nourished his people in a supernatural way (John 6:32–35).

Our Rock of Salvation promised the victorious saints a white stone. The *stone (psephos)* was a small round stone used by the ancient courts.[11] The courts of justice used black pebbles to condemn and white pebbles to acquit.

THE WHITE STONE

I lived my life on earth.
I tried to follow my God.

Sometimes I had problems.
Yet, Jesus gave much grace.
One day I got sick and died.
Satan came and condemned.
Jesus dropped a white pebble.
Not guilty—Not guilty—Not guilty.

YOU ARE SPECIAL TO GOD

Our Lord promises...*a new name written on* a white stone. He means fresh or new in kind. God created each of his children in a special way. The Creator builds each person as a one-of-a-kind model. The Almighty Creator does not copy parts from one person to make another person.

When I admire the different trees in the forest or the city parks, I never see any that look bad. Some are young, and some are old. Some are healthy, some are sick, and yet each tree is beautiful. Our Father God admires each of his created people. Our God yearns for each of his beautiful creations to turn to him, so that he can put a new and unique name on their white stone.

Everyone walks alone with his or her God. People who have a close bond with God know it. Many people have salvation with their Lord, and it's...*known only to him who receives it*. One person cannot walk in another person's shoes to receive salvation. As Christians, we should not try to judge someone else's relationship with God. Perhaps, we should refine our own union with the Savior (Matt. 7:1–5).

CHURCH IN THYATIRA

Thyatira, a garrison town for Rome, lay thirty miles NE of Sardis on the road to Pergamum. The Greek colony of Thyatira was an active commercial center filled with trade guilds. To find business success in the city, people needed to belong to a trade guild. The trade unions worshiped false gods, and they practiced immoralities.

The residents of Thyatira used the natural resources of the area to make a living. The art of dyeing purple and scarlet cloth gave the city their principle trade. Lydia, who was from Thyatira and a dealer in purple cloth, was Paul's first convert at Philippi (Acts 16:14). The Bible didn't say who started the church at Thyatira. Many commentators suggest that Lydia went back to her home and began the Christian Church.

[18]**"To the angel of the church in Thyatira write: These are the words of the Son of God, whose eyes are like blazing fire and whose feet are like burnished bronze. [19]I know your deeds, your**

love and faith, your service and perseverance, and that you are
now doing more than you did at first (Rev. 2:18, 19, NIV).

The Lord identifies himself as the Son of God with eyes like blazing
fire. We see a picture of a Righteous God of fire and purity. His eyes know
all things. Jesus looks into the depth of our minds and hearts with his eyes
of understanding.

Jesus gave the Thyatira Church a good approval rating. He said their
works, their love, their faith, their ministry, and their perseverance were
better than when they started. The church would have looked ideal if Jesus
had stopped here. He continued to speak.

> [20]Notwithstanding I have a few things against thee, because thou
> sufferest that woman Jezebel, which calleth herself a prophetess,
> to teach and to seduce my servants to commit fornication, and to
> eat things sacrificed unto idols. [21]And I gave her space to repent of
> her fornication; and she repented not. [22]Behold, I will cast her into
> a bed, and them that commit adultery with her into great tribula-
> tion, except they repent of their deeds. [23]And I will kill her chil-
> dren with death; and all the churches shall know that I am he
> which searcheth the reins and hearts: and I will give unto every
> one of you according to your works (Rev. 2:20–23, KJV).

Jesus warned the Christians at Thyatira not to tolerate the woman
Jezebel who called herself a prophetess. Jezebel, the wife of king Ahab of
Israel, symbolized an evil woman. She supported 450 prophets of Baal and
400 prophets of Asherah (1 Kings 18:19). Jezebel also killed the Lord's
prophets and led the people of Israel into Baal worship (1 Kings
16:31–33).

The Lord named her Jezebel to reveal her as a type of evil person. The
Church of Thyatira permitted her to lead the Christians astray from the
true Gospel of Christ. Jezebel *seduced* (*planao*) them: she deceived them
from the truth.[12] She then led the Christians into worship of idols, and the
pleasures of immoral actions.

WORSHIP THE TRADE-GUILD GOD

The trade guilds of Thyatira worshiped their local gods in their meetings. If the Christians wanted a good job, they needed a trade guild. When
you belonged to a guild, you worshiped their god. After they sacrificed food
to their god at the union meeting, the members ate the food. Then the real
fun began. If a person walked out, the other members ridiculed him.

In this difficult situation what must a Christian do? If he quits the union, he loses his position and his standing in society. He may have to suffer want, hunger, persecution. On the other hand, if he remains in the guild and attends the immoral feasts,...he denies his Lord.[13]

The prophetess Jezebel gave the members a solution. She encouraged them to stay in the guilds. Jezebel probably told them that they could witness to the other union members and participate in their parties. Our Lord had a different viewpoint from Jezebel.

The Lord gave Jezebel time to repent, but she would not. It was easier to go along with the community standards. The Son of God, who searches hearts and knows everything, promised to throw Jezebel on a sickbed of suffering. God also promised tribulation and trouble to those who worshiped idols with her.

The Lord said...*I will kill her children with death*. Children (*teknon*), in the NT meaning, pointed to disciples of a teacher.[14] Jesus used double words for kill and death. The word for kill meant to kill or destroy the body. Death (*thanatos*) meant "the death of the body with implied future misery in hell."[15] This implied the danger of their loss of physical life and their loss of future spiritual life in Heaven.

Jezebel, which calleth herself a prophetess...suggested an example of female leadership in the Christian Church. The Thyatira Church appeared to have accepted her role as teacher and prophet in the church. The church permitted her to teach and to deceive his servants. If Lydia started the church, than her prestige would have helped other women.

God used many women in leadership positions throughout the Old and New testaments. Jesus always treated women with much respect. Our Lord has always loved women, and he desires to see them blossom in the ministry he gives them.

I have attended several Bible studies and prayer meetings over the years. On average, the women seem to understand and seek the ways of God more than men. God at times looks for a man but cannot find one. He then raises up a woman to take the call.

[24]But unto you I say, and unto the rest in Thyatira, as many as have not this doctrine, and which have not known the depths of Satan, as they speak; I will put upon you none other burden. [25]But that which ye have *already* hold fast till I come. [26]And he that overcometh, and keepeth my works unto the end, to him will I

give power over the nations: [27]And he shall rule them with a rod
of iron; as the vessels of a potter shall they be broken to shivers:
even as I received of my Father. [28]And I will give him the morning star. [29]He that hath an ear, let him hear what the Spirit saith
unto the churches (Rev. 2:24–29, KJV)

Jesus continued speaking to his children in Thyatira who didn't follow
the evil Jezebel. The Lord of mercy said that he would not put any other
burden upon his true followers. Our Father knows the hearts of his children. He knew that the Christians of Thyatira were near the end of their
endurance.

Jesus asked his righteous saints to...*hold fast till I come.* They needed to
continue the race of salvation so that they could pick up the prize when
Jesus came (1 Cor. 9:24).

RULE WITH OUR SHEPHERD—JESUS

To victorious Christians, the Lord gives power and authority to rule
over nations with God. To *rule* (*poimaino*) means "to feed or tend a flock or
to nourish as a shepherd does."[16] Christians rule with...*a rod of iron.* The
rod of iron indicates a staff used by shepherds, or a scepter of authority used
by kings. Jesus gives his servants power to feed and nourish his little lambs
much like Psalm 23.

The Almighty gives his Christian Church authority to rule...*as the vessels of a potter shall they be broken to shivers.* This passage gives us an interesting view of the authority we have in the name of Jesus Christ.

The metaphor for *vessels* (*skeuos*) means "a person or body with a soul
living in it."[17] Potter represents vessels made of clay or the earth. *Broken to
shivers* (*suntribo*) means "to bruise, or to put Satan under foot and trample
on him as a conqueror would."[18] It appears that the Lord wants his Church
to use his power to rule over people of the earth who belong to Satan.

The Lord's people should shepherd and nourish other members of his
Church. The Church should also take authority over Satan and his kingdom through prayer. Our Savior offers his same power to us...*even as I
received of my Father.* God lives in us. He wants us to activate his power
residing in us. In this process, the Church should bruise Satan's power over
people in the world and nourish them into God's kingdom. The Lord then
promises the morning star to his victorious saints of Thyatira.

NOTES

1. Ray Summers, *Worthy Is the Lamb* (Nashville: Broadman Press, 1951), p. 107.
2. Holds, *krateo*, G2902. Use strength to retain, keep. Dominion.
3. Hard work, *kopos*, G2873. Toil, pains, trouble, grief.
4. Nicolaitanes, *Nikolaites*, G3531. Conquest over people.
5. Tribulation, *thlipsis*, G2347. Pressure, anguish, persecution.
6. William Hendriksen, *More Than Conquerors* (Grand Rapids: Baker Book House, 1939) Pp 80.
7. Rich, *plousios*, G4105. Metaphor: Much Christian purity, integrity, and eternal riches.
8. Tried, *peirazo*, G3985. Entice, tempt, test.
9. Second death, *thanatos*, G2288. Death, separation from God.
10. Hear, *akouo*, G191. To hear with various senses. Understand.
11. Stone, *psephos*, G5586. Smooth pebble, white for acquittal.
12. Seduce, *planao*, G4105. Deceive, Go astray from truth or virtue.
13. Hendriksen, *More Than Conquerors*, p. 88.
14. Children, *teknon*, G5043. Child, offspring, spiritual pupils or disciples.
15. Death, *thanatos*, G2288. Death of a body. Metaphor—implied future misery in hell.
16. Rule, *poimaino*, G4165. Tend as a shepherd, feed and nourish.
17. Vessels, *skeuos*, G4632. Implement, metaphor—a man or woman with a soul living in their body.
18. Broken to shivers, *suntribo*, G4862. Break or bruise. To put Satan under foot, as a conqueror, and trample on him.

CHAPTER 3

Letters to the Churches

Sunflowers Seek

I worked in North Dakota in 1984. On a warm summer evening, I camped beside a large sunflower field. I noticed the sunflowers were all turned toward the west at the setting sun.

I woke the next morning before sunrise and looked at the sea of yellow flowers. I was surprised to find that every sunflower had turned toward the east. They were ready to face the rising sun.

Even the humble sunflowers knew they should turn and face the rising sun to receive nourishment, light, and energy. The church at Sardis also needed to repent, turn, and face the risen Son. Then the Son would have given them his spiritual food, his light of revelation, and his energy from the Holy Spirit.

An Epitaph for Sardis

The city of Sardis lived in its past glory and richness. The city stood on a hill with cliffs on three sides. Although Sardis had excellent natural defenses, enemies invaded and conquered the city twice in its history. Because of their pride in the past, the people of Sardis didn't use lookouts to check for approaching enemies.

The old city, dating back to 1,200 B.C., was important in ancient times, but later declined in value. A large earthquake devastated Sardis in

A.D 17. The residents never fully rebuilt the decaying city. Several hundred years later, the citizens abandoned Sardis and left it to the birds and the animals.

> [1]"To the angel of the church in Sardis write: These are the words of him who holds the seven spirits of God and the seven stars. I know your deeds; you have a reputation of being alive, but you are dead. [2]Wake up! Strengthen what remains and is about to die, for I have not found your deeds complete in the sight of my God. [3]Remember, therefore, what you have received and heard; obey it, and repent. But if you do not wake up, I will come like a thief, and you will not know at what time I will come to you." (Rev. 3:1–3, NIV).

Jesus identifies himself as the One…*who holds the seven spirits of God and the seven stars.* Revelation 5:6 shows us the slain Lamb who has seven eyes. John calls the seven eyes of the Lamb the seven Spirits of God that go into all the earth. The number seven, pointing to perfection and fullness of the Spirits, indicates the Holy Spirit of God.

At the end of each letter, Jesus asks us to hear what the Spirit says to the churches. Seven letters—seven Spirits; all together, they represent the wisdom the Holy Spirit gives to the Christian Church. The Holy Spirit of God sees all, knows all, and understands our hearts and thoughts.

GOD DISCERNS ALL (PS. 139)

God searches me and knows me.
He watches every move I make.
Before I speak, he hears.
Before I think, he knows.
The Lord protects my going and coming.
Where can I hide from the Almighty God?
The Creator covers the earth and the skies.
His Spirit roams from Heaven to the earth.

ALIVE BUT DEAD

Jesus said…*I know your deeds; you have a reputation of being alive, but you are dead.* The Sardis Church looked successful. They kept busy doing many good works. The decaying city of Sardis seemed similar to the Church of Sardis because both followed past glories and works. Jesus called the church dead. Unless these people repented and turned to Jesus Christ, he saw them as spiritual corpses.

The church in Sardis had not been at war with Rome. There is no indication in the Bible, or out of it, that she was having any trouble with the prominent group of Cybellian worshipers which lived there. No slanderous Jews attacked her. In her peace she seems to have drifted into a coma and on into death.[1]

Jesus said to the Sardis Church…*Wake up! Strengthen what remains and is about to die*. The Lord wanted the people of Sardis to recognize their loss of spiritual understanding of his will. Most people in the church appeared self-satisfied and unaware of the potential danger that faced them. Somehow, God's people had taken their eyes off Jesus, and they then grew out of harmony with God's leading.

Your Deeds Not Perfect

Jesus didn't find their…*deeds complete*. In God's eyes, their works didn't achieve his purpose. Their actions left gaps in the Lord's plan for the community. The Sardis Christians probably did it their way and didn't pray and seek the Lord's will. They worshiped on a regular schedule; and yet, they needed to strengthen their faith in Jesus, seek his will, and cling to him.

Our Savior told the Sardis Church to remember, obey, and repent. The Sardis Christians needed to remember their lost condition and their lack of hope before their salvation. Jesus Christ reached down and gave them eternal life. His love, grace, and mercy saved them from destruction, but now Jesus was calling them to remember and repent.

Our Father deeply loves each of us, but he expects us to return his love. Why does the Creator of the universe desire our love? Why does a self-sufficient Infinite Spirit crave an intimate union with his children? The Bible doesn't give us all the answers. Nevertheless, the Triune God longs to for us to say, "I love you Father: I love you Jesus: I love you Holy Spirit."

Return to God

Our Father looks at our heart attitude. When a redeemed saint takes his eyes and thoughts away from Jesus, then our God calls him back. The Lord wants us to surrender each day of our lives. Jesus yearns for the opportunity to share his life with us (2 Thess. 2:13–16).

God has a special love for each person on earth. He sees each of us as his favorite person on earth. The Lord contains so much love that he can love each person as his favored one. I am the Father's favorite child, and you also are the Father's favorite child. God thinks of each of us as his little darling.

Our Hope of Glory gave the Sardis Church five specific actions to take to come back where he wanted them. He said to wake up, strengthen, remember, obey, and repent. If they did not follow his instructions, would they go to Heaven? Only the Lord knows the answer to this question. Everyone is responsible for his or her relationship with God. Jesus reminds the Sardis Church and us to, "Remember where we came from."

The Lord promises to...*come like a thief*, and we do not know when he will come. This applies to the end of the Age and to each individual life on earth (Luke 12:16–20). God doesn't tell us how many days we will live on earth. He tells us to prepare ourselves for Jesus and then wait.

> **⁴Thou hast a few names even in Sardis which have not defiled their garments; and they shall walk with me in white: for they are worthy. ⁵He that overcometh, the same shall be clothed in white raiment; and I will not blot out his name out of the book of life, but I will confess his name before my Father, and before his angels. ⁶He that hath an ear, let him hear what the Spirit saith unto the churches (Rev. 3:4–6, KJV).**

The Lord told the Sardis Church they had a few members who had a living faith in God. They kept themselves clean: they hadn't...*defiled their garments*. Not defiled (*moluno*) meant "not polluted, stained, or contaminated."[2] This pointed to OT priests who wore undefiled garments for their ministry to God.

> ³ᵇthat they are to make garments for Aaron, for his consecration, so he may serve me as priest. ⁴³Aaron and his sons must wear them whenever they enter the Tent of Meeting or approach the altar to minister in the Holy Place, so that they will not incur guilt and die. This is to be a lasting ordinance for Aaron and his descendants. (Exod. 28:3b, 43, NIV).

The priests wore seven separate garments. The holy garments sanctified them for ministry to God in the Holy Place. The seven garments set them apart and made them holy unto God. The priests could then serve in the Temple.

Because the priests wore the specified holy garments, they did not die when they entered God's presence in the Temple. The Almighty looked at them through the garments he had specified them to wear. The priests and their families considered it exceedingly important to wear the right holy garments in front of the Sovereign God (Lev. 10:1–7).

Jesus Gives Holy Garments

The OT priesthood and laws preview our covenant with God today. When we trust in Jesus for salvation, he covers us with his righteousness. Our Holy Redeemer gives us undefiled garments that make us worthy (Phil 3:9; Eph. 6:10–18). Isaiah says that the Lord clothes us with garments of salvation. He covers us with robes of righteousness (Isa. 61:10).

Our Savior promises that we...*shall be clothed in white raiment; and I will not blot out his name out of the book of life.* Jesus Christ guarantees us that if we win the victory we shall go to Heaven with him forever and ever. Amen! Amen!

"Father, we thank you for your overwhelming grace and compassion that comes to each of us. We thank you Lord because you cover us with your perfection and forgive us. Precious Lord, we look forward to that moment when we see your True Glory."

Love, Trust, and Obey

The Lord only desires three simple actions from Christians. He wants us to love him, trust him, and obey him. As we try to love, trust, and obey him, our Father will work out the details in our lives.

Think of a person stranded on a hidden island in the ocean. He has all the necessities such as food, shelter, and clothing, and yet something is missing. No one else lives on the island. After a few years, most people would have an intense craving for a friend. He or she would love to reach out and touch someone.

Our Lord Jesus desires our friendship: he reaches out to each of us. Jesus wants us to crave his intimate love even more than the lonely person on the island. Our Father wants to love us, and just let us love him in return. Our Prince of Peace wants to take our hand and lead us through the rocky fields and the sandy beaches of life.

Philadelphia

The name Philadelphia meant brotherly love. The area around Philadelphia produced many grapes. People in Philadelphia worshiped the grape god Dionysus. A large earthquake in A.D 17 also devastated the city. Philadelphia was located on the fault line, and this caused many earthquakes for years. Much of the population moved out of the city because of the devastation.

⁷"To the angel of the church in Philadelphia write: These are the words of him who is holy and true, who holds the key of David.

What he opens no one can shut, and what he shuts no one can open. **⁸**I know your deeds. See, I have placed before you an open door that no one can shut. I know that you have little strength, yet you have kept my word and have not denied my name" (Rev. 3:7, 8, NIV).

THE OPEN DOOR

Jesus identified himself as the One...*who is holy and true, who holds the key of David.* This refers to the coming Messiah from Isaiah.

²²And the key of the house of David will I lay upon his shoulder; so he shall open, and none shall shut; and he shall shut, and none shall open (Isa. 22:22, KJV).

Jesus overcame the forces of Satan and opened the door of Heaven for us. When Jesus opens the way to Heaven for us, nothing can shut it except our own actions. Jesus shut the door to protect our spirits from Satan's kingdom of darkness.

The Lord knew their deeds. He encouraged the Christians of Philadelphia because they didn't have much strength. Although, they kept his Word and didn't deny his name. Our God of mercy offered them his free gift certificate to open the door to Heaven. The gift of our Savior allowed them to walk through the open door.

Jesus Christ paid for the gift certificate by his shed blood on the cross. All people need to do is accept his free offer and redeem the prize of eternal salvation.

⁹"I will make those who are of the synagogue of Satan, who claim to be Jews though they are not, but are liars—I will make them come and fall down at your feet and acknowledge that I have loved you. ¹⁰Since you have kept my command to endure patiently, I will also keep you from the hour of trial that is going to come upon the whole world to test those who live on the earth" (Rev. 4:9, 10, NIV).

The Creator tells the Christians in Philadelphia that he loves them. He says that the people of Satan's synagogue would...*fall down at your feet and acknowledge* my intense love for you. The Lord of Power promises us that people who harass and persecute us will fall at our feet in Heaven. The Almighty will turn everything around in the future. The Lord will upset the value system of the world and equalize all things.

Jesus Christ destroyed Satan's power when he rose from the grave. God then exalted his Son to the highest place in the universe (Phil.

2:8–11). Every knee shall bow to Jesus, and all that speak shall confess that Jesus Christ is Lord. Someday when Jesus returns, he will require everyone to recognize him as the King of Kings.

THE HOUR OF TEMPTATION

Our Lord recognized that they had patiently endured. He promised them that they would not undergo...*the hour of trial.* Jesus told them that the trials would happen in the...*world to test those who live on the earth.* We sense that Jesus permits temptations and trials to test Christians who live here on earth. The God of Love protects our spirit, and yet he permits trials to affect our physical and mental lives.

The Almighty loves every person on earth. His unchanging love stands firm throughout the ages. God permits trials to draw people to him and to help them persevere. When we endure temptations, we need to learn self-control and set our hope on the grace given to us through Jesus Christ (James 1:2–5; 1 Pet. 1:13).

The Christians of Philadelphia struggled under persecution from people who called themselves Jews. God didn't consider them Jews because their hearts didn't follow the Jewish heritage of listening to God. If they would have followed the Law, then they would have put God first and not attacked his children (Exod 20).

> [11]"I am coming soon. Hold on to what you have, so that no one will take your crown. [12]Him who overcomes I will make a pillar in the temple of my God. Never again will he leave it. I will write on him the name of my God and the name of the city of my God, the new Jerusalem, which is coming down out of heaven from my God; and I will also write on him my new name. [13]He who has an ear, let him hear what the Spirit says to the churches" (Rev. 3:11–13, NIV).

OUR PLACE IN HEAVEN

The Almighty again promises his Church that if they hang on and win the victory, he will give them a *crown* (*stephanos*).[3] The crown indicates eternal blessings that God gives as a prize to the genuine servants of God.

Our Savior is...*coming soon.* John wrote this some 1900 years ago. Soon or quickly means immediately. A few hours before Jesus was arrested and crucified, he gave words of comfort and promise to his disciples.

> [1]Let not your heart be troubled: ye believe in God, believe also in me. [2]In my Father's house are many mansions: if *it were* not

so, I would have told you. I go to prepare a place for you. ³And if I go and prepare a place for you, I will come again, and receive you unto myself; that where I am, *there* ye may be also (John 14:1–3, KJV).

After our Redeemer rose from death on the cross, he returned to Heaven and prepared a place for all his present and future children. Our Savior came back each time one of his disciples died and escorted them to his home in Heaven. Jesus also came back for each of his followers at Philadelphia as they died.

The Savior of the World comes back today to meet each saint after his or her physical death. Our Faithful and True God then authenticates their gift certificate of redemption. If it is genuine he takes them right through the open door into Heaven. Our All-Wise God who richly supplies then takes them down mansion avenue: he helps each saint pick a special home for eternity.

Jesus encouraged the Christians to hold on because he would make them...*a pillar in the temple of my God*. This had a special meaning to the God's elect at Philadelphia. The city sat on a fault line; earthquakes shook them year after year. None of the buildings remained permanent. Our Eternal Creator promised them a permanent place in his Temple in Heaven. Life in Heaven is not for a short time: life in Heaven lasts forever. That is a long, long, time.

DESTINATION—HEAVEN

Our Lord promises that he would...*write on him the name* of his God, the name of the city, and his new name. When I mail a package, I always write on the package the name of the person, the address of the city, and my name so it doesn't get lost. Our Father doesn't take a chance on any of his children losing their way to Heaven. He identifies them with his name, the name of the city New Jerusalem, and the name of the sender Jesus Christ.

CHURCH IN LAODICEA

Laodicea had an abundance of wealth by the standards of that time. The city prospered from banking, a medical school, and black wool clothing. Laodicea had many banks that controlled much wealth. The medical industry produced drugs, including a well-known eye salve that helped eye infections. The area raised black sheep famous for their black glossy wool. The city made high quality carpets and black clothes. The black wool clothing symbolized world prosperity.

¹⁴And unto the angel of the church of the Laodiceans write; These things saith the Amen, the faithful and true witness, the beginning of the creation of God; ¹⁵I know thy works, that thou art neither cold nor hot: I would thou wert cold or hot. ¹⁶So then because thou art lukewarm, and neither cold nor hot, I will spue thee out of my mouth (Rev. 3:14–16, KJV).

TRUE AND FAITHFUL—AMEN

Jesus Christ calls himself the True and Faithful Witness and the Amen. The word *Amen* (*amane*) means "verily or truly" at the beginning of a speech or prayer.[4] At the end of the prayer, it means "so it is, or may it be fulfilled." The word *Amen* comes to the Christian Church from the Jewish synagogues.

Scholars moved the unique word from Hebrew into Greek, into Latin, into English, and into other languages. The word *Amen* sounded the same in every language. *Amen*, as a universal word, meant faithful or absolute trust. When Jesus called himself "the Amen," people around the world understood who he was and is.

NOT COLD—NOT HOT

Jesus told the Christians at Laodicea that they were...*neither cold nor hot.* He saw their spiritual temperature as lukewarm. It appeared that the church was self-satisfied, complacent and had lost their zeal and excitement for their Savior. Evidently, Jesus considered them Christian in name only.

The Faithful Witness knew their works and their hearts. He knew what they considered important in life, and he knew it was not himself. The Lord warned the church that he was going to...*spue thee out of my mouth.* Many commentators applied the meaning of this to the poor drinking water of Laodicea. The water tasted bad when lukewarm. If people weren't used to the water, they sometimes spewed it out.

Jesus referred to their poor water when he said that their actions left a bad taste in his mouth. If one of us bites into some rotten food, we want to get rid of it. Jesus felt similar; he wanted to eject their actions and change them into his image.

THE ICEHOUSE

When I was a small boy, we had an icehouse. This happened before electricity came to the farm, and before my parents purchased a new gas refrigerator.

On those cold winter days, families would get together for an ice cutting party. We would go to a local reservoir and harvest blocks of ice. We then hauled the ice back to the icehouse and covered the ice with sawdust.

I was only about three or four years old, but I remember going to the icehouse and stirring around in the sawdust until I found a block of ice. After I uncovered it, my dad would then carry the block of ice to the icebox. The ice kept our food cold and gave us pleasure when we used it in our drinks. On those hot summer days, we often made homemade ice cream, which doubled our pleasure.

Jesus looks at the Laodicean Christians and says that he wants them either hot or cold. Our Sun of Righteousness reaches down into the sawdust pile of the world. He stirs the sawdust until he finds a person frozen in their attitude toward God. The Holy Spirit then begins to blow his heat of love, understanding, and mercy on the frozen child of the world.

The Lord feels double pleasure when the cold child begins to warm up to him. Jesus Christ loves to melt our cold, cold hearts in his icebox of Love.

> [17]Because thou sayest, I am rich, and increased with goods, and have need of nothing; and knowest not that thou art wretched, and miserable, and poor, and blind, and naked: [18]I counsel thee to buy of me gold tried in the fire, that thou mayest be rich; and white raiment, that thou mayest be clothed, and *that* the shame of thy nakedness do not appear; and anoint thine eyes with eyesalve, that thou mayest see. [19]As many as I love, I rebuke and chasten: be zealous therefore, and repent (Rev. 3:17–19, KJV).

Paul mentioned the Laodiceans in his letter to the Colossians written thirty years before John's vision (Col. 2:1–8). Paul encouraged the Christians of Laodicea to unite their hearts in love. He wanted them to have riches from understanding the mystery of God. He told them that all treasures of wisdom and knowledge came from Jesus Christ. Paul pointed the way to true riches through Christ.

> How strange that God's people in such a place were destitute of spiritual graces. There was plenty of money, but they were poor; there was plenty of the finest clothing on earth, but they were naked; there was healing for many in the medical school, but they were blind.[5]

The Laodicean Christians thought of themselves as rich in material goods, but they didn't have riches in spiritual understanding. Jesus said they were...*wretched, and miserable, and poor, and blind, and naked.* The Laodiceans had riches of the world, but they lacked spiritual riches and blessings of salvation.

BUY GOLD, WHITE CLOTHES, AND EYE SALVE

Our Savior recommended that they buy from him...*gold tried in the fire.* Malachi wrote about the coming Lord who would come like a refiner's fire. Malachi said the Lord would refine and purify men like gold until they brought offerings in righteousness (Mal. 3:1–3). Our Holy Savior wanted the Laodiceans to buy refined gold from him so he could give them goodness and purity.

Jesus advises the Laodiceans to buy...*white raiment, that thou mayest be clothed.* If they didn't accept white garments of righteousness from Jesus, then they would show up at Heaven's gate clothed in the nakedness of sin.

In verse 4, Jesus promised a few of the Sardis Christians that they would wear white raiment because of their undefiled garments. The OT priests used linen breeches to cover their nakedness when they served God (Exod. 28:42). Like the Sardis Church, this church needed to put on clothes of holiness from Christ. The covering, from the blood of Jesus, would have removed the shame of sin and nakedness (Col. 1:14; Heb. 9:14).

The Lord said...*anoint thine eyes with eye salve, that thou mayest see.* Their medical school was famous for its eye salve remedy. Jesus said to anoint the eyes of the mind or understanding. The Lord wanted them to see, perceive by their senses, the danger they had drifted into.

HE CHASTENS US WITH LOVE

The Author of Eternal Salvation says...*As many as I love, I rebuke and chasten: be zealous therefore, and repent.* Jesus Christ loves all of his children even when they disobey him. When a Christian walks on a different path then the Lord wants him to, he opens himself to a rebuke. The word *rebuke* (*elegcho*) means "to reprove or to convict someone of sin."[6] The word *chasten* (*paideuo*) means "to train a child sometimes with discipline."[7]

The Lord exposes our wrongs and trains us to walk on right paths because he loves us. He can only do this if we remain open to him and repent. If we stiffen ourselves against change, he may rebuke and chasten us in increasing amounts. To repent means to change one's mind and turn toward God. Jesus speaks to the Laodicean Church and asks them to listen and change their minds and hearts.

The Christians in the Laodicean Church stood on a bridge that went to the Promised Land. They could hear calls from both ends. The world said, "Come back and enjoy yourself." Jesus stood at the other end near the doorway to Heaven. They needed to make up their mind; pleasure for a few years in this world, or eternal joy in Heaven.

> [20]Behold, I stand at the door, and knock: if any man hear my voice, and open the door, I will come in to him, and will sup with him, and he with me. [21]To him that overcometh will I grant to sit with me in my throne, even as I also overcame, and am set down with my Father in his throne. [22]He that hath an ear, let him hear what the Spirit saith unto the churches (Rev. 3:20–22, KJV).

The Church of Laodicea was so corrupt that Jesus did not commend them, as he did the other six churches. However, Laodicea also had a few people who listened to the Spirit.

Jesus says…*Behold, I stand at the door, and knock.* Our Savior stands on the outside of many people in the world. Jesus stands, waits, and listens for life stirring inside. He wonders whether the person will open and welcome him. Jesus stands outside and waits because he knows that some will drive him away. The Lord is happy when a person responds to his knock.

This image of Jesus, standing at the door of our hearts, gives comfort to many people in the world. The Lord calls to us each day of our lives. He speaks with compassion and waits for us to open our door wide to him.

If we hear his voice and open the door, he comes into us and gives us living water, living bread, and the living wine of the Holy Spirit. We return our love, our life, and our hearts to him as we take his nourishment. Then Jesus gives us more of himself and we return more of ourselves.

Do You Hear Him Knocking

I was busy walking.
Then I heard knocking,
But I kept on walking.
Then my heart weakened.
I invited him into my house.
He brought me bread and wine.
Then he invited me to his House.
I'm so glad I heard him knocking.

God's Really Busy

I was talking to several men at a lunch break a few years ago. Bill, a young man, about twenty-two, told us that he had gone to see a psychiatrist because he felt tormented. He explained that sometimes he didn't connect with himself or to other people. The psychiatrist old Bill to change jobs and get a girl friend. Bill didn't want to change jobs, but he thought a girlfriend would be okay. Bill said, "I've tried everything. I went to confession; I even asked my mother what to do."

After listening awhile, I asked Bill if he had tried Jesus Christ. Bill looked at me and said, "I would like to, but God's really busy!"

Jesus uses many methods to attract our attention to him. Sometimes he even rebukes and disciplines us. We can be certain that the Omnipresent and Unlimited God is never to busy. He always hears the cries of our hearts. He always answers when he hears: all we need to do is think of him and call. "Thank you, Lord, for your patience in drawing us."

Notes

1. Jim McGuiggan, *The Book of Revelation* (Lubbock, Montex PC, 1976) p. 62.
2. Defiled, *moluno*, G3435. To soil, defile, contaminate.
3. Crown, *stephanos*, G4735. Wreath, metaphor–eternal blessing given to servants of God.
4. Amen, *amane*, G281. Worthy, surely, so be it.
5. Coffman, *Revelation*, pp. 87, 88.
6. Rebuke, *elegcho*, G1651. Admonish, convict, reprove.
7. Chasten, *paideuo*, G3811. Train up a child, discipline, teach.

CHAPTER 4

Throne in Heaven

THE COLORS OF ALMIGHTY GOD

Many people see the Lord like a window of stained glass against the night sky. They can't see the beautiful image of God without the Light of Revelation. The bright colors and likeness of God remain trapped in the glass. When morning comes, children of Light look at the stained glass against the risen Son. The beautiful colors and images explode from the glass. In this vision, we see wonderful pictures of our Father and our risen Savior.

JOHN SEES THE THRONE

John's in a cave on the island of Patmos worshiping the Lord. As he prays and gives glory to his God, something begins to happen. John watches a door swing open that leads to the Throne of God and he hears a voice vibrating like a trumpet. The voice says, "Come up to my place."

The Almighty God picks John up and puts him right in front of his Throne of Authority. John looks around and sees an intimate view of Wisdom, Revelation, and Power. He beholds the Everlasting God. Do you suppose that John was excited?

John observes twenty-four elders encircling the Throne. John sees four strange creatures that surround the Throne. Finally, he notices a Lamb that appears slain. This is the Lamb who won victory over death. This is Jesus

Christ: crucified to death, buried in a tomb, risen to life, and ascended to the Father in heaven. Only Jesus Christ is worthy to take the scroll and open the seven seals.

PREVIEW OF THE VISIONS

Jesus Christ begins a new vision in chapter 4. The first vision introduces us to Jesus and the seven churches. The second vision reveals God the Father, God the Son, and God the Holy Spirit as different members of the Godhead. Each person of the Trinity plays a different role in the creation of the earth and the redemption of man.

The seven seals show us the past and future history of world events. Each seal pictures a different view of the Gospel Age. The first six seals illustrate Jesus Christ proclaiming the Gospel and Satan's attack on the Christian Church. God then seals his people against the spiritual ravages of Satan's kingdom. The Christian saints have a difficult and bitter struggle; but in the end, our merciful Father assures them victory.

The seventh seal unfolds into the seven trumpets. At the seventh trumpet, the Temple of God opens and we see the ark of his covenant. Later we see the seven bowls of wrath. On our walk through the Apocalypse, we see three more woes added to the trumpets.

God does not give us all the keys to understand the Revelation of Jesus Christ. Mystery still surrounds many of the symbols and the pictures. The Lord leads people in different directions when they study the book. I may understand the Book of Revelation one way, while other people may interpret it in a different way.

Jesus gives the second vision to John in chapters 4, 5, 6, and 7. We will treat the four chapters as one continuous vision. This vision sets the stage for the last five visions in the Revelation of Jesus Christ.

> **[1]After this I looked, and there before me was a door standing open in heaven. And the voice I had first heard speaking to me like a trumpet said, "Come up here, and I will show you what must take place after this" (Rev. 4:1, NIV).**

A GIFT TO US

John is in the Spirit when he looks at…*a door standing open in heaven. Look* (*eido*) means "to perceive with the eyes or any of the senses."[1] John saw these visions with his eyes; John also perceived and understood them with all of his other senses. In order for John to see these visions with such clarity, God must have fine-tuned each of his senses.

Our Lord gave John a special gift and told him to share the gift. The gift of Christ gave the Christian Church a different spiritual viewpoint of the Gospel Age than we find in the other NT books.

The Prince of Peace told John to...*Come up here.* John entered the inner sanctum of our God of Peace. The Lord removed John from the earth and placed him next to the center of compassion, love, and mercy. A tremendous peace must have flooded John's mind and spirit.

JESUS INVITES JOHN INTO HEAVEN

A voice spoke to John...*like a trumpet.* God and Israel used trumpets in the OT to announce important events. Israel used them when they marched around Jericho, and the walls fell down (Josh. 6). The Almighty God used trumpets when he summoned Moses up on Mount Sinai to receive the Ten Commandments (Exod. 19:16–19). When John heard the trumpet sound, this indicated that God was going to reveal something big.

Jesus Christ invited John to look at spiritual events from God's perspective. Our Savior wanted to show John...*what must take place* throughout the Gospel Age. John gave us a glimpse of God's view of the redemption of fallen man on earth.

> ²**And immediately I was in the spirit: and, behold, a throne was set in heaven, and** *one* **sat on the throne.** ³**And he that sat was to look upon like a jasper and a sardine stone: and** *there was* **a rainbow round about the throne, in sight like unto an emerald (Rev. 4:2, 3, KJV).**

JEHOVAH ON HIS THRONE

John looked; then suddenly...*behold, a throne was set in heaven.* John saw the Almighty God, sitting on his Throne, in the spiritual center of the universe. Paul saw this God, Ezekiel saw this God, Isaiah saw this God, and Moses saw this same God. All through history, the unchanging God has revealed himself to his prophets.

> ²⁶Above the expanse over their heads was what looked like a throne of sapphire, and high above on the throne was a figure like that of a man. ²⁷I saw that from what appeared to be his waist up he looked like glowing metal, as if full of fire, and that from there down he looked like fire; and brilliant light surrounded him. ²⁸Like the appearance of a rainbow in the clouds on a rainy day, so was the radiance around him. This was the appearance of the likeness of the glory of the LORD. When I

saw it, I fell face down, and I heard the voice of one speaking (Ezek. 1:26–28, NIV).

The prophet Ezekiel saw a vision similar to the one that John saw. The Almighty God brought Ezekiel near his Throne. Ezekiel fell on his face because of the awesome holiness of the Lord. Ezekiel felt, saw, and experienced the power and the Majesty of God. The Lord touched Ezekiel's spirit, mind, and emotions. Ezekiel experienced the timeless and changeless I Am.

THE TEMPLE OF GOD

John...*was in the spirit* when God took him to Heaven. We do not know whether the Holy Spirit took John's physical body or only took his spirit; still, John traveled there! John enjoyed the same Holy of Holies that Moses did when he went into the thick cloud of God on the top of Mount Sinai (Exod. 19 and 24).

> [17]And the sight of the glory of the LORD was like devouring fire on the top of the mount in the eyes of the children of Israel. [18]And Moses went into the midst of the cloud, and gat him up into the mount: and Moses was in the mount forty days and forty nights (Exod. 24:17, 18, KJV).

God then told Moses to build a Sanctuary so that he could dwell among them (Exod. 25:8–9). Moses used skilled craftsmen to construct a model of the Sanctuary in Heaven. When we study the OT Sanctuary, this helps us understand God's Throne.

THE OT TABERNACLE

Moses built the Sanctuary inside a tent that contained two compartments (Exod. 25:10–21). A thick woven veil separated the Holy of Holies and the Holy Place in the tent. The Ark of the Testimony stood in the Holy of Holies. The Ark contained the two stone tablets of the Ten Commandments.

The mercy seat, made out of a pure gold, rested on top the Ark of the Testimony. A Pair of cherubim stretched their wings over the top of the mercy seat. The Almighty God hovered above the mercy seat in the Holy of Holies. Moses met and spoke with the Creator in the Holy of Holies (Exod. 25:22).

Moses built a beautiful Sanctuary from the finest materials. They made the Sanctuary as perfect as skilled craftsmen could produce, and yet it was only a copy of the genuine Temple of God.

Our Father used the OT Tabernacle to begin drawing his people back to him. He forgave their sins through the sacrifice of animals, which pointed toward the coming Messiah.

WHO ARE YOU, LORD?

I wonder if John asked the question, "Who are you, Lord?" I have asked this question, just as others have asked, "Who are you, Lord?"

The Almighty reveals much about himself in the Holy Scriptures. However, because the Lord lives in a different dimension or spiritual place, we only understand part of what he reveals.

We glimpse the Lord's fingerprints in his creation. He displays his perfection in the stars and the earth. All the systems work together in unison to fulfill his plans. When we look at a delicate fern leaf, we recognize the precision of his creation.

The Almighty God finished his creation in six days. He then stopped and admired his masterpiece: he recognized its perfection (Gen. 1:31).

I can only answer the question, "Who are you, Lord?" with another question. "Who am I without him?"

He's everything to me. He's my Savior, my Creator, my friend, and my first love. Without the Lord, there's no hope, no love, no peace, and no future. The Lord says, "I am, because I am." We as God's children can only say, "We are, because he is."

WHO IS LIKE GOD (ISA. 40)

God sits enthroned above the earth.
He stretches the heavens as a canopy.
He measures the seas with his hands.
He weighs the mountains on his scale.
Who can give wisdom to All-Wisdom?
No one helped him design the universe.
No one gave God Truth and Revelation.
Who can understand the mind of God?

4And round about the throne *were* **four and twenty seats: and upon the seats I saw four and twenty elders sitting, clothed in white raiment; and they had on their heads crowns of gold. 5And out of the throne proceeded lightnings and thunderings and voices: and** *there were* **seven lamps of fire burning before the throne, which are the seven Spirits of God. 6aAnd before the throne** *there was* **a sea of glass like unto crystal (Rev. 4:4–6a, KJV):**

In Revelation 21, an angel shows us the New Jerusalem or the bride of the Lamb. The city comes down from God out of Heaven. We see the names of the twelve tribes of Israel written on the twelve gates of the Holy City. On the twelve foundations of the wall, we see the names of the twelve apostles to Jesus Christ.

> Around the central Throne John sees twenty-four thrones, and upon these thrones twenty-four elders, probably representing the entire church of the old and the new dispensation. Think of the twelve patriarchs and the twelve apostles.[2]

Number Twelve in the Bible

The Revelation of Jesus Christ uses numbers to give meaning and understanding. God uses the numbers three, four, and twelve throughout the Bible. They have a special meaning in Revelation. The multiplication of three times four gives you twelve. The number three symbolizes the Trinity. The number four pictures the four directions of a compass.

Many Christians believe that twelve symbolizes the universal church of God. In the OT, the twelve tribes develop into the nation of Israel. The twelve apostles begin the NT Christian Church. The twelve tribes plus the twelve apostles portrays the complete Church from the beginning of time to the end of time.

Twenty-four Elders

The twenty-four elders sat on thrones around God's Throne. They sat in the Sovereign Lord's presence. Jesus pointed to this scene at the last Passover meal with his disciples. He said they would sit with him on twelve thrones (Luke 22:29, 30).

Each of the twenty-four elders had a golden *crown* (*stephanos*) on his head.[3] The golden crowns indicated exalted rank or eternal blessings given as a reward to servants of Christ. The elders wore brilliant *white* (*leukos*) clothes that dazzled with whiteness.[4]

Whom the elders represent does not seem important when we see where they sit. They sit with our Lord. Each redeemed child of the Father also desires a chance to sit with the twenty-four elders.

Around the Throne

Seven lamps burn in front of the Lord's Throne. Jesus identifies the lamps as the Seven Spirits of God. The Seven Spirits represent the Holy Spirit who helps us understand the Scriptures and gives us light and revelation.

In the Tabernacle, they kept the seven lamps burning in the holy place before the holy of holies. These were the light-givers. Because of these everything was visible. The seven lamps here represent the Holy Spirit. He is the Revealer. He makes the things clear.[5]

"**Thank you, Father** for giving us a glimpse of your Throne in John's vision. We thank you, Lord, for the wisdom and insight from the Holy Spirit. Thank you, Lord, for your Word and the assurance of our eternal destiny. We look for that time when we can gather around your Throne and praise you day and night forever and ever. Amen!"

> [6b]In the center, around the throne, were four living creatures, and they were covered with eyes, in front and in back. [7]The first living creature was like a lion, the second was like an ox, the third had a face like a man, the fourth was like a flying eagle. [8]Each of the four living creatures had six wings and was covered with eyes all around, even under his wings. Day and night they never stop saying: "Holy, holy, holy is the Lord God Almighty, who was, and is, and is to come" (Rev. 4:6b–8, NIV).

DID GOD LAUGH THAT DAY?

Does God have any humor? If you don't believe that our Lord has a sense of humor, just look at the description of the four living creatures. They look strange! Each one looks different: one like a lion, one like a calf, one like a man's face, and one like a flying eagle. Perhaps the Creator couldn't decide what to do that day.

He made them all different. Then the Maker covered them with eyes to help them see. He then gave them each six wings and covered the wings on both sides with many eyes to improve their vision. "Now, honestly," if someone made a statue similar to the four beasts, you know that some might believe the artist was a little strange.

Yes, our loving Father has joy in his creation. He paints a beautiful landscape on earth, and then he fills it with thousands of different plants and animals. Some of the plants and animals appear different; we may wonder why? Everything the Lord creates has a unique purpose.

The God of Love created us in his image. I'm sure he laughs with us in many situations. Some Christians understand God only as serious and judgmental, but my Lord is loving, generous, peaceful, and full of joy.

THE FOUR BEASTS—CHERUBIM

God created the living creatures, cherubim in the OT, as his highest order of created angels. When saints saw visions of the Throne, they always saw the cherubim. God has used cherubim to minister to mankind throughout the history of the Bible.

The Creator stationed a cherub at the gate to Garden of Eden. The cherub kept Adam and Eve away from the tree of life after their fall (Gen. 3:24). Skilled craftsmen wove pictures of Cherubim into the veil covering the entrance to the Holy of Holies (Exod. 26:31). Two cherubim spread their wings over the Ark of the Covenant in the Holy of Holies (Exod. 25:10).

The living beings always served God around his Throne. When the King of Glory called Isaiah, he saw the same living beings or seraphim that John saw.

> [1]In the year that king Uzziah died I saw also the Lord sitting upon a throne, high and lifted up, and his train filled the temple. [2]Above it stood the seraphims: each one had six wings; with twain he covered his face, and with twain he covered his feet, and with twain he did fly. [3]And one cried unto another, and said, Holy, holy, holy, is the Lord of hosts: the whole earth is full of his glory (Isa. 6:1–3, KJV).

John gives us a picture of cherubim who have eyes...*in front and in back* and all around. The highest angels can see all that happens on the earth and in Heaven. In the Bible, cherubim spend most of their time ministering to the Supreme God. Day and night they cry,..."*Holy, holy, holy is the Lord God Almighty, who was, and is, and is to come.*" This gives us a glimpse of the future glories that we shall encounter in Heaven.

> [9]**And when those beasts give glory and honour and thanks to him that sat on the throne, who liveth for ever and ever,** [10]**The four and twenty elders fall down before him that sat on the throne, and worship him that liveth for ever and ever, and cast their crowns before the throne, saying,** [11]**Thou art worthy, O Lord, to receive glory and honour and power: for thou hast created all things, and for thy pleasure they are and were created (Rev. 4:9–11, KJV).**

GOD OF MAJESTY

We see the Omniscient God who lives forever in these verses. We see a God of Majesty who always was and always will be. The Sovereign God created and made everything we can touch, see, smell, and understand.

The cherubim cry holy, holy, holy, and give glory to God. The elders worship the Almighty God falling prostrate and giving praise to the Everlasting Majesty. They *cast* (*ballo*) their golden crowns toward the Throne, and they don't even care where the crowns land.[6]

The elders pronounced...*glory and honour and power* to the Lord. They spoke praise, blessings, adoration, and gratitude to their awesome Creator. The elders held a privileged place with the Lord, and they thanked him for his wonderful grace.

HOW I FEEL ABOUT THE LORD

In a small way, I understand what the elders and the cherubim felt at the Throne. When I pray and worship God, I often sense the presence of Jesus standing close to me.

I have felt the perfect Love and holiness of God. At times, all I could do was whisper, "Jesus, Jesus, Jesus, Holy One." Then say, "Glory, Glory to the Lamb, praise his Holy name."

I have never seen Heaven, but when Jesus reveals his Love to me, I can only thank him in gratitude and praise. After an experience with the Lord, I often think about Heaven. I look forward to going to that bright city and joining the other saints.

How can I explain the closeness of the Holy Spirit? I would prefer an experience with the Lord over any other experience the world has to offer. I've tried most of what the world has, but there's nothing that can compare to the love and peace of Jesus. Life appears different when the Holy Spirit touches my spirit. God gives me assurance of his love and his ability to take care of any problems. He gives me peace that reaches from today through all eternity (John 14:27).

RAISED ON A FARM

I can see the Lord's guidance through my life when I look back on it. I was born in 1943 at Sturgis, South Dakota. I lived on a farm and ranch in western South Dakota for the first twenty-one years of my life. I had loving parents and three brothers. It was a good place to grow from childhood into manhood.

I attended Sunday school and went to a Lutheran Church, until I was old enough to say, "I don't want to go anymore." I was typical of many young people, who have no interest in the church or God.

In 1964, I married my beautiful wife, Linda, and we moved to Oregon. Soon, the Lord gave us two special children, Wanda and Lisa. For the past twenty-seven years, I have worked as a plumber in the Portland, Oregon, area.

MONEY WAS IMPORTANT

I had many goals and desires when I was young. I wanted to make much money and accumulate many material possessions. For years, I worked overtime jobs so I could afford the lifestyle we chose. I enjoyed exciting hobbies. I rode dirt motorcycles in the beautiful Oregon hills. In the middle seventies, I learned how to fly and flew airplanes for several years.

We had many interests through the years. Some were good, and we still do them. Others were temporary, and we left them behind. I've experienced much over the years, and found that not everything gives fulfillment. I always searched for something, but that something always seemed to be missing.

BORN AGAIN

In 1975, at the age of 32, I accepted Jesus Christ as my Lord and Savior. Over the next few months, as I read the Bible and learned about God, life began to make sense. The Holy Spirit gave witness to me. I knew that God was real: I knew that I would live with him forever. It is a comfort to know that when I die, I shall go to Heaven to be with my Lord.

I joined a Lutheran Church and studied the Bible: this helped me learn more about God. Over the years, I have found that the Faithful Witness always kept his promises. God fulfilled my life and gave me peace. He helped us through difficult times of problems and troubles.

The Lord gave Linda and me happiness through the seventies, but I still felt something was missing. Through a series of events in my life, God called me into a deeper walk with him. Seven years after I was born again, God filled me with the Holy Spirit in 1982.

BAPTIZED WITH THE HOLY SPIRIT

After God released his Spirit in me, Jesus drew me into a close personal friendship. I sensed the deep love that Jesus has for his children. Over the years, my love and understanding of the Lord increased. As I developed my relationship with the Savior, my interests changed. God gave me new desires to do his will rather than what I wanted to do.

The Bible came alive: the Holy Spirit helped me understand its fullness and richness. My understanding of the sacraments in the church increased. The Lord's Supper and Holy Baptism have a special meaning.

THE PROMISE OF OUR FATHER

The Baptism of the Spirit and Holy Baptism indicate two different events in the Bible. I understand and believe that a person receives the Holy

Spirit when he or she is baptized with water and the word. The Christian Church baptizes in the name of the Father, the Son, and the Holy Spirit.

Some ask, "What does it mean when God fills you with the Spirit?" It's called the Baptism of the Holy Spirit, being filled with the Spirit, or the release of the Spirit.

After Jesus rose from the grave, he appeared to his disciples. Jesus breathed on them and said, "Receive the Holy Spirit." (John 20:22). Jesus also told his disciples to wait "for the promise of my Father" (Luke 24:49). The promise of the Father, the Holy Spirit, then came at Pentecost (Acts 2). Our Lord breathed the Holy Spirit into his disciples soon after his Resurrection. The Holy Spirit later baptized them with the Holy Spirit of power at Pentecost.

ONGOING WORSHIP EXPERIENCE

The Baptism of the Spirit was the most profound experience of my life. When I accepted Jesus as my personal Savior, that was important for my eternal destiny. It also helped to change my life. However, when God filled me with his Holy Spirit, that ongoing experience changed my outlook on the values of this world.

The Holy Spirit, through the years, came into my mind and rewired some of the circuits. He put up signs on some well-used paths that said, "Not important, do not use." On other dusty paths, he put signs that said, "Priority, go this way." Through this process, the Lord changed my thoughts on what is important and what is not important in this world. This didn't happen all at once: it took years and will go on until Jesus takes me to his house.

From my perspective, the filling of the Spirit helped me to release myself to the Lord. From that time on, God could accelerate the changes he wanted in me.

GOD DESIRES A CLOSE WALK

God starts drawing a person to himself by giving them a desire for a deeper relationship with his or her Lord. The individual then spends more time praying, reading the Bible, and asking for a closer walk with Jesus. The important ingredient here is asking.

God responds, when someone asks, by giving the person more desire for the Lord. This exchange goes on until the Lord leads the person to that place where he wants him. Along this path, the Lord releases the Spirit in the person. Sometimes the release happens dramatically. In other people, the release of the Holy Spirit comes slowly over several months or years.

The Baptism of the Spirit helped me to focus on Jesus for a closer walk with him. When we give as much of ourselves as we can to God, he responds by giving us more of himself. This in turn helps us give more of ourselves to God.

INTIMATE IN GOD'S CIRCLE

This ongoing experience with the King of Glory resembles a circle. The exchange will go on and on until someone breaks the circle. The Lord never breaks it—only people break the circle. When the circle separates, our God of Love tries to put the ends back together again. Our God will go to extreme measures to join the ends of our broken ties with him.

God not only works with individual people in this way; he works with individual churches to draw them to himself. The process works in similar ways. Today in the late nineties and on into the next century, we live in special time. Our Rose of Sharon seeks to draw all of his children closer. The doors to the Kingdom of God stand wide open.

The Lord desires to give the Baptism of the Spirit to each of his children. Not every child of God wants an intimate relationship with the Lord. Many Christians enjoy church and fellowship with other Christians, but they stand away from God. They may not want any changes in their lives, or perhaps they fear God.

BAPTISM DIFFERENT FOR EVERYONE

The immersion in the Holy Spirit influences God's children in different ways. God uses individual gifts for different purposes. There is only One Spirit; Jesus desires to activate it in our lives. All of God's children have salvation: they will all go to the same Heaven. The Baptism of the Holy Spirit does not give anyone special privileges with God.

Many things change as a person draws near to Jesus. For many, the Lord cuts the strings to their billfold or checkbook for work in the Kingdom of God. Attitudes change and Christians begin to put the Lord first in their life. Jesus puts more love and caring for others in his followers. The Lord helps his children share abilities, lives, and possessions with people as the he leads them. As this happens, our King of Glory then embraces them with love and mercy.

NOTES

1. Look, *eido*, G1492. To know or to perceive with senses.

2. Hendriksen, *More Than Conquerors*, p. 104.
3. Crown, *stephanos*, G4735. A wreath or eternal blessings.
4. White, *leukos*, G3022. Brilliant light or dazzling white. Garments of angels or saints in heaven.
5. McGuiggan, *The Book of Revelation*, p. 80.
6. Cast, *ballo*, G906. To throw without caring where it falls.

CHAPTER 5

The Scroll—the Lamb

THE FATHER'S SON

Long ago a father had a son. The boy grew, and the father was proud of him. When the child matured, the father taught him all he needed to know. The young man wanted to please his father, and he did everything right.

The boy loved and obeyed his father. The young man carried all our troubles on a long walk up a hill. The father's Son died on a tree on a hill. The land darkened because the Father's tears covered the sun. As he wept and quivered, the earth shook.

After three days the Father, armed with unlimited energy, walked into the tomb and breathed life into his Son. Then the Son went to his Father's house to live forever. The Father was so happy with his Son that he made him the King of Kings and Lord of Lords.

Miracle of miracles: when the Father's Son died on a tree, he died to set us free. He has died for you and me.

The Father's Son still lives; perhaps, you know him. His Father calls him Jesus.

The second vision of Revelation continued into chapter 5. John looked at the Almighty sitting on a throne. As John's vision widened, he saw a scroll and a Lamb. The vision increased to show thousands upon thousands of angels until finally every creature on earth sang praises to the Lamb.

¹Then I saw in the right hand of him who sat on the throne a scroll with writing on both sides and sealed with seven seals. ²And I saw a mighty angel proclaiming in a loud voice, "Who is worthy to break the seals and open the scroll?" ³But no one in heaven or on earth or under the earth could open the scroll or even look inside it. ⁴I wept and wept because no one was found who was worthy to open the scroll or look inside (Rev. 5:1–4, NIV).

THE CREATOR HELD A SCROLL

John viewed the Holy God who held a book or a scroll in his *right hand* (*dexios*), which symbolized his Authority.[1] The Lord held a book written on both sides, and seven seals covered it. The sealed book contained a record of God's future spiritual work on earth. The time span covered the cross through the final coming of Jesus Christ.

The sealed book offers us a preview of the unfolding history of the Christian Church and the world. Revelation does not tell us all the details of the Gospel Age. It only gives us previews and highlights of coming events, much like movie previews. The Revelation of Jesus Christ doesn't tell the whole story, but it entices us to read more.

The powerful angel shouted...*Who is worthy to break the seals and open the scroll?* They could not find anyone worthy. Then John wept and wept! The question—why did John weep? God placed John in his immediate presence (Rev. 1:10). In this privileged position, John could feel, sense, and see what the Lord felt for his children.

The Creator yearned for the freedom to hug his children. The evil of sin separated the Creator from his creation (Rom. 3:10–12, 23). Because the Almighty is untainted by sin, he could not come into the presence of sin (1 Pet. 1:15, 16).

John wept because someone needed to break the curse of sin and death for mankind. John knew what Jesus had completed on the cross, but in this vision, time went back to before the cross.

THE FALL OF MAN

God created man and woman in the beginning, and he put them in the Garden of Eden. He created them in his image—perfect, without sin. The Lord then placed them in charge of all things on the earth. The Creator gave Adam and Eve one rule.

¹⁶And the Lord God commanded the man, "You are free to eat from any tree in the garden; ¹⁷but you must not eat from the

tree of the knowledge of good and evil, for when you eat of it you will surely die" (Gen. 2:16, 17, NIV).

The old serpent enticed Eve to eat fruit from the tree; she then gave some fruit to Adam. Adam also disobeyed God and ate from the tree of the knowledge of good and evil. Because of their disobedience, the Lord opened their eyes to sin. They destroyed the perfect union they had with their Creator, and suddenly they knew separation for the first time.

A rich apple collector searched the world for a perfect apple. He found a rare pair of matched apples. The collector put the perfect apples in a cold display case is his home. He then called all his friends to see his find.

The apple collector left for six weeks. He returned home to look at his pride and joy. In the warm case, he found two rotten apples.

Adam and Eve hid from God when he came walking in the garden (Gen. 3). God asked them if they had eaten from the tree. Adam then blamed Eve, and Eve blamed the serpent. Did you ever do something wrong and then try to blame someone else? You can thank Adam.

THE PRICE OF SIN

When Adam and Eve disobeyed God, they lost paradise, innocence, and a privileged relationship. They also gained suffering, toil, and death. When they ate the fruit, they sinned against God and all men, women, and children. Their original sin passed down through every generation of mankind until today.

What could the rich collector do with his apples? If he put his prize with other apples, their decay would have tainted the whole box. They seemed worthless. Adam and Eve seemed offensive to the Creator. The sin of the first man tainted all men and women. The perfect creation seemed worthless, except for the Creator's mighty Love.

I do not believe we can fully grasp the results of Adam's sin. Adam and Eve fell from holiness into the corruption of sin. The Lord God gave Adam everything on the earth. When he ate the fruit, Adam, in essence, told his Creator, "I don't need you."

Adam is responsible to God for his sins, just as we are responsible to God for our sins (Rom. 3:22–25). Sin is an act against God's grace and love for us. Because of God's Holiness, sin requires punishment. Without the grace of God, we would have no end but eternal death (Rom. 6:23).

GOD'S FIRST COVENANT

The Creator began to draw his children back to himself in the OT. He used the sacrifice of animals at the Tabernacle of Moses. Once a year on the Day of Atonement, the high priest sacrificed a lamb for himself and a lamb for the people. The high priest then sprinkled the blood of the sacrificed lambs on the mercy seat where God dwelt (Heb. 9:7).

The people of Israel could approach the Lord because the high priest sprinkled the blood of the sacrifice on the mercy seat. Through the blood of the slain lamb, God then forgave the people for their sins.

THE NEW COVENANT

God found fault with the OT covenant. He looked for another way to forgive sin because of his intense love for his people. (Heb. 8:7). The Lord used the first covenant of Moses to point the way to a superior covenant. In the new and better covenant, God put his laws on their minds and hearts. He then forgave their evil and did not remember their sins anymore (Heb. 8:10, 12).

John wept because he saw the lost condition of man. Our Father longed to have a close communion with us. Unity with him was impossible because we were living in a state of tainted decay. The first covenant didn't bring man to the state of holiness that God wanted for his children.

John sensed that man could not help God obtain a spiritual relationship. There was no hope in the old covenant. That's the reason God needed a Redeemer to open the scroll and break its seals.

> **⁵Then one of the elders said to me, "Do not weep! See, the Lion of the tribe of Judah, the Root of David, has triumphed. He is able to open the scroll and its seven seals." ⁶Then I saw a Lamb, looking as if it had been slain, standing in the center of the throne, encircled by the four living creatures and the elders. He had seven horns and seven eyes, which are the seven spirits of God sent out into all the earth (Rev. 5:5, 6, NIV).**

THE SLAIN LAMB

An elder said to John, "Stop weeping! The Lion of Judah and the...*Root of David has triumphed.*" The word *triumph* (*nikao*) meant "to win the victory or overcome."[2] The prophet Isaiah referred to the future Messiah as the Root of Jesse who was David's father (Isa. 11:1, 10). David was Jesus' ancestor by blood through the tribe of Judah.

Jacob, the father of Israel, blessed his twelve sons. When Jacob blessed Judah, he called him a lion's cub and told him that the scepter would not leave the tribe of Judah (Gen. 49:8–11). The people of Israel understood the Lion of Judah and the Root of David as well-known OT names for the coming Messiah.

> The Lion represents absolute strength and bravery; the Lamb, a religious symbol, represents absolute goodness. The characteristics of the Lamb are significant. It stood as "one slain." The word indicates the wounds received in cutting the throat of the young lamb sacrificed on the altar. Christ is here pictured in his atoning sacrifice.[3]

The slain Lamb stands…in the center of the throne where the Almighty God sits. The Lamb has…seven eyes, which are the seven spirits of God. The eyes represent the Holy Spirit. We see a picture of the Father, the Son, and the Holy Spirit united as the Holy Trinity.

The slain Lamb displays…seven horns: the number seven points toward fulfillment and perfection. The horns (keras) describe strength, courage, and a mighty deliverance.[4] The slain Lamb fulfills his roll as Messiah by delivering people from bondage, sin, and death.

TRUE MAN—TRUE GOD

Jesus Christ left his position as True God in Heaven and came to earth to live as a man in the flesh. God left paradise to live like you and me. He suffered cold and heat and earned a living with hard labor. Only out of vast love for his children did Jesus Christ come down to earth. The Lord did not need to come. God could have gone on with the old covenant of sacrifice, but it was not complete (Heb. 8:1–13).

Mary, a young virgin woman, was the mother of Jesus (Luke 1:26–31). The angel Gabriel told Mary that the Most High God would come over her and she would give birth to the Son of God (Luke 1:35).

Mary raised Jesus like any other child of the time. Mary's husband, Joseph, also treated Jesus as his own son. Joseph taught Jesus how to support himself with the carpenter trade. When Jesus Christ was thirty years old, he began his ministry that led to his new mission as Savior of the world.

JESUS THE PERFECT LAMB

As True God and true man, the Redeemer understood all the problems that people have in this world. He experienced the same temptation, pain, and problems that we experience, but he never sinned (Heb. 4:15). Jesus was God, and yet he was a man made of flesh, blood, and bones (John 1:14).

The Lord volunteered to strip himself of Almighty Power when he came to earth. Jesus lived as a man and endured all types of temptation to sin. He obeyed the Father as a servant, and in humility he endured death on a cross (Phil. 2:5–8). God considered Jesus the perfect Lamb of sacrifice (1 John 3:5).

I have always felt that Jesus knew exactly who he was from the time of conception. Otherwise, he would have strayed from purity. There had to be an awareness of who he was, and what he had to do.

Even when Jesus was a baby, he probably thought: "I Am the Savior; I cannot sin. I must remain pure, so that my Father can substitute my Holiness for their sins. My Father needs to look through my sinless body at the people. Then he will not see their sins: he will only see my perfection" (1 John 1:7).

Christ Jesus was about thirty-three years old when the Romans crucified him to death. After three days, the life-giving Creator raised his crucified Son to life. The Father then brought him into Heaven and sat him at his right hand on the Throne.

The elder told John that the Lamb had…*triumphed*; he was worthy to open the scroll and break the seven seals. This happened years before, and yet John looked at the moment when the victorious resurrected Christ returned to the Throne. God transcends time, and he could put John when or where he wanted to.

BLOOD COVERS SIN

The inheritance of Adam's disgrace brought sin to all people. Sin brought death to all people because all sinned (Rom. 5:12). Because the Creator is a God of absolute Holiness, he couldn't come into the presence of sin or look on evil (Hab. 1:13; Ps. 5:4). This prevented a close union with his children on earth.

Jesus shed his perfect blood for our sins when he died on the cross. The shed blood perfectly satisfied God's demand for our holiness. The Creator considered the blood of Jesus an acceptable sacrifice for our sins. Because of the covering of his blood, Jesus can now present us to God as holy, blameless, and without sin (Col. 1:19–23).

THE BLOOD PURIFIES

Linda and I live in a 100-year-old home. The front door contains a stained-glass window with small red panes around it.

I stood at the front door last summer and watched Linda walk up the front walk. She wore a red pantsuit. I happened to look at her through the red glass: Linda's clothing appeared as fresh fallen snow. When we look at a red object through a red glass, the object turns white.

I thought to myself, this is how the Lord sees us. When God looks through the red blood of Jesus Christ, he pictures our sins as white and pure.

> Come now, and let us reason together, saith the Lord: though your sins be as scarlet, they shall be as white as snow; though they be red like crimson, they shall be as wool (Isa. 1:18, KJV).

This was good news. The Father didn't remember our sins when we trusted in Jesus for eternal life. He only saw the holiness and perfection of his Son. On the cross Jesus said, "It is finished." He completed his work for the salvation of man. Jesus paid the full price for our redemption by his blood. He returned to his Father, and his Father crowned him King!

THE GLORY OF SALVATION (ISA. 12)

The Lord was angry—Then he turned away.
Then he returned with grace, Love, and mercy.
Behold, our Almighty God gives us salvation.
We shall trust and not fear, for he redeems us.
The Lord comforts us and gives us strength.
We shall draw from the well of salvation.
In joy, we shall sing Praises to the Lord.
Shout for joy—Great is the Holy One.

⁷He came and took the scroll from the right hand of him who sat on the throne. ⁸And when he had taken it, the four living creatures and the twenty-four elders fell down before the Lamb. Each one had a harp and they were holding golden bowls full of incense, which are the prayers of the saints (Rev. 5:7, 8, NIV).

John witnessed an important event in the history of the world. He saw the moment when the risen Christ came back from the grave and presented himself to the Father. John saw the return of the living triumphant Christ.

The Lamb went up to the Father...*and took the scroll from the right hand.* After the King of Glory took the scroll, the four cherubim and the twenty-four elders fell down and worshiped the Lamb. This scene in Heaven pointed to Glory and Majesty of the living Christ, whose name towers above every other name.

GOD CONSIDERS PRAYER IMPORTANT

Each of the elders holds a golden bowl filled with…*incense, which are the prayers of the saints.* The golden bowls of incense symbolize of the prayers of God's children here on the earth. God considers our prayers so precious that he keeps them in golden bowls.

God didn't reveal prayers until Jesus gained victory and returned to the Father in his Revelation. The Almighty waited until the victory celebration of the risen Savior before he brought out the prayers of the saints. What do you think our Father was trying to say to us by this act?

I understand that our prayers endure longer than most other actions that we do. It appears that the Lord puts the highest priority on prayers. God hears our prayers, and yet many people don't understand the importance of them.

God uses prayer as a key to bring salvation, deliverance, and healing for men, women, and children. Prayer opens the gate that leads us into Heaven. Someday we shall join the other saints and rejoice with our Savior over answered prayers.

> [9]And they sang a new song: "You are worthy to take the scroll and to open its seals, because you were slain, and with your blood you purchased men for God from every tribe and language and people and nation. [10]You have made them to be a kingdom and priests to serve our God, and they will reign on the earth" (Rev. 5:9, 10, NIV).

The words…*they sang a new song* pointed to the salvation of the Lord. The word *new* (*kainos*) meant "fresh in form or recently made." It's a new and different nature when compared to the old.[5] They sang a new song to the Lamb because he was slain for us. By his blood, Jesus Christ purchased our salvation and redeemed us from spiritual death.

REDEEMED BY HIS BLOOD

The Father desired oneness with his children.
Sin raised a barrier between God and man.
Our sinfulness disgusted the Holy Creator.
The Father sent his only Son to purify us.
Jesus liberated our freedom by the cross.
Our Redeemer exchanged his life for ours.
Jesus smashed the barrier to union with God.
Thank you, Lord, for your Redeeming love.

Our Union—Our Holiness

We have a union with God: by this union, we have eternal life. No one on this earth or in Heaven has the strength to break the bond between our Father and us. Satan cannot break it, nor can any other power on earth or in Heaven. Nothing can separate us from God's love in Christ Jesus (Rom 8:37–39). We have a free will, and only we can break our union with God. We can break it if we harden our hearts to God and to his Word.

The Miracle of Our Holiness

A few years ago, I worked with a Southern Baptist pipe fitter. We talked about the Lord and the churches. I could never get him to express his feelings about his Savior. Then one day I said, "Jesse, when God looks at me through the blood of Jesus he sees me as perfect."

Jesse wouldn't talk to me for two weeks. He acted as if I was unclean. Finally after several weeks we began to talk once more. Jesse told me that we're all sinners, and no one's perfect but Jesus Christ. It's true: Jesse's right!

Everyone's born into sin and remains a sinner until they die. Only Jesus Christ walked on this earth as perfect. Each of us sins, and we cannot save ourselves. Only the blood of Jesus can cover our sins.

Jesse finally permitted me to explain what I meant when I said, "God sees me without sin." God is Holy, and it's a true miracle that he sees his children as holy. When God looks at us through the shed blood, he sees us as perfect. God doesn't see our sin: he only sees the perfection of our Savior.

> [21]God made him who had no sin to be sin for us, so that in him we might become the righteousness of God (2 Cor. 5:21, NIV).

> [21]Once you were alienated from God and were enemies in your minds because of your evil behavior. [22]But now he has reconciled you by Christ's physical body through death to present you holy in his sight, without blemish and free from accusation (Col. 1:21, 22, NIV).

Our God of Grace says, in both the OT and the NT, that he doesn't remember our sins after we ask him to forgive us (Isa. 43:25; Mic. 7:19; and Heb. 10:17). If we believe that the Bible's true, we need to accept God's entire Word.

Why Do Christians Hold On to Sin

Some Christians go through life saying, "I'm a Christian saved by grace—I'm a Christian saved by grace!" Then they think about their sins and don't forgive themselves. Some of the Father's children see him as a stern judge waiting to punish them. They don't understand the love, grace, and mercy that the Savior offers us.

Jesus came to give us truth. He told his disciples that the truth would set them free (John 8:32). So Christ came to free us from death, bondage, and sin. Paul said that we need to accept freedom in Christ; we should not go back to slavery under sin and the Law (Gal. 5:1).

Why then do some Christians hang on to their past sins? When a person asks our Faithful God to forgive his sins, from that time on the Lord doesn't see any of his past sins. Our forgiving God sees our record clean, without even a smudge. When God looks at us, he only sees the perfection and righteous of Jesus Christ. Praise the Lord! Hallelujah! Amen!

Jesus said on the cross: "it is finished." Why then does anyone want to take the saving grace and work of Jesus Christ, and believe that it's not sufficient for their BIG SIN (Gal. 3:1–5)? God said "it is finished," so don't doubt it.

> [11]And I beheld, and I heard the voice of many angels round about the throne and the beasts and the elders: and the number of them was ten thousand times ten thousand, and thousands of thousands; [12]Saying with a loud voice, Worthy is the Lamb that was slain to receive power, and riches, and wisdom, and strength, and honour, and glory, and blessing. [13]And every creature which is in heaven, and on the earth, and under the earth, and such as are in the sea, and all that are in them, heard I saying, Blessing, and honour, and glory, and power, *be* unto him that sitteth upon the throne, and unto the Lamb for ever and ever. [14]And the four beasts said, Amen. And the four *and* twenty elders fell down and worshipped him that liveth for ever and ever (Rev. 5:11–14, KJV).

REJOICING AT THE THRONE

John's vision of the Throne widens out; he sees and hears the glorified chorus at the Throne. He beholds an unlimited (*murias*) number of angels singing with the twenty-four elders and the four living creatures.[6] They sing praises to the Lamb. The angels, the beasts, and the elders give a sacred concert of praise and adoration to the Lord!

They said, the Lamb's Worthy to receive…*power, and riches, and wisdom, and strength, and honour, and glory, and blessing.* The seven parts of this blessing gave it perfection.

All of creation, on earth and in Heaven, belongs to the Lamb, who sits at the right hand of our Father on the Throne. All creatures in Heaven will sing praises, honor, and glory forever and ever.

When we all get to Heaven, the Bible says we will walk on streets of gold and live in big houses. The glory of the Lord will surpass our expectations. Eyes cannot see the glory of the Almighty, nor can ears hear the glorious praises. One thing we know: when we get to Heaven, we shall see our Savior face-to-face. Then we shall sing praises to him for all eternity and thank him for his abundant grace. Amen! Amen!

NOTES

1. Right hand, *dexios*, G1188. Right hand or side. Metaphor of authority.
2. Triumphed, *nikao*, G3528. To win the victory or overcome.
3. Summers, *Worthy Is the Lamb*, p. 135.
4. Horns, *keras*, G2768, Symbol of strength and courage, gives mighty deliverance.
5. New, *kainos*, G2537. Recently made, fresh, new in kind.
6. Ten thousand, *murias*, G3461. An innumerable multitude.

CHAPTER 6

Six Seals

THE BLACK BALL

I recently talked with a man named Bruce who told me about a vision that drew him closer to God. Bruce grew up in a church and considered himself a Christian. As a young man, he began to experiment with drugs and put God on a shelf.

The Lord gave Bruce a vision while he was at a party using LSD. He saw a black ball bounce around the room that contained sparks and twinkling lights. The ball bounced from wall to wall and sometimes rested on individual people. When the ball covered their heads, the sparks and lights jumped back and forth through the person's head.

Bruce began to pray and seek understanding of the meaning of his vision. He felt the sparks and flashing lights represented people, or their spirits, trapped by the evil of Satan. The sparks symbolized people that couldn't come away from the black cloud because of their lifestyles and world desires.

The black ball moved from person to person in the room but didn't come near him. God had sealed Bruce by his Baptism and early commitment to his Savior. Although he walked away from God, the Lord protected him. He didn't permit the Devil to touch his spirit with the blackness of death.

Because of this vision, Bruce began to understand the overflowing grace of God. He changed his lifestyle and quit drugs. Bruce has stayed close to Jesus Christ for the past twenty years. Some people have considered him radical in his Christian walk. Our Lord hasn't considered him extreme; he would view him as one of his true servants.

The Devil uses hallucinogenic drugs to draw many people into his camp and trap their spirits in the evil black balls of life. Bruce believes that the lights of the people in the black ball represent the evil and hopelessness of Satan's kingdom. The lights of people shine bright, and then blackness may overwhelm them. Their lights go out!

INTRODUCTION TO THE SEALS

On our walk through the Revelation of Jesus Christ, we come to a muddy trail. Many people journey through the Book and leave numerous footprints. The footprints from different teachings blend until they seem hard to identify.

God uses symbolism in Revelation to conceal the meaning to some, and to give the true meaning to others. Most scenes in the Book of Revelation point to pictures and stories in the rest of the Bible. We shall try to discern what Jesus means from stories and practices in the Bible. We also shall look at the Greek words, and check what they mean in the rest of the NT.

Because God inspired his Word, the Bible interprets itself it. Topics in Revelation reveal themselves to us by what the rest of the Bible says. The Word of God always stays in harmony with itself. When we use this method to explain the Revelation of Jesus Christ, the book makes sense.

THE INTERPRETATION OF REVELATION

Christians usually agree on the meaning of the first five chapters of Revelation. Most people use symbolism in the Bible to understand the first five chapters. As an example in chapter 4, the OT names for the coming Messiah reveal Jesus Christ as the slain Lamb. If we interpret part of the Book of Revelation using symbolism from the Bible, we should use the same method of interpretation for all of it.

Jesus Christ gave his Revelation to John in the same format. Therefore, he evidently wants us to understand it by using the same format all the way through it. A computer programmer would not use one format for the first third of a program and then change formats. The last part of the program would look like a jumbled mess.

Chapters 6, 8, and 9 of Revelation cover the seals and the trumpets. They seem difficult to understand. Nevertheless, we need to grasp the meaning of the seals and the trumpets to help us understand the rest of the book. The reading for these chapters isn't as light as some books, and yet if we go through it, God will bless us.

I **explain** the meaning of the seals and the trumpets from stories and principles in the Bible. I use Greek and Hebrew lexicons to check meanings of the original words. John used the Greek language to write Revelation. The people of the time understood meanings that our English doesn't show. Only by prayer and meditation on God's Word can we hope to understand the Revelation of Jesus Christ.

THE LAMB REIGNS

The second vision of the Throne, the Lamb, and the seals continued into chapter 6. John witnessed the slain Lamb returning to the Throne of his Father. The Eternal God invited Jesus Christ, Savior of the World, to sit at his right hand on the Throne. The Almighty gave Christ all power and all authority in the heavens and on the earth (Col. 1:18). The Lamb began his reign by the Power of the Throne.

The Lamb takes the scroll from his Father and opens the first seal. Each seal gives us a different picture of the Christian Church during the Gospel Age.

> [1]And I saw when the Lamb opened one of the seals, and I heard, as it were the noise of thunder, one of the four beasts saying, Come and see. [2]And I saw, and behold a white horse: and he that sat on him had a bow; and a crown was given unto him: and he went forth conquering, and to conquer (Rev. 6:1, 2, KJV).

THE WHITE HORSE

John watches the Lamb open the first seal. He hears one of the four cherubim thunder...*Come and see.* The living beast calls forth the first of four horsemen who ride from the seals. Out comes a rider on a white horse. Jesus Christ rides the white horse as he proclaims the Gospel throughout the world!

Some believe that the white horse represents the Antichrist, but the symbolism does not point that way. The white color (*leukos*) always symbolizes holiness, purity, and righteousness.[1] It never points toward Satan or his kingdom. John uses the same white color in the Apocalypse for the robes worn by the saints, for the hair of our Lord, and the horse that the Word of God rode (7:13, 1:14, and 19:11).

The rider wore a...*crown* given to him by his Father. The *crown* (*stephanos*) symbolized "royalty and victory."[2] The word often denoted a garland that circled the head by twisting or twining. Jesus, on the night he was crucified, wore a crown (*stephanos*) of thorns twisted around his head (Mark. 15:17).

This crown in the NT refers to the believer's crown of life, crown of glory, or the crown that Jesus Christ wears. In Revelation, the dragon and the beast wear different crowns (*diadema*), meaning "a kingly ornament."[3]

JESUS OVERCOMES

Jesus the King of Glory rides the white horse from the first seal...*conquering, and to conquer*. You could ask, "Why would Jesus go out conquering?" To answer that, we need to understand what the word conquering means.

They only translate the word (*nikao*) as "conquer" in this verse.[4] In the other twenty-seven verses of the NT, (*nikao*) means "to overcome, to prevail, or to win the victory." Jesus Christ leads his saints in ministry to overcome the world, to prevail against the forces of darkness, and to win the victory of eternal life.

THE LAMB RIDES

We saw John weep in chapter 5 because no man was found worthy to open the seals. Man's nature decayed from sin: no one was worthy to save mankind. Man needed a Savior, and God needed a way to proclaim the Gospel. The Holy Lamb rose from death and broke the bondage of sin. This cleared the way for him to mount that white horse and ride. Hallelujah to the Lamb! Ride on, Ride on!

The rider on the white horse holds...*a bow* (*toxon*), used only once in the Bible.[5] The word (*toxon*) comes from the base word (*tikto*), which means "to bring forth, to bear, to produce fruit from the seed, or to give birth."[6]

> [1]Listen to me, you islands; hear this, you distant nations: Before I was born the LORD called me; from my birth he has made mention of my name. [2]He made my mouth like a sharpened sword, in the shadow of his hand he hid me; he made me into a polished arrow and concealed me in his quiver (Isa. 49:1, 2, NIV).

In this prophecy, Isaiah refers to the coming Redeemer and Holy One of Israel (Isa. 49:6, 7). The verse above speaks of our Savior as a polished arrow. The first seal gives us a picture of Jesus Christ riding a white horse and holding a (*toxon*) to bring forth his Church. The Lord sends out arrows of the Holy Spirit and uses them to draw people to himself.

THE FISHERMAN

Before I was a Christian, I enjoyed the sport of archery. I used a bow to shoot targets and sometimes to fish with. The special arrows that I used for fishing had a barb and a string attached. If I got lucky and hit a fish, I could draw the fish back to me. Then we had a tasty meal.

The rider on the white horse also uses special arrows to draw people to himself (John 6:44). The power of prayer activates the special arrows that he uses. The Lord uses a line that won't break to play children of the world on his gentle fishing tackle. The Arm of the Lord lightly tugs; he then gives slack so the child can run with it. Our Lord uses much patience to draw men, women, and children.

The bow, held by our Savior, isn't a weapon of war and destruction. Jesus Christ uses the bow as an instrument to bring forth and produce Christians for our God. "Father, I thank you for drawing each of us to you. Lord, we thank you for your patience, kindness, and your abundant Love. Holy Spirit, we thank you for activating the arrows that drew us. Amen!"

KINGDOM OF HEAVEN ADVANCED BY PRAYER

John the Baptist ushered in a new way to advance the Kingdom of God. Jesus said that the Kingdom of Heaven advances by force through forceful men (Matt. 11:12).

The Devil tries to control the world and its people. He still has limited power, even though Jesus Christ destroyed his power when he rose on that first Easter morning (1 John 3:8). Satan's kingdom tries to force its influence on every person that it can. He wants to rule over all the earth.

Why does God permit Satan to control people, and why does God permit so much evil in the world? People have asked this question throughout the age. I will give my thought on this subject.

Satan led Adam and Eve into sin. He then began to force his dominion over the earth. God gave this same dominion to Adam after the creation (Gen. 1:28). Satan caused the fall of man: he then believed that he had a right to man's rule over the earth. Although Satan didn't have a claim to Adam's control, he took it (John 12:31; 1 John 3:8).

Jesus Christ rides the white horse into areas of darkness. He brings light to all who accept it. Prayer is the key that brings the white horse to an area or to an individual.

PRAYER POWER

The Father, the Son, and the Holy Spirit wrestle people away from the kingdom of darkness (Acts 26:17, 18). They move individuals from darkness into the Kingdom of Light by our prayers. Jesus won the war against Satan on the cross, but we battle against the forces of darkness for our salvation (Eph. 6:12–18). The Lord is not playing a game. The stakes are high because men's, women's, and children's souls are at risk.

When we pray for an individual, God intensifies his work in the person's life for their salvation. The disciples and the women pray constantly in the upper room (Acts 1:14). Then on Pentecost the Holy Spirit answered the prayers by adding 3,000 people to his church (Acts 2:41).

God forcefully advances his kingdom by forceful means. The Almighty God uses our prayers as a catalyst that activates the power of the Holy Spirit. I don't understand everything in the spiritual world, but I know that God works through people. The prayers of God's children open the door to spread his kingdom. When we understand the importance of prayer, our prayer ministry should increase.

> [3]**When the Lamb opened the second seal, I heard the second living creature say, "Come!" [4]Then another horse came out, a fiery red one. Its rider was given power to take peace from the earth and to make men slay each other. To him was given a large sword (Rev. 6:3, 4, NIV).**

THE FIRE RED HORSE

The rider on the red horse travels over the earth. He takes harmony and security away from people and nations. The red horseman causes wars and fighting between people of different races and cultures. The red horseman brings strife and disharmony to our streets and country.

The word for *fiery red* (*purrhos*)only appears twice in the NT.[7] John uses it here and in Revelation 12:3 to describe the red dragon. (*Purrhos*) comes from the Greek word (*pur*), meaning "fire."

JESUS CONTRASTED WITH SATAN

Satan rides the fiery red horse. The Bible shows us a dreadful contrast between the riders on the white horse and the red horse.

> [10]The thief cometh not, but for to steal, and to kill, and to destroy: I am come that they might have life, and that they might have it more abundantly (John 10:10, KJV).

Jesus is light; Satan is darkness. Jesus is good; Satan is evil. Jesus is innocent and Holy; Satan is immoral and polluted. Jesus gives eternal life; Satan gives eternal death.

During the eighties, Linda and I lived northwest of Portland. We lived in a house located among the tall Douglas fir trees. We raised a few chickens for the eggs. In the spring of the third year, a coyote found the chickens and began to kill them.

Early in the morning, she would boldly sneak into the yard. The coyote then snatched one and ran like the devil, disappearing into the trees with her prey. While the chickens were there, the coyote was faithful, because she came every other day to pick up a victim.

Satan's kingdom of darkness compares to the ways of the coyote. The Devil attacks the redeemed children of God when they are sleepy or their defenses are low. Like the coyote, Satan is sneaky and bold. The coyote and Satan both wait patiently for an opportunity to attack their victim. The coyote hunts for food because he's hungry. The Devil plunders and kills because he hates the children of Light.

THE RED HORSE SLAYS CHRISTIANS

Satan persecutes people in many ways. Some attacks by Satan give people subtle harassment. Satan attacks other people with deadly harm. The cross limits Satan's power over Christians, but sometimes God permits Satan to attack them. Why God gave the red horseman authority to take peace from the earth remains one of the mysteries of the Gospel.

> We believe that this horse and its rider refers to religious persecution of God's children rather than to war between nations; to slaughter and sacrifice rather than to warfare. Believers are slaughtered "for his name's sake."[8]

The red horseman displays a special agenda for the followers of Jesus Christ. In the first seal, John shows us a picture of Christ and his Church spreading the Gospel throughout the earth. When Jesus Christ proclaims the Gospel, the Devil always follows with persecution of the Church. He hates the Savior and his elect. Satan is headed for the lake of fire, and he wants to drag as many people with him as God permits.

The rider on the red horse help men slay each other. John is the only writer who uses the word *slay* (*sphazo*) in the NT.[9] The Bible uses a different Greek word for the common word meaning to kill. *Slay* (*sphazo*) means "to slaughter, sacrifice, or bring death by violence."

John always used slay to indicate slain or slaughtered Christians except where the beast had a fatal wound (Rev. 13:3). The beast used the healed wound (*sphazo*)to imitate the sacrifice of Christ. Cain slew his brother (1 John 3:12). The Lamb was slaughtered or sacrificed (Rev. 5:6, 9, 12; 13:8).

SWORD SLAUGHTERS CHRISTIANS

The...*large sword* (*machaira*) was a knife or a short sword used to kill and butcher animals.[10] The word *large* (*megas*) meant "big in space and in dimensions."[11] The largeness of space that the sword occupied pointed to a sword covering the whole world. The writer of Hebrews used the same sword when he talked about the terrible conditions that the followers of Jesus had to endure.

> [37]They were stoned, they were sawn asunder, were tempted, were slain with the sword: they wandered about in sheepskins and goatskins; being destitute, afflicted, tormented; (Heb. 11:37, KJV).

The persecution of the saints in this verse gave us a picture of the hostility of the world toward the Christian Church. The rider on the red horse...*was given a large sword* to massacre Christians. Throughout the Gospel Age, the people of the world have sacrificed millions of holy saints. In some countries today, the red horseman has continued his ride of slaughter. The methods of Satan have never changed; only the times and the places change.

In conclusion, when the rider on the red horse rides, he looks for the redeemed children of Jesus Christ. He's...*given power to take peace from the earth* and the Church. The Devil uses his power to sacrifice the chosen elect of the Almighty God, but God promises each of his sacrificed children a special place in front of his Throne (Rev. 7:9–17).

> [5]When the Lamb opened the third seal, I heard the third living creature say, "Come!" I looked, and there before me was a black horse! Its rider was holding a pair of scales in his hand. [6]Then I heard what sounded like a voice among the four living creatures, saying, "A quart of wheat for a day's wages, and three quarts of barley for a day's wages, and do not damage the oil and the wine!" (Rev. 6:5, 6, NIV).

THE BLACK HORSE

In chapter 1, Jesus Christ told John to send his vision to the seven churches. The members of these seven churches understood the purpose of the black horse and rider. The black horseman moved among the seven churches that John wrote to, just as he moves among portions of the Lord's Church today.

The question, "What's the black horse?" The prophet Ezekiel gives us an example of enemies attacking OT Jerusalem from the outside. This causes famine and high prices for food and water (Ezek. 4:1–16).

Ezekiel gave a prophecy about the future of Jerusalem. He told the people that enemies would come from the outside and attack Jerusalem. Because food was scarce during the siege, people weighed it with scales and sold it at high prices (Ezek. 4:10, 16). Outside forces caused the food and water shortage in Jerusalem, and yet outside the city walls there was an abundance of food (2 Kings 25:1–3).

The black horse used economic persecution against the saints of God in most of the seven churches. As a Christian, you could not profess your faith and keep the good jobs. The Roman government oppressed the Christian people in many ways. Sometimes they forfeited their homes and property and had to fend for themselves. The people in power hated the children of Christ. The government forced the Christians to buy food and staples on the black market at high prices.

THE SCALES AND THE YOKE

The Greek word *zugos*, used for a...*pair of scales*, literally means "to join with a yoke."[12] The Bible used *zugos* for "yoke" in the rest of the NT. Jesus told us to submit to his yoke and we would find rest for our souls (Matt. 11:29).

The rider on the black horse holds scales that could also serve as a yoke. The scales symbolize scarcity of food and staples needed to live. The scarcity comes because the child of God joins or yokes himself to Jesus. The black horseman rides by a Christian and holds up his yoke. He says, "If you join yourself to Jesus Christ, then I will bring problems and scarcity to your life."

The third seal shows us a picture of economic oppression and food shortages. Most commentators believe famine caused this, and yet oil and wine seem abundant.

GOD TAKES CARE OF OUR NEEDS

A voice from one of the four living creatures says..."*do not damage the oil and the wine!*" What message does the Lord give us from this statement? The word for...*do not damage (adikeo)* means "do no wrong, do not injure, do not sin, and do not offend anyone."[13]

Christians may pay a high price for following their Lord, Jehovah. Oppression from the world tempts Christians to make life easier by dishonest means. The Lord wants his children to live a superior life. He doesn't want them to lie, steal, cheat, or do anything that would offend other people.

Jesus, our God of provision, promises us that he will take care of our needs (Matt. 6:24–33). When he says don't damage (*adikeo*) the oil or the wine, Jesus encourages each of us. Jesus speaks to his Church and tells them to let their light shine and to trust him. The love of our Father will transcend any oppression or problems that we may encounter.

ECONOMIC PREJUDICE

In every country, the Devil's disciples can cause economic hardship on Christians. If we follow the teachings of the Bible, the business world looks down on us. We lose opportunities for monetary advancement because of high moral standards. When we speak our Lord's name at our jobs, the other workers and employers may discriminate against us.

The righteous face subtle bias today: people talk behind your back and may speak a negative remark. At other times, bias blatantly raises its head into the open. A Christian always needs to pray for the guidance of the Holy Spirit before witnessing to others. Otherwise, the black horse and rider may ride your way.

> **7When the Lamb opened the fourth seal, I heard the voice of the fourth living creature say, "Come!" 8I looked, and there before me was a pale horse! Its rider was named Death, and Hades was following close behind him. They were given power over a fourth of the earth to kill by sword, famine and plague, and by the wild beasts of the earth (Rev. 6:7, 8, NIV).**

THE DEATH HORSE

John sees a pale greenish yellow horse that looked like a corpse. Death rides the horse, and…*Hades was following close behind him.* This gives us a gruesome picture of many forms of death in the world. The death rider has fulfilled this prophecy throughout the world's history.

The pale horse shows us death from strife, starvation, sickness, and wild beasts. These types of death happen in all countries: they will continue until the return of Jesus Christ. They affect Christians and non-Christian alike.

The Savior gives the rider of death authority over only one fourth of the earth. He's limited in the destruction and death that he can cause.

Natural disasters and wars only cover a part of the earth at any given time in history.

> ⁹And when he had opened the fifth seal, I saw under the altar the souls of them that were slain for the word of God, and for the testimony which they held: ¹⁰And they cried with a loud voice, saying, How long, O Lord, holy and true, dost thou not judge and avenge our blood on them that dwell on the earth? ¹¹And white robes were given unto every one of them; and it was said unto them, that they should rest yet for a little season, until their fellowservants also and their brethren, that should be killed as they were, should be fulfilled (Rev. 6:9–11, KJV).

Angels and saints wait with trembling anticipation until the Lord fulfills his Word. The martyrs cry...*How long, O Lord, holy and true* will you wait to judge the people who murdered us. They give each of them white robes: Jesus never misses any. They exchange the perfect robe of Jesus for their own filthy clothes (Zech. 3:4).

SOULS UNDER THE ALTAR

We see a picture of the martyred saints under God's altar in Heaven. Because they stay under the altar in the Holy One's presence, the martyrs must think like the Lord. The saints ask the Lord how long before the judgment begins.

Our God of righteousness will judge and repay the evil that happens in this world (Rom. 12:19). Because of the Lord's holiness, he must avenge the wrongs committed on this earth.

The altar in verse 9 pointed to the golden incense altar in the tent of the Tabernacle. The altar stood before the curtain in front of the Holy of Holies (Exod. 30:1–10). The priests sprinkled blood from a sacrificed bull on and around the altar of incense. (Lev. 4:3–12). The slain souls remained under the golden altar where the blood was sprinkled. In a sense, they resembled an offering to the Lord.

HOW MANY MORE, LORD?

A voice says to the souls under the altar...*that they should rest yet for a little season* until God works out his plan of redemption for all his children. No one knows the full number of saints and the full number of years, except the Everlasting Father.

The Lord has plans for people yet unborn in this world. Because of Satan's agents, some of the unborn will join the souls under the altar before they leave the security of the womb. The law and the courts say it's okay to slay the unborn child. Yet, Jesus weeps over each of his children who will never fulfill their destiny here on earth.

All of Heaven and Christians on earth have waited for the Second Coming of Jesus Christ. Jesus told the Church that he would stay with us until the end of the age. Jesus has stayed with each of his children when they died for his Gospel.

Our Lord walks with each of us through our life on earth. When the life on earth ends early, the heart of God mourns with the family. Before Jesus comes back, he wants the full number of his children home in Heaven. Many saints have wondered about this mystery. Why does the Almighty God let the Devil's people persecute Christians?

THE CHURCH SUFFERS WHEN WITNESSING

During times of pressing by Satan's evil kingdom, the Church's witness increases for Christ. In hard times, the Holy Spirit gives more help to the followers of Christ (Rom. 8:26).

When Christians smile and hold their heads up during difficult times, their friends and relatives look at them with wonder. They don't understand their calmness. Some people may ask, "How can you smile and feel at peace when the world's crumbling around you?" This gives a golden opportunity to tell the Gospel story. The Bible gives us a partial reason of why the Lord lets his children suffer.

> [17]Now if we are children, then we are heirs—heirs of God and co-heirs with Christ, if indeed we share in his sufferings in order that we may also share in his glory. [18]I consider that our present sufferings are not worth comparing with the glory that will be revealed in us (Rom. 8:17, 18, NIV).

Paul saw the glories of Heaven before he wrote these words (2 Cor. 12:1–6). He said he went to Paradise and saw unspeakable things. Paul knew what waits for us in Paradise when he said that we could not compare our suffering on earth to our future majesty in Heaven.

The Father wants all of his children to have the correct...*season* of time. Then they can go with us to that glorious land, where we shall eat from the tree of life and drink the living water forever. Praise to the Lamb! Hallelujah! Amen!

> [12]**And I beheld when he had opened the sixth seal, and, lo, there was a great earthquake; and the sun became black as sackcloth of hair, and the moon became as blood; [13]And the stars of heaven fell**

unto the earth, even as a fig tree casteth her untimely figs, when she is shaken of a mighty wind. [14]And the heaven departed as a scroll when it is rolled together; and every mountain and island were moved out of their places (Rev. 6:12–14, KJV).

The fifth seal shows us the slain souls crying out to the Lord for justice: the sixth seal begins that justice. The time of grace has expired. The day of the Lord comes.

THE DAY OF THE LORD

The disciples asked Jesus when he would return, and what sign would precede the end of the age (Matt. 24:3). One of the signs the Lord gave us was a fig tree. Jesus said that when the leaves grew on the fig tree that the end was near, or that the kingdom of God was near (Matt. 24:32; Mark 13:28; Luke 21:31).

What did the Lord say to us? Jesus told us in Revelation that...*the stars of heaven* fell to the earth like green figs blown off by a mighty wind. Our Lord spoke of the fig tree in the Gospels and in Revelation when he referred to the end of the age. In the sixth seal, he used the fig tree that dropped green figs to illustrate the falling stars of heaven.

THE STARS OF HEAVEN

The Bible shows: the black sun, the heaven rolling up, the falling stars, and the fig trees to symbolize the end of the age and the day of the Lord. The Bible gives many references to these symbols and events (Joel 2:10, 31; Matt. 24:29). The English language doesn't explain Bible meanings with the picture language that the Hebrew does.

> [4]All the stars of the heavens will be dissolved and the sky rolled up like a scroll; all the starry host will fall like withered leaves from the vine, like shriveled figs from the fig tree. [5]My sword has drunk its fill in the heavens; see, it descends in judgment on Edom, the people I have totally destroyed. [8]For the LORD has a day of vengeance, a year of retribution, to uphold Zion's cause (Isa. 34:4, 5, 8, NIV).

Isaiah paints us a word picture, of the day of vengeance or judgment that points to the sixth seal. The Hebrew word for *stars* (*tsaba*) means "host of angels or an organized army."[14] Isaiah says the (*tsaba*), or host of angels, will be *dissolved* (*maqaq*), meaning "to decay and pine away."[15]

The starry host *will fall* (*nabel*): this indicates "fading away because of disgrace, or to wither."[16] The (*tsaba*) will wither like shriveled figs that fall from a fig tree. Isaiah says that the Lord's sword has drunk its fill in the heavens. This gives us an indication of the fallen angels fading at Jehovah's judgment.

Both Isaiah and John picture the same events in their descriptions of the day of the Lord. Jesus says that the stars he held in his right hand were the angels of the churches (Rev. 1:20). Therefore, in Rev. 6:13 the stars of Heaven falling to the earth point to heavenly beings.

The stars or the fallen angels begin to decay as they wither away. The fallen angels do this because of the disgrace from loosing the battle with the Lord, Jehovah. The...*stars of heaven* or fallen angels appear as shriveled...*untimely figs* because they never blossomed to their fullest. They fall short of their destiny because they rebelled against the God of Heaven!

GOD GIVES LIGHT

The phrase "*sun became black*" gave us a picture of the light or the sun leaving the earth. This always seemed backward to me. If the sun went black, then we wouldn't see...*the moon became as blood*. We wouldn't see the moon because the moon's light comes from the sun. Isaiah wrote about the glory of the Lord shining on the people of God.

> [19]The sun shall be no more thy light by day; neither for brightness shall the moon give light unto thee: but the LORD shall be unto thee an everlasting light, and thy God thy glory. [20]Thy sun shall no more go down; neither shall thy moon withdraw itself: for the LORD shall be thine everlasting light, and the days of thy mourning shall be ended (Isa. 60:19, 20, KJV).

In this image of new heavens and a new earth, we won't need the sun any longer. Isaiah says the Lord shall be our everlasting light because the sun will expire. The Bible says the sun goes black at the end of the age because we have a new heaven and a new earth. God then gives us his spiritual light that lasts forever.

Ultimately, we see the Holy City, the New Jerusalem coming out of Heaven (Rev. 21). It shines with the glory of God. The New Jerusalem doesn't need the sun or the moon to give it light because the glory of the Lord gives light (Rev. 21:23).

The Almighty Creator exists in a different dimension then earth. Heaven is a spiritual place; the same physical laws of earth don't apply there. We call our environment the natural realm on earth. The new Heaven and the new earth will exist in a spiritual realm. No one understands the difference between the new Heaven and the earth today. As children of the Father, we can only accept the Scriptures by faith.

THE GLORY OF ZION (ISA. 60)

Arise and shine—our Light has come.
Darkness covered the earth and people.
The Lord came and his Light revealed.
We lift up our eyes to view the Light.
We run to our Redeemer and Savior.
The Lord brought us to his Holy City.
The sun and moon will rise no more.
The Lord gives Everlasting Light.

[15]**And the kings of the earth, and the great men, and the rich men, and the chief captains, and the mighty men, and every bondman, and every free man, hid themselves in the dens and in the rocks of the mountains;** [16]**And said to the mountains and rocks, Fall on us, and hide us from the face of him that sitteth on the throne, and from the wrath of the Lamb:** [17]**For the great day of his wrath is come; and who shall be able to stand (Rev. 6:15–17, KJV)?**

END—THE DAY OF WRATH

Everyone will know it when Jesus returns. The people will see their own wretchedness in the light of the Savior's Holiness. In an instant, the lost will know what lies ahead. How terrible for the Devil's children!

Jesus shows us seven classes of people that cover all types of humanity. On that last day they try to hide from the Lamb's…*wrath to come*. No one can stand up to the Lamb unless they have exchanged their vile clothes for robes of righteousness. Without Jesus, it's too late! It's finished! Amen! Amen!

NOTES

1. White, *leukos*, G3022. Brilliant light, sign of innocence and purity.
2. Crown, *stephanos*, G4735. Wreath or garland, eternal blessing given to servants of God.
3. Crowns, *diadema*, G1238. Kingly ornament, A blue band.
4. Conquer, *nikao*, G3528. Overcome, rrevail, gain victory.
5. Bow, *toxon*, G5115. A bow, from G5088.
6. Bring forth, *tikto*, G5088. Be delivered, produce fruit.
7. Red, *purrhos*, G4450. Red. From pur, 4442. Fire.
8. Hendriksen, *More Than Conquerors*, p. 120.

9. Slay, *sphazo*, G4969. To butcher, slaughter, slay, kill.
10. Sword, *machaira*, G3162. Knife, war, judicial punishment.
11. Large, *megas*, G3173. Exceedingly great, large in dimensions or space.
12. Pair of scales, *zugos*, G2218. Coupling together, yoke, submission to authority.
13. Damage, *adikeo*, G91. Do wrong, unjust, offend.
14. Stars, *tsaba*, H6635. An army organized for war.
15. Dissolved, *maqaq*, H4743. To melt, be corrupt, pine away.
16. Fall, *nabel*, H5034. To fall away, dishonor, to fade away.

CHAPTER 7

144,000 Sealed

WHO IS HE

I worked several years as a plumber for Portland Public Schools. Two of the other plumbers had lunch in the employee lunchroom at one of the schools. One day the principal came in with a woman TV reporter who was doing a story on school programs. The principal introduced the reporter to all the people in the room except the two plumbers.

The TV reporter asked the principal, "Who are they?" The principal ignored her and kept talking. Again the lady asked, "But, who are they?"

Finally, the school principal said, "Oh...they're nobody."

The principal could have said, "They are maintenance men" or given them any title, but not, "They're nobody." We could think of Jesus, who worked with his hands as a carpenter, setting in the room when the school principal came in. She probably would have looked at him and said, "He's nobody."

We should thank God that he doesn't consider his children as nobodies. Chapter 7 reveals to us how important we stand in God's eyes. He seals and protects his own and helps them stand against the forces of evil in this world.

In chapter 6, we saw the Devil's kingdom persecute the Christian Church. God in his mercy and love added an important element to the second vision. After these things indicates an elapse of time or something new. As the first part of the vision faded away, Jesus began a new theme. The Lord wanted to tell his children that he's still on the Throne, and that he's still in control of their destinies.

> ¹And after these things I saw four angels standing on the four cor-
> ners of the earth, holding the four winds of the earth, that the
> wind should not blow on the earth, nor on the sea, nor on any tree.
> ²And I saw another angel ascending from the east, having the seal
> of the living God: and he cried with a loud voice to the four angels,
> to whom it was given to hurt the earth and the sea, ³Saying, Hurt
> not the earth, neither the sea, nor the trees, till we have sealed the
> servants of our God in their foreheads (Rev. 7:1–3, KJV).

FOUR ANGELS

John saw four angels holding back the four winds of the earth. The winds came from the earth and blew over all the parts of the earth. The four winds caused some form of spiritual destruction as they blew.

The Lord revealed that he controls the natural and spiritual forces on the earth. These angels held back the winds of evil from Satan, who wanted to bring spiritual destruction to God's people with the winds.

Where the four winds come from isn't as important as what the Lord is doing in this picture. The angels hold the winds from blowing on God's children throughout the Gospel Age. In this postscript, Jesus goes back to the beginning of the Age to give his bondservants his seal of protection. *Another angel*...comes from the Savior with a message of mercy for each of us.

SERVANTS OF CHRIST

An angel comes from the East, or from the rising sun, to tell the four angels not to let the winds go. The angel tells them to hold the winds until the living God seals each of his bondservants. Who are the servants of God?

The word for *servant* (*doulos*) refers to Christians throughout the NT. Paul calls himself a (*doulos*) of Jesus Christ (Rom. 1:1).[1] Jesus calls John and the readers of Revelation his servants or (*doulos*) (Rev. 1:1). The NT contains at least seventy-five verses referring to Christians as (*doulos*).

> The notion that the 144,000 are literally fleshly Jews can exist
> only in those who are unaware that the church of Jesus Christ
> is the true and only Israel of God, beside which there is no
> other. The NT witness to this truth is extensive and over-
> whelming.[2]

The Lord has always sealed and protected his children. He saved Noah and his family from the flood that destroyed the earth. An angel brought Lot out of Sodom and Gomorrah when God destroyed the city (Gen. 19). God sealed and saved the Hebrew firstborn when the angel of death passed over their homes (Exod. 12).

MARK OF THE BLOOD

The God of Salvation told Moses to have each Israelite family slaughter a perfect lamb on Passover. They then took the blood from the sacrificed lamb and put it on the sides and the tops of their doors. The Israelite people then ate the lamb for their Passover meal. (Exod. 12:1–13).

God told Moses that he would pass through Egypt on Passover to kill the firstborn of both men and animals. The Lord promised Moses that when he saw the blood he would not let the death angel kill anyone. The destroyer could not cross the mark or the seal of the blood.

> [12b]I *am* the LORD. [13]And the blood shall be to you for a token upon the houses where ye *are*: and when I see the blood, I will pass over you, and the plague shall not be upon you to destroy *you*, when I smite the land of Egypt. [23]For the LORD will pass through to smite the Egyptians; and when he seeth the blood upon the lintel, and on the two side posts, the LORD will pass over the door, and will not suffer the destroyer to come in unto your houses to smite *you* (Exod. 12:12b, 13, 23, KJV).

The death angel killed the firstborn of each family in Egypt. The Israelites then left Egypt to go to the Promised Land. Israel marched away in full view of all the Egyptian families who were burying their firstborn (Num. 33:4). This reveals the other side of the Passover and the Exodus from Egypt. Millions of Egyptian mothers wept for their firstborn. Each family in Egypt lost someone to the destroyer. Our God's full of compassion and mercy, but don't trample on his grace and his people (Ps. 145:8).

THE OT COVENANT

God used circumcision as a sign to mark his people in the OT. God made an everlasting covenant of circumcision with Abraham. If anyone refused circumcision, he was cut off from the people and God (Gen. 17:9–14).

Abraham was 99 years old when God renewed their agreement (Gen. 17:1). God again told Abraham that he would have a child with Sarah, have numerous descendants, and become the father of many nations. The

Lord then told Abraham to circumcise himself, at 99 years, and all the males in his household (Gen. 17).

The God of Love used many physical signs to work with his people in the OT covenant. He used a physical sign on the flesh to identify his children. The mark of circumcision pointed to the NT seal and spiritual mark of life.

The Mark of Jesus Christ

Jesus gives us a mark of life and righteousness. He gives the spiritual mark by his shed blood through the power of the Holy Spirit. Jesus Christ anoints us with his seal of ownership and gives us the Holy Spirit to guarantee our salvation (2 Cor. 1:21, 22). God the Father adopted us as his children through Jesus Christ. Our Father forgives our sins and redeems us through the blood of his Son (Eph. 1:3–8).

God gives the Holy Spirit through Holy Baptism (Matt. 3:11; Mark 1:10). He seals us with the promised Holy Spirit that marks us and guarantees our salvation (Eph. 1:13, 14). God seals his saints to protect them against the spiritual forces in this world.

Our Father wants spiritual children to fill Heaven. In chapter 6, the slain souls under the altar ask the Lord how long until the end. The Lord, the angels, and the saints wait and wonder how long before the end. I think the Lord's ready for the end also. As soon as they reach the full number, the end will come. The Father sitting on his Throne probably asks, "Jesus are all the children home yet?" Then later he may ask again, "Son have all of our children come home?"

> **4And I heard the number of them which were sealed: *and there were* sealed an hundred *and* forty *and* four thousand of all the tribes of the children of Israel. 5Of the tribe of Juda *were* sealed twelve thousand. Of the tribe of Reuben *were* sealed twelve thousand. Of the tribe of Gad *were* sealed twelve thousand. 6Of the tribe of Aser *were* sealed twelve thousand. Of the tribe of Nepthalim *were* sealed twelve thousand. Of the tribe of Manasses *were* sealed twelve thousand. 7Of the tribe of Simeon *were* sealed twelve thousand. Of the tribe of Levi *were* sealed twelve thousand. Of the tribe of Issachar *were* sealed twelve thousand. 8Of the tribe of Zabulon *were* sealed twelve thousand. Of the tribe of Joseph *were* sealed twelve thousand. Of the tribe of Benjamin *were* sealed twelve thousand (Rev. 7:4–8, KJV).**

144,000—TRUE CHURCH OF GOD

John heard the number of 144,000 people sealed to the Lord. Who were the 144,000? Some Christians have believed that they represent the twelve tribes of Israel. If this were the true Israel, then why did these things happen?

The identity of ten tribes disappeared several hundred years before Jesus Christ. Judah and Benjamin, the last two tribes, lost their national identity when Jerusalem fell to the Romans in A.D. 70. The Lord omitted the tribes of Ephraim and Dan and counted Manasses twice through Joseph.

> The 144,000 of the first consolatory vision represent not Jewish Christians only but the whole body of believers....The number "12," a sacred number of religious significance, is first multiplied by itself and then by a thousand, the number used to signify completeness. The resultant 144,000 is used to represent absolute completeness.[3]

The 144,000 symbolize the total number of God's people throughout the ages. God sealed his people in both the OT and the NT. God reveals his mercy by the sealing of the 144,000. The Lord wants to protect his children from the spiritual forces of darkness coming in later chapters.

THE SEAL OF HOLY BAPTISM

The Almighty God seals his children by Holy Baptism, the Word of God, and faith. The power in baptism doesn't come from anything we do. The power in Holy Baptism comes from God working through the water and the Word (Gal. 3:26, 27). The Holy Spirit goes into a child when he's baptized in the name of the Father, the Son, and the Holy Spirit. God then considers the baptized child as one of his own. In a spiritual sense, we become his property.

My parents decided to have their children baptized when I was four. They took us four boys to church, and the pastor baptized us. We then attended Sunday school. My parent's decision to take us to church shows the leading of the Holy Spirit through the power of prayer.

HOLY BAPTISM SHIELDS FROM EVIL

God used Holy Baptism to seal and protect me from the forces of evil. Throughout my life, the Holy Spirit kept me away from occult influences. I never had any interest in horoscopes, ouija boards, or any form of witchcraft.

I walked away from God in the late teens and through the twenties, and yet he was always with me. Jesus continued to draw me to himself even when I didn't trust him for eternal life. Because my parents baptized me at an early age, I have a relationship with Jesus Christ today. Without the connection of Holy Baptism to draw me, I probably wouldn't have come to the Lord. I know how I thought and felt about life. I thank God and praise him for his everlasting love, grace, and mercy.

The Lord seals people through Holy Baptism. Many Christians believe it's important to have their children baptized as quickly as they can. The power from baptism comes from God's grace and the work of the Holy Spirit, not from our own works. Jesus commanded us to go, to teach, and to baptize all nations. The all in nations include the children (Matt. 28:19).

CIRCUMCISION—HOLY BAPTISM

Christians believe that Holy Baptism in the NT replaces circumcision in the OT. Paul says that Christ himself circumcises us. God buries us with him in baptism, and we rise with him through faith (Col. 2:11, 12). This points toward baptism replacing OT circumcision.

Abraham circumcised himself and his people by faith. The sign of circumcision gave him a seal and covenant by faith. They circumcised themselves as adults because it was a new covenant from God. This made Abraham the father of all who walk in faith (Rom. 4:9–12).

After the initial circumcision, they circumcised baby boys on the eighth day of life. They didn't wait until adulthood because God considered circumcision a seal or sign. They only circumcised once. They did not recircumcise themselves as adults. When the Creator saw the circumcision, he considered the people his.

They baptized the adults in the name of the Father, the Son, and the Holy Spirit at the beginning of the NT covenant. In the early Church, they baptized adults because it was a new command as circumcision was a new command when it began.

Because the Holy Spirit works through Holy Baptism as a pledge to God, it only works once (1 Pet. 3:21). God recognizes my baptism as a young child, and I was never baptized again. Nevertheless, the Holy Spirit lives in me, and Jesus lives in me through the Holy Spirit.

The Bible revealed that they baptized everyone in the families (Acts 16:15). Not everyone in each family had accepted the Lord at the same time. Therefore, they must have baptized many people in the households who had not committed their life to Jesus Christ. This indicated that God wanted people and children baptized as a sign or seal to him. They baptized by faith and by the command of Jesus (Matt. 28:19).

Because Abraham circumcised babies by faith, we also baptize our children by faith. Jesus seals us with the Holy Spirit that comes from his power working within us from Holy Baptism.

PAUL BAPTIZED THE CHILDREN

Paul and Silas were in jail when an earthquake shook open the prison doors (Acts 16:26). After the earthquake, the jailer thought the prisoners had escaped and prepared to kill himself. Paul told the jailer not to kill himself because they had not escaped.

> [30]And brought them out, and said, Sirs, what must I do to be saved? [31]And they said, Believe on the Lord Jesus Christ, and thou shalt be saved, and thy house. [32]And they spake unto him the word of the Lord, and to all that were in his house. [33]And he took them the same hour of the night, and washed *their* stripes; and was baptized, he and all his, straightway (Acts 16:30–33, KJV).

Paul baptized all the members of the jailer's family. The word *all* includes his children. God sealed the jailer and his whole family that night when they were baptized. The jailer committed his life to Jesus Christ, but not every family member accepted Jesus as their personal Savior that night. The Holy Spirit brings members of a family to salvation one by one. Nevertheless, Paul baptized everyone whether they believed or not. This indicates that the Lord also wants us to baptize our children.

In Acts 2:38, Peter told the people to repent and be baptized. In verse 39, he said the promise was for them and for their children also.

Our Father of Love uses the power of the Holy Spirit through Holy Baptism to protect us from evil. Infant baptism is important to your children. The Holy Spirit lives in each of them and helps keep them in the family of God.

Holy Baptism begins the sealing process for many people. Baptism works, together with the Word and faith, to seal us unto the Lord. Baptism gives us the Holy Spirit, which guarantees us an inheritance of redemption from spiritual death (Eph. 1:13, 14). Infant baptism helps bring us to the Lord. Nevertheless, everyone as an adult remains responsible for his or her personal salvation through Jesus Christ.

[9]After this I beheld, and, lo, a great multitude, which no man could number, of all nations, and kindreds, and people, and tongues, stood before the throne, and before the Lamb, clothed with white robes, and palms in their hands; [10]And cried with a loud voice, saying, Salvation to our God which sitteth upon the throne, and unto the Lamb. [11]And all the angels stood round about the throne, and *about* the elders and the four beasts, and fell before the throne on their faces, and worshipped God, [12]Saying, Amen: Blessing, and glory, and wisdom, and thanksgiving, and honour, and power, and might, *be* unto our God for ever and ever. Amen (Rev. 7:9–12, KJV).

THE FEAST OF INGATHERING

Jesus again shows us a different scene of an unnumbered multitude of people standing before the Throne and the Lamb. No man can count the number of people because there are so many. Only the Lord can keep track of that mass of humanity. They come from every nation, every ethnic background, and every class of people on earth. God does not miss any of his children: he makes a list and counts it twice.

This scene shows us the victory and celebration of God's saints who come through the tribulation. We see the joy of Christians in Heaven after enduring trials through their life on earth. This reflects God's company of people that make up his universal Church from the OT and the NT. The Bible gives us the hope of eternal life. This scene reveals the result of our hope.

These verses pictured the OT Feast of Tabernacles or feast of the ingathering (Exod. 23:16; Lev. 23:34–36). The Israelites celebrated the harvest of their crops in this feast each year. The feast lasted seven days, and they lived in booths made of tree and palm branches. The celebration also reminded them of their deliverance from Egypt when they lived in tents.

All Israel looked forward to the ingathering of the harvest because they celebrated with festive joy. The harvest feast pointed to Heaven where the saints celebrated the joyous ingathering of God's children. In these verses, they gave thanks, praise, and honor to the Almighty for his love and grace of Salvation.

WELCOME TO HEAVEN

Our Father forgives our sins if we ask him in the name of Jesus Christ (Heb. 9:24–28, Eph. 1:3–7). Our Savior redeems us by his death and

Resurrection on the cross. Salvation through the shed blood of Jesus Christ seems so simple. God makes us holy and gives us eternal life because he declared it so. We only need to accept the free gift and let the Holy Spirit guide us through the rest of our lives.

Some Christians try to help the Lord gain salvation through their works. Yet, we cannot earn salvation. The Almighty does want us to work in a church and serve him. Nevertheless, we should ask ourselves why we do it. Do we work to gain a higher place in Heaven, or do we work out of love for our Savior?

God gives us the opportunity and the choice to accept his gift of life. We should then trust him, obey him, and allow him to lead us in every part of our life. Some ask, "How do we commit our lives to Jesus Christ? We should repent of our past sin and decide to turn toward God. All one needs to do is say a prayer similar to this.

"Father, I know that I am a sinner and cannot save myself. I believe that Jesus died and rose again for my sins. Father, forgive me for all my sins in the name of Jesus Christ. I accept your gift of salvation. I want to live the rest of my life for you. I thank you for forgiving my sins and giving me life forever."

MERCY, GRACE, AND SALVATION

I looked beyond the daily sunsets.
I recognized my sin and poverty.
I saw the Lord's favor and love.
I recognized Jesus as Lord of all.
By his Light, I followed my path.
I closed my eyes at the last sunset.
The angels came and escorted me.
Glory to God—He let me in.

[13]And one of the elders answered, saying unto me, What are these which are arrayed in white robes? and whence came they? [14]And I said unto him, Sir, thou knowest. And he said to me, These are they which came out of great tribulation, and have washed their robes, and made them white in the blood of the Lamb (Rev. 7:13, 14, KJV).

An elder asked John who the people in the white robes were? John then gave the question back to the elder. The elder explained that the people came through the great tribulation on earth, and that Jesus washed their robes white in his blood.

The *white* (*leukos*) robes revealed the saint's purity and innocence.[4] The blood of the Lamb covered and purified their sins. Because the saints wore garments that our Redeemer made white, they could stand in the presence of Almighty God.

PUT ON THE FULL ARMOR OF GOD

The Lord offers us holy garments and powerful armor to help us through difficult times and tribulation. The Holy Spirit inspired Paul to write about one type of protection that the Lord gives us.

> [14]"Stand firm then, with the belt of truth buckled round your waist, with the breastplate of righteousness in place, [15]and with your feet fitted with the readiness that comes from the gospel of peace. [16]In addition to all this, take up the shield of faith, with which you can extinguish all the flaming arrows of the evil one. [17]Take the helmet of salvation and the sword of the Spirit, which is the word of God. [18]And pray in the Spirit on all occasions with all kinds of prayers and requests. With this in mind, be alert and always keep on praying for all the saints" (Eph. 6:14–18, NIV).

Our Father wants us to understand that we don't need to fear the Devil's schemes. Paul recommends that we use God's Almighty power and put on the entire armor. The Word of God says we don't struggle against the people in this world. Our conflict comes from Satan's kingdom: rulers, authorities, powers of darkness, and spiritual forces of evil in the heavenly realms (Eph. 6:10–12).

The Lord encourages us to put on his full armor; not just part of it, but all of it. God's armor helps us stand against the aggression from the kingdom of darkness. The Bible says that we should do everything we can to stop the Devil's harassment. After this, we need to stand firm with all seven pieces of the armor on us and around us (Eph. 6:13).

Each item of the armor plays an important role in our protection. We may not understand what each does, but the Lord knows and acts upon our faith when we speak his Word. The Word will sprout and mature in our lives when we voice it (Mark 4:26–30). As the Word grows, our attitudes and actions change for the better. This results in Jesus Christ pushing the Devil away from us (2 Thess. 3:3).

PRAY FOR PROTECTION

Each morning after I wake up, I ask my Father to forgive me for my sins in the name of Jesus. I then say the Lord's Prayer and put on the full armor of God. For many years after I began to follow Jesus, I didn't do this. When I began to consider writing this book, the intensity of Satan's harassment increased. Our God of grace revealed through the Bible and personal experience that if I did this each day, my walk through life would stay on level roads.

I always start at my feet and work up to the top of my head when I put on the armor of God. I say, "I put on the Gospel of peace on my feet and the belt of truth around my waist. I put on the breastplate of righteousness and the helmet of salvation on my head. I hold up the shield of faith so that the Devil and his kingdom cannot touch me. I pick up the sword of the spirit so I can speak, think, act, and write the Word of God. I ask you, Lord, to keep me alert and help me to pray for everything and everyone that I should pray for."

I have more freedom in Jesus since I started repeating the Lord's Prayer and putting on the full armor of God every day. God says he will not let us be tested or tried by more than we can stand. He will always give us a way out (1 Cor. 10:13). The Lord's Prayer and the Armor of God give us two methods that we can use. They help protect us from troubles and desires of the world.

TOOLS FOR PROTECTION

The Almighty God gives us many tools in the Bible to use for protection. Automobiles of today have built-in safety for passengers. We call the protection seat belts. In order for a seat belt to work, we need to put it on or activate it. A seat belt does not help if we crash, and it rests on the seat.

Likewise, the full armor of God does not help us in a crash with demonic forces if we do not put it on. When we come into the Kingdom of God, the Lord gives us his armor. Nevertheless, most of the pieces of armor listed here need reinforcing.

From a personal outlook, I don't like to live on the edge of endurance day after day. I prefer praying ten minutes a day. This builds a spiritual hedge and helps me enjoy the marvelous freedom that our King of Glory gives. "Thank you, Jesus, for your tools of protection that give us freedom and peace."

> [15]Therefore are they before the throne of God, and serve him day and night in his temple: and he that sitteth on the throne shall dwell among them. [16]They shall hunger no more, neither thirst any more; neither shall the sun light on them, nor any heat. [17]For the Lamb which is in the midst of the throne shall feed them, and

shall lead them unto living fountains of waters: and God shall wipe
away all tears from their eyes (Rev. 7:15–17, KJV).

The multitude of God's children stand before his Throne. They...*serve
him day and night in his temple.* Because of their joy and thanksgiving to the
Lord, the saints worship and serve their God forever and ever. The *temple*
(*naos*) means "Holy Place or Holy of Holies where the Throne of the
Almighty sits."[5] The saints have every right to come into the Holy of
Holies where God is because Jesus purified them with his blood.

God Covers Us

This view of Heaven shows that all the barriers that separate us from
God are gone. God loves his people so much that he...*dwells* (*skenoo*) or
"spreads his protection over them."[6] He says no more hunger, thirst, nor
any sun or heat. The Lamb will feed us and lead us to living waters. We
won't need the sun anymore because the Light of the World will give us
light. God the Father...*shall wipe away all tears from* our eyes.

This picture of Heaven also points to the Kingdom of God here on
earth. God reaches out to each of us here on earth and spreads his tent over
us. He not only dwells with us: he lives in us by the power of the Holy
Spirit. Jesus prayed that we would be one with him and one with the Father
(John 17:21).

If we hunger and thirst for righteousness, Jesus fills us with spiritual
food and gives us living water here on earth. The Almighty gives us his
light and leads us to fountains of life giving water. He feeds us food and
gives us spiritual nourishment during our temporary life on earth. When we
shed tears, our Father holds us, takes our tears, and gives us peace.

Of course, trials and tribulation come, but someday we will stand in
victory before our God. After we will leave this earth, we will enter the
Glory of Heaven and stand with the King of Kings. All praise and glory to
the Almighty Savior. Hallelujah! Amen!

Notes

1. Servants, *doulos*, G1210. A slave or bond servant.
2. Coffman, *Revelation*, p. 147.
3. Summers, *Worthy Is the Lamb*, p. 150.
4. White, *Leukos*, G3022. Bright light.
5. Temple, *Naos*, G3485. A sacred place, sanctuary.
6. Dwells, *Skenoo*, G4637. To occupy, symbol of protection.

Chapter 8

Four Trumpets Bring Plagues

God's Protection and Grace

Linda and I spent an unscheduled night at the hospital in the fall of 1980. The next day we went to my brother's house. On the way, we stopped at the airport to look at the remains of an airplane my family and I had flown in the day before. As we drove up to the twisted wreckage of the Cessna 177, I was shocked!

I thought, "How could it be that the four of us lived." As I walked around the ball of scrap aluminum, I knew that the Almighty God had intervened. He sent his angels to protect us. Because of our Father's love and mercy, he saved my family from physical death and injury.

I have looked back at that moment as a point of change in my life. I further sought the will of Jesus Christ in my life after the airplane accident. He led me on a long walk of deeper understanding and faith. I had accepted Jesus as my Savior years before, but I knew the Holy Creator wanted more from me. I began the process of deeper commitment to Jesus after I realized how quickly life could end.

Mystery of the Trumpets

The crash of the Cessna 177 was a hard place in my life. The vision of the trumpets is a hard or a difficult place in the understanding of Revelation of Jesus Christ. I found chapters 8 and 9 the most puzzling part

"He has delivered us from such a deadly peril, and he will deliver us. On him we have set our hope that he will continue to deliver us" (2 Cor. 1:10, NIV).

"We wait in hope for the LORD; he is our help and our shield"
(Ps. 33:20, NIV).

of this book to research and write about. The spiritual resistance to understanding and writing about the trumpets was intense.

The Bible gives us pictures and principles that point to each trumpet. It helps us comprehend the trumpets when we look at the spiritual meanings of the OT stories and customs. If we pray for understanding and check the references, the Holy Spirit will help us discover the meaning of the trumpets. However, the trumpets remain mysterious and ominous. Yet, if we struggle through them, God will give us blessings and wisdom from the Bible.

Our Lord began the third vision of Revelation with chapter 8. The first vision showed Christ working in the midst of his churches. He sent letters to seven churches and told them what he wanted them to do.

In the second vision, we saw the Almighty God on his Throne. The slain Lamb was in the midst of the Throne. The Lamb opened six seals that revealed the attack of Satan on the Christian Church. Then our loving Father sealed his children. The third vision dealt with the trumpets, the mighty angel, and the two witnesses.

TRUMPETS OF WARNING

The people of the world have rejected Jesus Christ. God decided to blow some trumpets to call them into repentance. Trumpets in the Bible warned people to repent after they sinned or rejected God.

The Creator used trumpets to warn of coming dangers throughout the Bible. In modern terms, the trumpets compared to a hurricane warning system. Just as people prepared for a coming hurricane, they needed to act when God blew the trumpet. The Almighty required them to repent and turn to him, or terrible events would happen.

God gave us a picture of the trumpets in the OT. He told the prophet Ezekiel to tell his people to put a watchman in place. The watchman's job was to blow his trumpet when he saw the sword of death coming (Ezek. 33:3–5). When the people ignored the trumpet, they were responsible for their own death. If the people listened for the trumpet and responded, then they saved their lives.

God blows trumpets of warning throughout the Gospel Age. Our Savior gives salvation and love to people who respond. If people ignore the trumpets of warning, then our Savior holds them accountable for their spiritual end.

> [1]**And when he had opened the seventh seal, there was silence in heaven about the space of half an hour. [2]And I saw the seven angels which stood before God; and to them were given seven trumpets (Rev. 8:1, 2, KJV).**

SILENCE IN HEAVEN

John witnessed an unusual moment in Heaven. The Lamb opened the seventh seal: everyone in Heaven quit praising God and talking. Why the silence?

Out of the seventh seal came the seven trumpets. Everyone in Heaven waited in anticipation of God's future actions. In spiritual timing, John's vision happened moments after the Resurrection of Jesus Christ. The citizens of Heaven had just watched a vision of Satan's kingdom attacking the Christian Church. They waited in silence to see what the Creator would do.

Then the seven angels...*stood before God* and received the seven trumpets. The third vision showed us the truth of God's promises in the Bible. Out of mercy and love, our Father stretched out his hand of grace to the world, but much of the world rejected him.

> ³**And another angel came and stood at the altar, having a golden censer; and there was given unto him much incense, that he should offer it with the prayers of all saints upon the golden altar which was before the throne. ⁴And the smoke of the incense, which came with the prayers of the saints, ascended up before God out of the angel's hand. ⁵And the angel took the censer, and filled it with fire of the altar, and cast *it* into the earth: and there were voices, and thunderings, and lightnings, and an earthquake (Rev. 8:3–5, KJV).**

GOLDEN ALTAR IN THE OT

The Lord told Moses to build an altar of incense and cover it with gold. The golden altar stood in the Tabernacle before the Veil that led to the Holy of Holies (Exod. 30:1–8). Aaron or an appointed priest burned sweet incense on the altar every morning and evening as an offering to the Eternal God.

Once a year, on the Day of Atonement, the high priest sacrificed a goat and a bull for himself. He filled a censer full of burning coals from the golden altar and then took sweet incense and the burning coals into the Holy of Holies. The high priest burned the incense in the censer of hot coals. The smoke from the incense flowed over the Lord who hovered above the mercy seat (Lev. 16:1–14).

God accepted the offering and sacrifice from the high priest when the cloud of incense covered the mercy seat. Because God approved the offering, the high priest did not die when he came into God's presence in the

Holy of Holies (Lev. 16:12, 13). God considered the incense offering most holy to himself (Exod. 30:7–10).

GOLDEN ALTAR IN THE NT

Another angel appeared with a golden censer and stood before...*the golden altar*. The angel offered much incense...*with the prayers of all saints.* The smoke and the prayers...*ascended up before God out of the angel's hand.* In the OT, the incense offering was holy to God (Exod. 30:34–38). This indicated that the NT prayers of the saints are most holy to God.

The angel then takes his censer, and...*filled it with fire of the altar, and cast it into the earth.* What does the fire from the altar represent? It appears that the fire cast to the earth symbolizes the answers to the prayers of the saints. It's true that we see some form of judgment, but God sends many answers to prayers. What type of answers do we see?

TYPES OF PRAYERS

In 166 verses on prayer in the NT, I did not find any verses where Christians asked God to hurt their enemies. In contrast, Jesus told us to love and bless our enemies.

> But I say unto you, Love your enemies, bless them that curse
> you, do good to them that hate you, and pray for them which
> despitefully use you, and persecute you (Matt. 5:44, KJV).

NT prayers covered many types. Christians prayed for: salvation (Rom. 10:1); the spread of the Gospel and harvest of souls (Luke 10:2, Col. 4:3); other peoples welfare (Col. 1:3); new physical life for a person (Acts. 9:40; Mark 5:23); deliverance from persecution (Acts 12:5); and health and healing (James 5:14; 3 John 1:2).

Christians also asked God for these gifts: more of the Holy Spirit and boldness (Acts 4:31), knowledge of God's will and spiritual guidance (Acts 1:24, 11:5), for forgiveness of sin and wickedness (Acts 8:22–24), more love (Phil. 1:9), more peace, and to ask God to grant their requests (Phil. 4:6).

The prayers of the NT reveal the love and compassion of God for his children. The saints asked God for more love, more boldness, and more of the Holy Spirit. They asked for the qualities of Jesus. If our Savior sends fire in answer of our prayers, he must send the fire of the Holy Spirit to bring salvation and deliverance.

JESUS CASTS FIRE TO THE EARTH

After mixing the prayers and incense, an angel took fire from the golden altar and...*cast it into the earth.* What does casting fire mean? Jesus told his disciples that he came to bring fire to the earth, and that he wished it were already kindled (Luke 12:49).

The Holy Spirit came in tongues of fire at Pentecost (Acts 2:3). John the Baptist said that One coming after himself would baptize with the Holy Spirit and with fire (Matt. 3:11). God declared that his Word was like fire and like a hammer that breaks rock (Jer. 23:29).

The Lord continues to send the fire of his Word to the earth. Jesus does this by the power of the Holy Spirit. Many Christians associate the Baptism of the Holy Spirit with fire in their lives. The fire of Jesus gives them more boldness to speak the Word of God.

The prayers of the first Christians asked for the spread of the Gospel and for salvation of other people. They asked for heath, deliverance, and healing. Their prayers also asked for God's favor and more of his fire in their lives.

Therefore, the angel took...*fire of the altar, and cast it into the earth* in answer to our prayers. Our Savior has continued to send his fire of the Holy Spirit upon the people of the world. Our Father sent the fire of his love and mercy to redeem his children throughout the world. He desires that all come to salvation (1 Tim. 2:4). "Father, I thank you for the fire of your Love that you send to people when we pray for salvation and deliverance."

> **6Then the seven angels who had the seven trumpets prepared to sound them. 7The first angel sounded his trumpet, and there came hail and fire mixed with blood, and it was hurled down upon the earth. A third of the earth was burned up, a third of the trees were burned up, and all the green grass was burned up (Rev. 8:6, 7, NIV).**

Hail, Fire, and Blood

The trumpets parallel the seals. They each give us a different viewpoint of how God works with man on earth. The seals reveal the Lord's Church during the Gospel Age. The trumpets portray the people of the world and their reaction to the Lord.

The first angel blows his trumpet. The Lord sends...*hail and fire mixed with blood* to the earth. Our God of grace sends a warning of hail, fire, and blood to the people of the earth. What should they do with God's warnings that he sends over the Gospel Age?

On Pentecost, Peter quoted the prophet Joel and told the people that God would show wonders in heaven and signs on the earth. The Lord would show blood, fire, and smoke (Acts 2:19). Jesus sends the fire of his

Word to burn out the chaff from among his people (Luke 3:17). The fire of the Holy Spirit burns out false gods and carnal desires.

The Lord mixes the grace of his shed blood with the fire of mercy to cleanse us from all sins. The shed blood of our Savior calls for repentance, but not everyone will repent.

BURN THE GREEN TREES

Our Redeemer mixed hail, fire, and blood and cast it on the earth. This blend from the Word of God burned up...*a third of the trees.* What spiritual meaning does the Bible show us?

The Lord cuts down trees that don't bear good fruit and burns them (Luke 3:9). In the OT, green trees represented places where people worshiped other gods and idols. The people of Israel used the shade under oaks and poplars to sacrifice and burn incense to other gods and images (Deut. 12:2; Jer. 3:6).

> Then shall ye know that I *am* the LORD, when their slain *men* shall be among their idols round about their altars, upon every high hill, in all the tops of the mountains, and under every green tree, and under every thick oak, the place where they did offer sweet savour to all their idols (Ezek. 6:13, KJV).

The Creator hated the symbol of the green trees because they represented places where his people worshiped other gods. The Bible contained fifteen references to green trees as places of idol worship. In addition, the people worshiped false gods under other types of trees (Hos. 4:13). The Word of God also compared evil men to green trees and to...*green grass* that withers away (Ps. 37:2, 35; James 1:10).

Jesus even spoke of people doing things in the green tree as he walked up the hill to his death (Luke 23:31). Every word Jesus spoke during his last hours of life was like a signpost that pointed to a spiritual truth. God detested the trees where his children worshiped other gods. This indicated that he wanted to destroy the symbols for worshiping other gods in the Gospel Age.

HAIL STOPS LIES

Often, the fire of the Holy Spirit and the grace of his shed blood fail to move unrepentant men. Our Savior the Chief Cornerstone then mixes hail, fire, and blood to get their attention.

> [16]So this is what the Sovereign LORD says: "See, I lay a stone in Zion, a tested stone, a precious cornerstone for a sure foundation;

the one who trusts will never be dismayed. [17]I will make justice the measuring line and righteousness the plumb line; hail will sweep away your refuge, the lie, and water will overflow your hiding place" (Isa. 28:16, 17, NIV).

This verse says that hail will sweep away the refuge and lies. The Rock of Ages uses hail to help remove the lies of Satan's kingdom. The hail helps Jesus bring people to repentance.

ALTARS OF HARD ROCKS

Hailstones appeared hard as rocks and symbolized hard times when they fell. In the OT, the patriarchs built altars to God out of rock and stone. They did this when they experienced God's presence or something special happened. Abraham built several altars to the Lord after God spoke to him or helped him (Gen. 13:4; 22:9).

NT Christians build altars to God with the hard places of their lives. The grief and trials that we endure in this life strengthen our faith (James 1:2–4). The trials and hard places of life help prove our faith. Our faith, more precious than gold, stands long like the rocks of an altar (1 Pet. 1:6, 7).

HAILSTONES OF GRACE

God sees Christians as living stones built into a spiritual house and priesthood. The spiritual sacrifices or stones of their lives become acceptable to God (1 Pet. 2:5). I believe that the hail mixed with the blood and the fire symbolizes the hard trials of people. These trials come to both Christians and non-Christians whom the Lord calls.

In the first seal, Christ sends the Gospel to his Church in the world. In the first trumpet, Christ sends the Gospel to the world in a different way. Jesus sends the fire of his Word, the grace of his shed blood, then mixes in a few hailstones or hard trials to draw people.

Jesus reaches out with his Word and his grace to help people repent and turn away from sin. When people do not respond to his love and grace, the Lord permits Satan to send a few hailstones to get their attention. Depending on the situation, the hail may increase in size and numbers until the hard stones pound the person flat. The person then crawls bitterly through life, or he turns to God and repents. The King of Glory will then shower his new child with favor and love.

A MAN CALLED DESPAIR

Fifteen years ago I worked with a man I shall call Despair. In this true story, Despair was fifty-one years old when I met him. We worked together as plumbing partners for six months, and we talked about life and the Lord.

The Holy Spirit gave Despair a special anointment when he was only fifteen years old. He lived in southern California and attended Pentecost Churches. The Lord called him into a preaching and healing ministry at a young age.

Despair ministered during his teenage years in the late nineteen forties. He traveled to different churches teaching, preaching, and healing. Sometimes, the special services lasted several weeks. God used Despair to bless people in the churches.

DESPAIR QUIT GOD

Because Despair was away from his family most of the time and didn't have any friends, he felt lonely. Despair told God that he didn't want to minister anymore at the age of twenty-one. He quit God!

Despair married, raised six children, drank much, and worked as a plumber. He told me that for the first fifteen years he kept thinking about returning to the ministry. He sometimes attended church during that time. When Despair quit going to church, the problems started.

He came from a large family of nine brothers and sisters. Three of his children and two of his brothers died in an automobile accident. Two years later he lost another child in a boating accident because they didn't use life preservers. When I met Despair, his wife has recently died from a heart problem. Over the months, he told me about many other problems that had confronted him in most areas of his life.

Despair didn't speak with love toward God—slowly his story emerged. The Lord led me to pray for him after we met. When I began to bind the power of Satan in his life, I struggled against strong resistance.

Over the months as I worked with him, Despair began to change. His bitterness seemed to retreat. He told me that the Bible was beginning to make sense again. One day he quit his job and went back to California. I have not heard from him or seen him since.

The God of Revelation involved me in this tragic story for some purpose. I don't know if Despair went back into some form of ministry or to church, but I believe that he was walking on the right path when he left. I shudder when I think how cruel life can be.

Our Father loves his children, but there's another side to him. A person invites much trouble into his life when he or she says yes to God and then takes back the yes. Then comes the hail of destruction. When a man or woman disobeys God, they step away from God's cover of protection.

The destroyer lurks in the shadows and waits for a nod from the Almighty (Job 1:6–12).

> **8And the second angel sounded, and as it were a great mountain burning with fire was cast into the sea: and the third part of the sea became blood; 9And the third part of the creatures which were in the sea, and had life, died; and the third part of the ships were destroyed (Rev. 8:8, 9, KJV).**

THE DESTROYING MOUNTAIN

The second trumpet compares with the second seal because outside forces attack people. Satan's kingdom attacks God's people and slays them with the sword in the second seal. Forces from the burning mountain, the second trumpet, cause the death of many people in the world. Jeremiah calls Babylon the...*great mountain burning with fire.*

> 24"Before your eyes I will repay Babylon and all who live in Babylonia for all the wrong they have done in Zion," declares the LORD. 25"I am against you, O destroying mountain, you who destroy the whole earth," declares the LORD. "I will stretch out my hand against you, roll you off the cliffs, and make you a burned-out mountain" (Jer. 51:24, 25, NIV).

BABYLON REFLECTS EVIL

God detested Babylon, and he hated what she stood for (Jer. 50:23–32). Babylon represented the evil that controlled people's actions and beliefs. She was an evil country that attacked and burned Jerusalem and the Temple. Babylon then took the people captive to another country (2 Kings 25:9). She oppressed the people and left Judah as a wasteland for 70 years (Jer. 25:11).

Babylon destroyed the people's access to God when she attacked Judah and burned the Temple. The Israelites worshiped and sacrificed to the One God at their Temple. In Babylon, the Israelites didn't have a Temple for worship. The Babylon authorities took away their ability to worship their God.

Jeremiah described Babylon as a country that influenced the whole earth. God told his people to flee out of Babylon so they would live. Jeremiah called Babylon the golden cup that made the nations act like a madman (Jer. 51:6,7). *Babylon (Babel)* meant "confusion."[1] Throughout the Bible, she has confused and drawn people away from God.

God worked through the Law and in the physical environment in the OT to develop a relationship with his people. God developed a relationship through spiritual qualities in the NT. Babylon attacked Israel by physical means in the OT.

The spiritual Babylon has attacked people in the spiritual environment for the NT. Babylon of the Gospel Age has symbolized the evil and corruption from Satan and his kingdom of darkness. Therefore, the great mountain...*cast into the sea...* described the powers of Satan attacking people in the world.

SEA POINTS TO PEOPLE

John conveyed the idea that the sea and the waters represent peoples, nations, and governments (Rev. 17:15). The verses in Revelation containing "sea" represent people and nations. The Devil comes down to the sea (12:12), then the beast comes out of the sea (13:1). Every living soul dies in the sea (16:3).

The verse 20:13 gives us an interesting concept. In the final judgment, only death and hell and the sea give up their dead. Where are all the dead who die on the land? Most people in the world die on land. The final judgment of chapter 20 does not mention the billions of people who rest on land. Therefore, the sea in Revelation appears to symbolize the nations of the world.

The second trumpet pointed to spiritual Babylon thrown into the sea of people and nations. One third of the *creatures* (*ktisma*) in the sea who...*had life, died.*[2] James 1:18 used creatures (*ktisma*) to indicate our creation as firstfruits. John used (*ktisma*) as all created beings, including men who praise the Lord (Rev. 5:13). It appeared that the creatures that died in the sea describe people in the sea of nations.

BABYLON SHED BLOOD

The life of a person or creature came from the blood in the OT covenant (Lev. 17:11). The sea that Babylon turned to blood gave us a picture of spiritual death in the NT covenant. People died a spiritual death when they continued to sin and worship other gods (Rom. 8:13). Because they worshiped other gods, the people died from their sins in both physical death and spiritual death. Therefore, Babylon polluted the sea of people by turning a...*third part of the sea became blood.* One-third part indicated that Babylon caused spiritual death for the entire Gospel Age.

The burning mountain destroys a...*third part of the ships.* The word *destroys* (*Diaphtheiro*) means "to corrupt or to change for the worse the mind and morals."[3] John uses ships to indicate the commerce of the world. The commerce gives us a picture of business, trade, and social relationships.

Babylon corrupts moral values, business honesty, and family importance. John shows us a picture of the corruption, decline, and death for one third of the people and nations. He reveals that corruption and spiritual death comes from Babylon. The powers of darkness assault the sea of nations throughout the Gospel Age.

The spiritual mountain of destruction fell on people and nations around the world. Babylon, indicating the evil of the Devil, polluted the people. They worshiped the creation instead of the Creator. Babylon enticed many people to worship money, success, power, sex, and self instead of Jesus Christ.

Worship the Creation (Rom. 1)

Our Majestic King shows his Infinite Spirit.
The Creator reveals himself by his creation.
Men and women know God, but deny him.
People think themselves wise, yet are fools!
They exchange God's glory for his creation.
God lets unholy desires rule their thoughts.
Men and women plunge into lust and greed.
They hate God—they run for the fires of hell!

[10]**And the third angel sounded, and there fell a great star from heaven, burning as it were a lamp, and it fell upon the third part of the rivers, and upon the fountains of waters; [11]And the name of the star is called Wormwood: and the third part of the waters became wormwood; and many men died of the waters, because they were made bitter (Rev. 8:10, 11, KJV).**

The third angel blew his trumpet. *There fell a great star from heaven*…burning like a lamp. Lucifer was the bright star that God cast to the earth (Rev. 6:13; 12:9). The star burned like a lamp because the Devil imitates the Light of Christ. Satan disguised himself as an angel of light (2 Cor. 11:14).

The *great (megas)* star, meaning "large in space or dimensions," points to a kingdom covering the whole earth.[4] (*Megas*) also refers to someone who oversteps God's bounds and with pride and arrogance tries to lower the Majesty of God:

TEST FOR UNFAITHFULNESS

The priests of the OT used bitter water to test a wife for unfaithfulness (Num. 5:11–31). When a husband suspected his wife of sleeping with another man, the priest required the wife to stand before the Lord. She had to swear with an oath that she had not cheated on her husband. Then the wife drank holy water with dust in it.

The holy water turned bitter if she had lied. This caused her thigh to rot and her abdomen to swell. If she told the truth, her thigh never wasted away, and her belly never swelled. This gave us a picture of the suffering that the bitter waters bring to the people of the world from the burning star.

> [27]If she has defiled herself and been unfaithful to her husband, then when she is made to drink the water that brings a curse, it will go into her and cause bitter suffering; her abdomen will swell and her thigh waste away, and she will become accursed among her people. [28]If, however, the woman has not defiled herself and is free from impurity, she will be cleared of guilt and will be able to have children (Num. 5:27, 28, NIV).

BITTER WATERS OF LIFE

God feeds wormwood to his people when they don't follow his laws. The Bible uses wormwood eight times when it talks about people who worship other gods and live immoral lives. He forces them to drink bitter water when they worship the god of Baal (Deut. 29:18; Jer. 9:15).

The Bible calls God's people the bride of Christ (Rev. 19:7). Christians, as the bride of Christ, go through a test of faithfulness to Jesus throughout their lives. The type of water we drink in the spiritual realms determines the outcome of our life. We may encounter bitter waters and wormwood if we don't remain faithful to Christ.

Satan offers people in the world three things: the lust of the flesh, the lust of the eyes, and the boasting for self (1 John 2:16). Many people on earth follow the delight of their eyes and the desires of their minds and bodies. Lusting after greed and pleasure turns sweet water bitter.

The Lord gives his people Biblical principles to live by. When people live outside the Lord's boundaries, the consequences from their actions can lead to pain and grief. Lust and corrupt lifestyles lead to illness and death of the body.

Jesus gives his people living water: Satan gives his people bitter water. Jesus gives his people truth and light: Satan gives his people lies and darkness. Jesus gives his people freedom and life: Satan gives his people bondage and death.

SUICIDE BRINGS BITTER WATER

Most of the bitter waters go to the people who follow the Devil. Sometimes the God of Love permits the bitter waters to spill over onto Christian families. It's difficult to live as a teenager today. They have tremendous pressures from all sides. Their friends pull one way: their families pull a different way. Satan attacks our children, and sometimes he wins the battle over the child.

Satan loves to kill children and disrupt families. When a child gives up and takes his own life, he hurts his parents, family, and friends. Linda and I know a Christian family whose teenage daughter Diana cut her wrists and died.

Some Christians believe that if a person commits suicide, the person's lost. What matters most in this situation depends on what God thinks. We live in a state of grace from God (1 Cor. 10:13; Eph. 4:7). Sometimes Christians die because of sin of drinking and driving. If people eat excessively or smoke for many years, this can cause physical death. Few would say that dying from a disease caused by the sin of excesses would cause the loss of salvation. In God's eyes, sin is sin!

DIANA—CHILD OF GOD

The Scriptures say train a child in the ways of God, and he will not depart from it (Prov. 22:6). Our Savior says that if someone confesses him before others, then he would confess the person before our Father in Heaven (Matt. 10:32).

God promises much in the Bible, and our God of Truth always honors his promises. We don't always understand events in this world, but God remains faithful to us and to his Word.

Diana always picked her friends with care. Her spiritual life was important to her. Diana's true friends were teenagers who had a relationship with the Lord Jesus Christ. Diana felt in her heart that the Lord told her to take her life. She believed that she was going to be with Jesus in Heaven.

A young lady goes to church, has a relationship with God, gets good grades in school, and then shortens her life. What do we do with this, and more important what does God do with it?

PRAYER AND GRACE

Christians live in a state of grace by God's love and mercy. Our Savior understands the cries of our hearts. Our faithful God will not let us endure temptation that's more than we can stand (1 Cor. 10:13). The Almighty God seals each of his children: he won't let them go.

Because prayer has mighty power, I believe children similar to Diana end up in Heaven. Diana received many prayers in her lifetime. Satan cannot touch a child of God unless the Lord permits it. I don't know why this happened, but I know the faithfulness of Jesus Christ. Events happen in the spiritual and physical realms that we don't understand. When something like this happens, believers in God can only trust that everything's OK.

The act of ending your own life brings serious consequences to parents, family, and friends. Our Father loves each of us and gives us the grace to make our own decisions even if they seem wrong.

"**Lord, we thank you** for leading us on the right paths of life. We thank you for helping us to cope with the big problems of life. Help each of us not to sit in judgment, because we probably don't have the pressure that breaks others. Lord, protect us from the powers of evil that try to destroy our life on earth. Thank you, Lord, for your wondrous grace, love, and mercy. Amen!

> [12]**The fourth angel sounded his trumpet, and a third of the sun was struck, a third of the moon, and a third of the stars, so that a third of them turned dark. A third of the day was without light, and also a third of the night.** [13]**As I watched, I heard an eagle that was flying in midair call out in a loud voice: "Woe! Woe! Woe to the inhabitants of the earth, because of the trumpet blasts about to be sounded by the other three angels"** (Rev. 8:12, 13, NIV)!

Darkness and Light

The fourth trumpet affected light. The angel *struck* (*plesso*) the sun, moon, and stars, meaning "to pound flat or to inflict with calamity."[5] It appeared that Jesus gave us a picture of the Devil pounding or pushing light aside with darkness (Acts 26:18; 2 Cor. 4:4). People who have followed Satan's values have lived in spiritual blindness and darkness (Isa. 42:16). People without God have not understood the Light of Salvation.

A person could not describe sunlight if they lived their whole life in a cave and never saw the sun. They wouldn't understand the gentle warmth, the life-giving qualities, and the cleansing ability of the rays of sunlight. People who reject Christ live in darkness. They cannot understand or describe him. They don't know about his gentle love, his life-giving nature, and his willingness to cleanse us from all sin.

Yes, the Devil desires to keep us in darkness. The prayers of Christians will help lift the darkness from people. Prayers bring the Holy Spirit who reveals the Light of the World. Jesus Christ calls himself the Light of the World (John 8:12). After a person begins to sense the Light, the Living God will then draw him or her to himself (John 12:32).

DESOLATION OR ABUNDANCE

A few years ago, Linda and I went on a vacation through Yellowstone National Park. We saw the beauty and the grandeur of that part of this wonderful country. We then drove through southern Idaho on the way back to Oregon. We traveled about 100 miles through a wasteland of lava flows. In many places, the grass didn't even grow.

We can compare the majesty of the mountains in and around Yellowstone Park with the desolation of a lava wilderness. This parallels the difference between living in spiritual light and living in spiritual darkness. One place gives us a productive place to live, while the other deprives us of the necessities of life. To live in the light and the love of Jesus Christ will last forever. To live in the darkness of this world lasts a lifetime, then misery comes and lasts forever.

GOD LOVES THE CHILD

Around the world, there's an ongoing genocide. People are killing God's children. The medical profession calls them fetuses: our Heavenly Father calls them his precious children.

The prophet Jeremiah confirmed that God considers each of us a real person when we begin life. God told Jeremiah that he knew him before he formed him in the womb (Jer. 1:4, 5, NIV). Each child, living in the mother's womb, desires life just as much as any adult. (Matt. 6:22, 23).

We are all children of the Heavenly Father, and the spirit within us longs to have fellowship with the Father. God gives each of us a spirit when he molds us in the womb. Emmanuel, God with us, loves his children: he doesn't want to see them murdered before birth. These children will never have the opportunity to mature. They will never get married and have babies of their own. They will never have the chance to serve God and work out their lives of destiny.

Jesus Christ wept when the people of Jerusalem didn't recognize him (Luke 19:41). I believe he weeps today each time someone sacrifices one of his little ones.

People abort their children for many reasons: for convenience, for financial reasons, for birth control, because they are young, or because they are afraid and don't know any better. Regardless of the reasons, the God of Love weeps for each of the unborn children. The child will never have the chance to make an impact in the Kingdom of Heaven.

Satan's the reason for throwaway children. He loves to kill and destroy. If he can kill a child in the womb, that child will never be a threat to him. If the child grew up and learned how to pray, the Devil would lose many people to the Lord. The murdered children will never have the privilege to walk the path of life that God gives him or her.

Woe—Woe—Woe

John watches an eagle cry...*Woe! Woe! Woe to the inhabitants of the earth.* Woe (*ouai*) stands for "an exclamation of grief."[6] The eagle expresses grief for the people of the earth because the next trumpet comes.

In this vision, John had already witnessed one third of the earth touched by fire, blood, and hail. He saw a mountain of fire turn the sea into the blood of death. John saw a burning star that turned sweet waters into bitter waters. Then one third of the light turned into darkness. Yet, the eagle cried Woe! Woe! Woe! Because more devastation comes.

Notes

1. Babylon, *Babel*, H894. Confusion, babylonia.
2. Creatures, *ktisma*, G2938. Thing founded, created thing.
3. Destroy, *diaphtheiro*, G1311. Destroy, corrupt, ruin. To change for worse minds and morals.
4. Great, *megas*, G3173. Great, large in space, authority, power.
5. Struck, *plesso*, G4141. To pound or flatten. To inflect with calamity.
6. Woe, *ouai*, G3759. Woe, exclamation of grief.

CHAPTER 9

The Fifth and Sixth Trumpets

MORE THAN ENOUGH

Several years ago, I went to the pantry to get some honey out of a two-quart plastic jug. I noticed that the lid was missing from the honey jug. When I picked the container up, I saw two large mice floating in the honey. I wondered how they had taken the lid off. I looked on the shelf and saw yellow grains of plastic and the round center of the lid.

The hungry mice chewed through the cap on the jug. The mice desired the sweet honey so much that they spent hours chewing a way into the forbidden honey. They then crawled through the opening and dived into the honey to their destruction. When I inspected the mice, they appeared to have a smile on their faces.

This true story illustrates how Satan uses lust and craving to entice people into hazardous situations. The fifth and sixth trumpets continue the same spiritual theme as the first four trumpets. Satan continues to attract unsuspecting people into lifestyles of havoc. The two trumpets increase the severity of God's judgment on godless people. Yet, the Lord still desires that people repent and turn to him.

TRUMPETS AND SEALS ARE SIMILAR

The first seal shows us Christ proclaiming the Gospel. Satan then attacks the Christian Church in the second, third, and forth seals. The fifth and sixth seals show us the result of the first four seals by revealing the Christian martyrs and the world's end.

In the first trumpet, Jesus proclaims the Gospel with the fire of the Holy Spirit and the grace of his blood. He sends the hail of tribulation when people don't respond to his grace and love. The second trumpet, Babylon, leads people away from God.

The third trumpet revealed Satan falling as the burning star. The Devil and his fallen angels attacked the people of the world with deception and darkness. The fourth trumpet covered the earth in spiritual darkness. The fifth and sixth trumpets repeat the message of the first four trumpets, but from a harsher viewpoint. They reveal Satan's desire to destroy all the people in the world.

Our God of mercy and compassion sent the first four trumpets in answer to the prayers of his children (8:3–5). Satan responded by hindering God's salvation plan. When people craved darkness, God permitted them to follow their desires. The Creator allowed the results of their evil to bring forth misery and finally death to those who rejected God.

> [1]**The fifth angel sounded his trumpet, and I saw a star that had fallen from the sky to the earth. The star was given the key to the shaft of the Abyss.** [2]**When he opened the Abyss, smoke rose from it like the smoke from a gigantic furnace. The sun and sky were darkened by the smoke from the Abyss.** [3]**And out of the smoke locusts came down upon the earth and were given power like that of scorpions of the earth.** [4]**They were told not to harm the grass of the earth or any plant or tree, but only those people who did not have the seal of God on their foreheads (Rev. 9:1–4, NIV).**

Demons Bring Spiritual Darkness

John saw the star representing Lucifer, which...*had fallen from the sky to the earth*. He saw the same star in the third trumpet. They gave the star...*the key to the shaft of the Abyss*. For some reason, the Almighty God permitted Satan power to open and shut the Abyss. Jesus Christ broke the power of Satan's kingdom by his Resurrection from the cross. Nevertheless, our Savior granted the Devil and his horde of evil spirits authority to molest people on earth.

God put multitudes of fallen angels and demons in the abyss. Satan chose to open the door to darkness, evil, and deception. He proceeded to let out a swarm of evil spirits that looked like smoke. The smoke caused spiritual darkness to cover the earth. The metaphor for *darkened (skotizo)* meant "to darken the understanding of the mind."[1] The demons darkened the spiritual eyes of people so that they could not see or recognize the Living God.

God permitted Satan to give the locusts power like scorpions. The Almighty told the Devil to only attack people who didn't belong to God. The Eternal God protected his children from the scorpions and serpents. This picture pointed to a time when the Israelites wandered in the wilderness for forty years. God protected them from fiery serpents and scorpions (Deut. 8:15).

The Bible used serpents to symbolize Satan (Rev. 12:9; 20:2). In the Garden of Eden, Satan deceived Eve by using the form of a serpent (Gen. 3:1). God also used serpents and scorpions to punish his people when they worshiped other gods, or they didn't obey him (Deut. 32:24; Num. 21:6).

AUTHORITY IN THE NAME OF JESUS

Jesus told the seventy disciples that Satan fell like lightning from heaven (Luke 10:18). The Lord gave the seventy disciples authority to trample on serpents and scorpions. Jesus gave them authority over the Devil's power and said nothing would hurt them (Luke 10:19). The cross of Christ also gave us authority over the power of Satan, just as the seventy disciples had control over him.

Just before Jesus ascended to Heaven, he told his disciples that all power and authority was given to him. The risen Savior told them to go, baptize, and teach everything that he had taught them. They were to do this for all people and for all time. Jesus promised that he would always be with them and us until the end of the Gospel Age (Matt. 28:18–20).

AUTHORITY FOR TODAY

The authority that the early church had in the name of Jesus Christ remains active today. Jesus Christ lives in each one of us; he gives us power to tread on scorpions, serpents, and devils (1 John 4:4). The Lord said that when someone stronger attacks the strong man, then the strong man or demon will loose his place of abiding (Luke 11:21–23).

We sometimes encounter problems from Satan's evil angels in our walk through life. We have the right and the authority to command them to leave us alone in the name of Jesus Christ. When we use the name Jesus Christ, his name always has more power than any devil or evil spirit (Mark 16:17, 18).

The mighty strength of Jesus Christ lives in each of us and gives us authority over Satan and his kingdom (2 Cor. 13:3). A problem arises when people don't use their authority because of lack of knowledge of their place in God's Kingdom. We have dominion in the name of Jesus that comes from his Resurrection Power.

COMMITMENT AND OBEDIENCE

It's important to follow Jesus and ask forgiveness for our sins daily. The Lord gives each of us that same control over demons that the early disciples had when we walk in obedience to him. When a child of God lets one leg dangle in the world, he or she won't have their full authority in the name of Jesus Christ. Our Father gives us many spiritual gifts, and yet we need to work to apply them.

Suppose you believe that someone hid a box containing 10,000 silver dollars in your back yard. What would you do? Would you dig it up, or would you forget about it and leave it there?

Our Savior offers each of us a way for more peace, more happiness, and more fulfillment. All we need to do is speak, "In the name of Jesus Christ, I bind your power, Satan. I command your spirits and influences to depart from me and go to Jesus."

Our Savior gives us his authority (John 14:12–14). Our authority lies in a box unless we take it out and apply it in his name.

OUR HOME REFINANCE

Linda and I decided to refinance our home a few years ago when interest rates were low. We received a letter offering to refinance our home at a competitive rate. After checking the costs and loan fees, we met with a loan officer on a Friday evening to start the loan process.

We signed the application papers and left feeling good. We returned home, and I reread the papers. Suddenly, I realized that the man had neglected to tell us about a three-percent loan fee charge. They added on the extra fee above all the other charges from the company. The contract said that they would charge the extra fee for ninety days even if we applied somewhere else. Actually the man lied, because I had asked him if there were any other fees. He said no!

After coming off the ceiling, I began to pray! I bound the power of Satan and any spirits involved. I also asked my Lord to take care of the problem. By Sunday afternoon after praying on and off through the weekend, I felt peace about it.

We didn't call the company. We just waited for their letter, but the letter never came. The papers we filled out and signed must have fallen through a crack. We waited ninety days until the agreement had elapsed;

then we went to another loan company. Because the interest rate had dropped one percent and the loan fees were less expensive; we saved a large amount of money over the life of the loan. The Lord's so good, and he always answers prayer. Thank God, he answered this one immediately.

> **⁵They were not given power to kill them, but only to torture them for five months. And the agony they suffered was like that of the sting of a scorpion when it strikes a man. ⁶During those days men will seek death, but will not find it; they will long to die, but death will elude them (Rev. 9:5, 6, NIV).**

The fifth seal shows us the martyrs under the altar in Heaven. The fifth trumpet may then give us a glimpse of men's and women's future in hell where they...*will seek death, but will not find it.*

The martyrs cry, "How long, Holy and True Lord, before you judge out killers." The people in hell cry, "How long will you force me to endure this. I can't take it any longer: just let me die."

They give each of the martyrs a white robe and then tell them to wait a little while for paradise. They give the people in hell: more pain, more regrets, more bitterness, and more darkness—then they tell them to wait forever and ever!

Some people call this misery or despair. Spiritual life will never end. The Bible says we will go to Heaven or go to hell. God leaves the choice to each of us. When a person seeks after the things of the world and doesn't choose God, he has already chosen. If a person seeks after Jesus, he shall find peace, rest, and happiness.

SPARKLING WINE—NEW WINE OF THE SPIRIT

The Lord only gives us what's good for us. Jesus tells us that if we ask for a fish, our father won't give us a serpent; or if we ask for an egg, he won't give us a scorpion. Jesus goes on to say that our Father in Heaven desires to give us the Holy Spirit or new wine. The new wine of the Spirit gives us peace, joy, love, and wisdom in this life (Luke 11:11–13).

The vulture cries Woe for the people affected by this trumpet. One type of Woe gives sorrow and confusion when lingering too long over the red sparkling wine (Prov. 23:29–35). When someone gazes to long at the smooth tasting wine in his or her cup, it will bite like a serpent and poison the life like a scorpion.

Their eyes will grow red: they will see strange things. The smooth red wine will stimulate their heart to speak in perversion. They will say, "Last night I had a wonderful time. I dreamed I had a fight, but I wasn't hurt. Give me another drink!"

⁷And the shapes of the locusts *were* like unto horses prepared unto battle; and on their heads *were* as it were crowns like gold, and their faces *were* as the faces of men. ⁸And they had hair as the hair of women, and their teeth were as *the teeth* of lions. ⁹And they had breastplates, as it were breastplates of iron; and the sound of their wings *was* as the sound of chariots of many horses running to battle. ¹⁰And they had tails like unto scorpions, and there were stings in their tails: and their power *was* to hurt men five months. ¹¹And they had a king over them, *which is* the angel of the bottomless pit, whose name in the Hebrew tongue *is* Abaddon, but in the Greek tongue hath *his* name Apollyon (Rev. 9:7–11, KJV).

The Devil and the Locusts

John calls the fallen star and the king over the bottomless pit Abaddon (*abaddon* in Hebrew) and Apollyon (*apolluon* in Greek).² These words mean place of destruction, ruin, destroyer, Satan, or the angel prince of the abyss. The Lord gave us these names to confirm that the falling star symbolizes Satan.

Jesus gives the Devil's name in both Hebrew and in Greek to stress the Devil's authority and power of evil. Satan controls a vast army of evil forces in this world, and he can only use his authorized power when the Lord permits him to (Job 1:6–12).

John describes supernatural life in these passages. When we look at the description in verses 7–10, we see spiritual killing machines. They appear like an immense army that no one can stop. John represents the locusts as only designed to hurt and destroy.

The Devil uses his demons to display his power and give desire for unholy lust. He waits to deceive his victims. He then uses the deadly teeth to rip up the unaware. They wear breastplates for protection and make loud noises that freeze their victims with fear. Satan uses the...*tails like unto scorpions* to torment his victims as long as permitted.

The destroyer leads his vast army of demons across the land seeking men and women who can't defend themselves. The demon locusts give us a picture of the Devil's true intentions for the people of the world. As children of the Father, we should thank and praise God because he surrounds us with supernatural protection.

Joel's Vision of Locusts Is Similar

God gave the prophet Joel a similar vision to the vision that he gave to John. (Joel 1:4–2:11). At the time of Joel, an enormous plague of locusts devastated the land of Judah. The plague caused famine and drought on the land by destroying the crops and even some of the trees. After the plague of locusts, Joel then received a vision from God about the future day of the Lord. In both visions, the locusts symbolized multitudes of destructive spiritual forces.

> ⁶For a nation is come up upon my land, strong, and without number, whose teeth *are* the teeth of a lion, and he hath the cheek teeth of a great lion. ⁷He hath laid my vine waste, and barked my fig tree: he hath made it clean bare, and cast *it* away; the branches thereof are made white. ¹²The vine is dried up, and the fig tree languisheth;…because joy is withered away from the sons of men. ²⁹They shall run to and fro in the city; they shall run upon the wall, they shall climb up upon the houses; they shall enter in at the windows like a thief (Joel 1:6, 7, 12; 2:9, KJV).

In Joel's vision, the locusts destroyed the vine. The vine symbolized Israel in the OT and the Christian Church in the NT. Jesus told us that he was the vine, and his people who lived in him were the branches (John 15:1–6). By stripping the vine, the Devil stopped the flow of nourishment from Jesus to his branches or children. This brought spiritual decline and sometimes death.

THE LOCUSTS STOP TRUTH

The locusts in Joel's vision ruin the vine and destroy the branches. This gives us a spiritual picture of Satan's horde of demons stopping the Light of the Gospel. The Light of Christ can't penetrate into smoke covered minds; this stops life-changing decisions. Nonbelievers don't repent and turn to the Lord. The demons of smoky darkness compel heathens to continue living a life void of God.

The Devil's locusts slowed the growth of the fig trees. Joel's vision gave us a picture of the locusts stripping the bark from the fig trees so that they didn't produce leaves and fruit on time. The leaves and fruit indicated the children of God.

Jesus said the tender branches and new leaves of the fig trees pointed to the end of the Gospel Age (Matt. 24:32). Because the demon locusts keep people from coming to God, they slowed the return of our Savior. Jesus doesn't want to return until the full number of his children repent and say, "Jesus is Lord."

The Holy Father desires that all repent. Every time the Devil entices

a person away from Jesus Christ, this affects the person's family for generations. A righteous man or woman leads many children, family members,
and friends to the Lord. A man or woman, who rejects Jesus and holy living, drags many children, family members, and friends down the path to
destruction (Prov. 7:10–27; 15:7–11).

Locusts like Savage Thieves

Joel wrote that the locusts run over the walls and go into the windows
like thieves. Jesus called himself the Good Shepherd and said that the thief
comes only to steal, to kill, and to destroy (John 10:10). The demon spirits destroy people, families, and relationships with the Lord.

Revelation pictures dreadful beings designed to cause pain and distress. They can only attack people whom our Lord hasn't sealed. The lion's
teeth rip and tear the spiritual life of victims who don't have the seal of
protection. Satan lures and deceives his victims with riches, lust, and pride;
then he destroys without remorse.

Satan has always coveted the opportunity to put people in situations
where they have no hope and long for death. When Job was in anguish, he
cursed the day of his birth and wanted to die, but he would not curse God
(Job 3:1–26; 2:10). Job was righteous and knew the Lord; he loved his God.
Job understood that even in his misery, he was far better off than someone
who had riches and health but didn't have God.

The Spirit Takes Away Fear

God doesn't give us a spirit of fear. He gives us power, love, and self-
discipline (2 Tim. 1:7). These words mean less until someone experiences
a situation where fear could reign.

In the late seventies, we rented a home to a family that lived there two
years and left the place in poor condition. One evening I met the man at
the house to discuss the cleaning deposit return. Although the condition
of the home didn't justify it, I gave him a check for one-half of the cleaning deposit.

As the young man walked away, he turned to me and said, "I'm gonna
kill you!" Suddenly, the Spirit came over me. I ran up to him nose to nose
and said, "Go ahead and kill me, but if you do, I will go to Heaven, and you
will go to hell and burn forever."

The smile he had on his face disappeared and terror replaced it. He
turned and ran down the street. The Spirit of God that came over me must
have helped him also because he ran super fast.

This was an unusual incident. I have never enjoyed confrontations and yelling at people. The Holy Spirit gave me tremendous boldness that night. I had no fear. This has only happened once, but the memory still lingers.

God's Spirit gives unlimited power to people and causes them to do things that they would not normally do. When persecution comes to the Church, we hear many stories about how God supernaturally delivers his children, or stays with them to the end. God protects his children; therefore, we should have no fear in Christ Jesus.

> 12One woe is past; *and,* behold, there come two woes more hereafter (Rev. 9:12, KJV).

THREE WOES

The vulture cried, "Woe, Woe, Woe," at the end of the fourth trumpet. The first Woe, covering the fifth trumpet, showed us the Devil attacking the people of the world with millions of demons. The demons darkened people's perception of the Almighty God. This caused them to walk away from the Savior and go to their destruction and spiritual death.

The second Woe comes in Revelation 11 when Satan attacks the witness of the Christian Church. The third Woe comes in Revelation 12 when the great dragon or Satan is cast to earth with his fallen angels. The powers of darkness then attack the Christian Church and the people in the world. Each of the three Woes involves the spiritual and physical attack by Satan's kingdom on earth.

> 13And the sixth angel sounded, and I heard a voice from the four horns of the golden altar which is before God, 14Saying to the sixth angel which had the trumpet, Loose the four angels which are bound in the great river Euphrates. 15And the four angels were loosed, which were prepared for an hour, and a day, and a month, and a year, for to slay the third part of men. 16And the number of the army of the horsemen *were* two hundred thousand thousand: and I heard the number of them (Rev. 9:13–16, KJV).

EUPHRATES RIVER BRINGS EVIL

The fifth trumpet reveals Satan's spiritual attack on the men, women, and children. The sixth trumpet characterizes foul spirits and black-hearted people who cross the Euphrates River. They spiritually and physically interact with people to keep them from repenting and turning to God.

God promised Abraham that the land of Israel would extend to the Euphrates River, which set their north and east borders (Gen. 15:18). When David and Solomon were kings, the border of Israel stretched to the Euphrates River. The people of Israel thought of the Euphrates River as a barrier to keep their enemies away from them. Armies from different countries came across the Euphrates to attack Israel (2 Sam. 8:3).

The city of Babylon sat next to the Euphrates River. Babylon represented all that was evil in the world to the Israelites. Babylonian armies came across the Euphrates and devastated Judah and their way of life.

The king of Babylon took people from Judah to his country for seventy years. John wrote the Revelation of Jesus Christ to people who knew what was...*bound in the great river Euphrates*. The people of Judah remembered their captivity. The countries on the other side of the Euphrates River only meant evil and suffering to them.

Physical OT—Spiritual NT

The OT shows us a picture of the physical enemies of Israel crossing the Euphrates River to attack them. The NT covenant reveals spiritual enemies of God who cross a spiritual Euphrates River boundary. Our Father seals his children, and in a spiritual sense, he doesn't let the four angels cross the Euphrates to assault his saints. This also points to the four angels holding the four winds in chapter 7. Because people of the world don't have divine protection, the armies of darkness put them at risk throughout the Gospel Age.

After the sixth trumpet blows,...*a voice from the four horns of the golden altar* says to release the four angels held at the Euphrates River. They gave the four angels the mission of killing one-third of the men, women, and children on earth. I wonder if our unchanging and compassionate God will give these four angels special treatment at the end of the age?

They prepared the angels to *slay* (apokteino) men.[3] In a spiritual sense, (apokteino) deprives spiritual life, which leads to eternal separation from God. When these men and women die on earth, they end up somewhere away from God for eternity. Unlike the spiritual lost, Christians with God go to eternal bliss for eternity.

How Long Is an Hour

The words of Jesus and John's writing indicated what an *hour* (hora) meant.[4] Jesus told his mother that his (hora) or hour had not come yet (John 2:4). Our Savior told the woman at the well that the (hora) was coming when true worshipers would worship the Father in spirit and in truth

(John 4:21, 23). Jesus referred to an hour as the short time of his ministry on earth and also as the full Gospel Age.

They prepared the four angels for…*an hour, and a day, and a month, and a year.* This gave us a sense of a long period of time that included every part of time. The number four implies all times of the Gospel Age and covers all parts of the earth. This points to the release of the angels throughout the Gospel Age. No one can escape their influence unless they have the saving seal from our living God.

John hears the number of the horsemen. The number is higher than all the people who lived in the known world at that time. Jesus gives the massive number to John to show the power and the vastness of evil. Satan's kingdom, of sinister spirits and treacherous people has much influence in this world. The Christian Church only overcomes evil by prayer, testimony, and by the blood of the Lamb (Rev. 12:11).

God Brings Deliverance

Hezekeah trusted the Lord God (2 Chron. 32).
Assyria sent an army to destroy Hezekiah.
Multitudes came against Judah (2 Kings 19).
Assyria raged against the Mighty God.
God said fear not—we have more then they.
An angel of God visits the Assyrian army.
Morning comes—Behold, 185,000 corpses.
God's deliverance comes in the morning.

> [17]**And thus I saw the horses in the vision, and them that sat on them, having breastplates of fire, and of jacinth, and brimstone: and the heads of the horses *were* as the heads of lions; and out of their mouths issued fire and smoke and brimstone. [18]By these three was the third part of men killed, by the fire, and by the smoke, and by the brimstone, which issued out of their mouths. [19]For their power is in their mouth, and in their tails: for their tails *were* like unto serpents, and had heads, and with them they do hurt (Rev. 9:17–19, KJV).**

Demonic Horsemen

John saw millions of lion-headed horses with riders that burned like fire. The breastplates of the riders glowed like dark fire resembling sulphurous brimstone. The lion heads of the horses expelled fire, smoke, and brimstone out of their mouths as they rode across the earth. The fire, smoke, and brimstone brought death to one-third of the people in their path. What do these verses mean today?

God rained the same fire and *brimstone* (*theion*) on Sodom and Gomorrah that the fiery monsters erupted out of their mouths (Luke 17:29).[5] David, the king of Israel, said that the Lord will rain snares, fire, and brimstone on the wicked and give them a cup of horrible tempest (Ps. 11:6).

The fire-breathing creatures cover the land. They swing their tails to torment anyone without the seal of the Deliverer. God must permit the demonic horsemen to bring a form of spiritual judgment on people who reject him.

The creatures have power (*exousia*) or authority in their mouths and snake tails to oppress people.[6] The (*exousia*) gives the demonic spirits and people freedom of choice to act in authority. The Bible also uses (*exousia*) to describe the powers of spiritual darkness that fight against Christians (Eph. 6:12; Rom. 8:38).

The power and harm came from the beast's tails that...*were like unto serpents, and had heads.* The heads of the serpents spoke words of harm and deception. That old snake Satan tempted Eve with words in the Garden of Eden. The cunning serpent asked Eve, "Did God say?" Then the devil lied and said, "You shall not die" (Gen. 3:1–6). The serpent deceived Eve because God gave her a free will, just as he gives us an ability to say yes and no.

GOD HATES FALSE PROPHETS

The Bible came from the Holy Spirit as God moved men to speak (2 Pet. 1:21). Throughout the history of the earth, many false prophets and teachers have told lies and heresies that came from demonic horsemen. Those lies have caused millions of people to turn away from God. The false teachers today and in the past lived in moral hypocrisy because they opposed God's Truth and purity. They lived a lifestyle of lust, pleasure, and deception (2 Pet. 2:1–22). Many well-known cult leaders, who led their disciples to destruction, have qualified for this label.

The Lord hates false prophets who lie and live in wickedness. God says he will feed them wormwood and make them drink bitter water (Jer. 23:14, 15). Our Faithful God promises to deliver the souls of his people from the lies of the false prophets who pollute the Word (Ezek. 13:16–23).

Millions live in bitterness around the world. They don't have God's seal of protection. Men and women without God's grace live in misery from the bites of the serpent and the heat of the brimstone.

Our Father loves each of these people so much that his Son shed his blood for their salvation. Some Christians read these verses and say God is judging the evil people: give it to them, Lord. Many of the non-Christians in the world would commit their lives to Jesus if someone prayed for them, or witnessed to them. No, our Father doesn't want to give it to them. He loves them. The Devil gives them more then enough.

Does God Make Mistakes

It's a mystery to me, why the God of Power gives Satan authority to harass people and keep them away from salvation? I know that the Lord gives free grace, but as I learn more about him, I realize that there's another side to his nature.

> [15]For he says to Moses, "I will have mercy on whom I have mercy, and I will have compassion on whom I have compassion." [16]It does not, therefore, depend on man's desire or effort, but on God's mercy. [18]Therefore God has mercy on whom he wants to have mercy, and he hardens whom he wants to harden (Rom. 9:15, 16, 18, NIV).

God permits the sly old serpent to harass and persecute individual persons, families, communities, and sometimes nations. It seems that the God of truth and justice does this in the Scriptures and from events around the world. I love the Lord, but when I don't know all the circumstances, I sometimes wonder why?

I don't know all the reasons why God lets people live a life of misery on this earth and then lets them continue to suffer in eternal death. The Lord says in Scripture…*I will have mercy on whom I have mercy.*

Salvation Payment

The Savior desires that all people be saved and to understand the truth of God. There's only one mediator between God and men: this is Christ Jesus our Lord (1 Tim. 2:3–6). Jesus offers himself as payment for every person's redemption and salvation.

Our Father permits his chosen children to suffer trials and tribulation while on earth. Perhaps he allows Satan to harass non-Christians to bring them to a point where they will repent and accept Jesus Christ.

God is Sovereign and perfect. The God of all knowledge must withhold some truth from us, about his mercy on some people and his hardening against other people. As his children, we need to trust his infinite love and judgment in every situation that happens around us.

[20]The rest of mankind that were not killed by these plagues still did not repent of the work of their hands; they did not stop worshipping demons, and idols of gold, silver, bronze, stone and wood—idols that cannot see or hear or walk. [21]Nor did they repent of their murders, their magic arts, their sexual immorality or their thefts (Rev. 9:20, 21, NIV).

The rest of mankind...*still did not repent* of their demon worship, of their riches, and of their idols. *Repent* (*metanoeo*) means "to change our mind for better."[7] A person should feel remorse for past sin. In the NT sense, repentance means a complete turnaround of lifestyle. People turn away from sin and seek the Holy God. Repentance gives us understanding that we cannot save ourselves, but we can only cling to God's mercy.

CONTROLLED ACCESS

When we traveled through the lava fields in southern Idaho, we saw several signs per mile on both sides of the road. The signs read, "Controlled Access, Entrances restricted or prohibited."

The authorities of Idaho didn't want people wondering around on the hazardous Lava. The state placed the signs along the road to protect the public. When people obeyed the signs and stayed off the lava, they were protected from unforeseen danger.

Many people carry spiritual signs around their necks that say to God, "Controlled Access—Entrance restricted or prohibited." Because they don't understand the goodness of God, they don't want him living around them or in them.

The unrepentant people desire a life of...*worshiping demons, and idols of gold, silver, bronze, stone, and wood.* People of the world desire a life of pleasure from sexual encounters, drugs and drinking, gaining riches, and the possession of idols. Yet, when the Lord invites them to repent, they reject him.

People who lust after the pleasures of the world seem similar to the two mice floating in the honey jar. The mice loved the honey and enjoyed it for a short time. Then they perished.

NOTES

1. Darken, *skotizo*, G4654. To obscure in darkness. Metaphor means to darken the eyes, understanding, and the mind.
2. Abaddon, *abaddon*, G3. A destroying angel, ruin, name of the angel

prince of the Abyss. Apollyon, *apolluon*, G692. A destroyer, Satan.

3. Slay, *apokteino*, G615. Kill, slay. Metaphor, to deprive spiritual life and bring eternal misery in hell.

4. Hour, *hora*, G5610. An hour, day, instant, and a season.

5. Brimstone, *theion*, G2303. Sulphur, brimstone.

6. Power, *exousia*, G1849. Authority, privilege, power of choice, authority and influence over mankind.

7. Repent, *metanoeo*, G3340. To change ones mind for better, to feel remorse for past sin.

The Mighty Angel

⌒

OUR FAITHFUL GOD

Many people enjoy the sounds and sights of the seashore. Near the shore, we can hear the waves crashing into the rocks and see the foaming surf. The sounds of the waves roar day and night. The waves come and come and come. The perpetual waves illustrate the faithfulness of our God. Like the endless waves, our faithful Father stays with us throughout our lives.

Chapter 10, in the vision of the trumpets, gave us hope. We witnessed the power and evil of Satan. Now the Creator revealed that he controls all.

> **[1]Then I saw another mighty angel coming down from heaven. He was robed in a cloud, with a rainbow above his head; his face was like the sun, and his legs were like fiery pillars. [2]He was holding a little scroll, which lay open in his hand. He planted his right foot on the sea and his left foot on the land, (Rev. 10:1, 2, NIV).**

THE MAJESTIC ANGEL

John sees a...*mighty angel coming down from heaven.* What an awesome angel! He comes from heaven robed with the clouds, and a beautiful rainbow circles his head. His face shines bright like the sun; his legs appear as pillars of fire. Is this Jesus or an angel?

John's description points to this angel as Jesus Christ the King of Glory. Because the symbols portray the angel as our Savior, I shall consider the angel as the real Christ.

Clouds surround the angel. Jesus spoke of returning in the clouds in the Gospels. He told the high priest that in the future he would see the Son of Man sitting at God's right side. Then he would see him come in the clouds (Matt. 26:64). If God gave us spiritual insight like John, we would see Jesus at God's right hand clothed with the clouds of Heaven (Dan. 7:13).

SYMBOLS POINT TO CHRIST

A bright rainbow circled the head of Jesus (Rev. 4:3). In the Bible, rainbows symbolized God's covenant with the people on the earth. (Gen. 9:11–17).

The prophet Ezekiel saw the same God of splendor and power that John saw. Ezekiel saw a bright figure like a man on a sapphire throne. The being looked like glowing metal and fire with a brilliant light around him. The radiance appeared like a bright rainbow around the glory of the Lord (Ezek. 1:26–28).

The angel's face was radiant like the sun. The face shining like the sun gave us a picture of Jesus as the Light of the World. Jesus took Peter, James, and John to a high mountain and transfigured himself before them (Matt. 17:1, 2). They saw his face shining like the sun, and his clothes looked as white as light.

JESUS CONTROLS ALL

Jesus…*planted his right foot on the sea and his left foot on the land.* This illustrates Jesus as the Mighty One who had all power and all authority over the land and the sea. After his Resurrection, the Father placed Christ far above all things. He gave Jesus the highest power and authority of any being in the universe. God appointed the slain Lamb over everything and made him the head of the Church (Eph. 1:21, 22).

This image of the Lord, with his feet on the land and on the sea, shows us a Creator who controls the destiny of the world.

HOLY IS THE LORD (PS. 95)

Sing with delight to our Redeemer.
Shout praise to our Rock of Salvation.
The Lord made the dry land and the sea.
The heavens proclaim the Creator's glory.
Justice and honor serve as his foundation.

He is exalted far above all other gods.
Let us bow down and worship him.
The Lord reigns—yes he reigns.

³and he gave a loud shout like the roar of a lion. When he shouted, the voices of the seven thunders spoke. ⁴And when the seven thunders spoke, I was about to write; but I heard a voice from heaven say, "Seal up what the seven thunders have said and do not write it down" (Rev. 10:3, 4, NIV).

John calls Jesus Christ the Lion from the tribe of Judah (Rev. 5:5). The...*loud shout like the roar of a lion* again points to the angel as the Lion of Judah or to Jesus Christ.

THE SEVEN THUNDERS

God gave Daniel a vision about a future time when the mystery would be finished (Dan. 12:4–9). The Lord told Daniel to shut up the words and seal the book until the end of time when all will be finished.

The voice from Heaven told John not to write about the seven thunders but to keep the message secret. No one on earth knows what was in the seven thunders. The God of Revelation may have other truths that he has not given us. Paul experienced a similar vision, in which the Lord didn't permit him to speak all he saw and heard.

> ¹ᵇI will go on to visions and revelations from the Lord. ²I know a man in Christ who fourteen years ago was caught up to the third heaven. Whether it was in the body or out of the body I do not know—God knows. ³And I know that this man— whether in the body or apart from the body I do not know, but God knows— ⁴was caught up to paradise. He heard inexpressible things, things that man is not permitted to tell (2 Cor. 12:1b–4, NIV).

WE SEE IN PART

The Lord has infinite wisdom. The environment that surrounds us limits our understanding. The dimensions of height, width, depth, and time restrict our thinking. God transcends time; he can look forward and backward through time, while we cannot.

Paul says we look through a dark glass, and we only see in part (1 Cor. 13:1). Some people believe they know everything about God and the Bible. Either they have a pride of inflated self-importance, or they really don't know very much.

I used to think I knew much about the Lord. As I learned more about him, I realized how little I do know about him. No, the Lord has not revealed everything to us. We will learn many things when we cross over the great divide between the physical world and the spiritual world. The many questions of, "Why God?" will be answered.

It's not important what the seven thunders contained. The Bible is a complete book, and it contains everything the Lord wants us to know and understand. The Almighty wants us to trust his Word and not doubt.

> **⁵Then the angel I had seen standing on the sea and on the land raised his right hand to heaven. ⁶And he swore by him who lives for ever and ever, who created the heavens and all that is in them, the earth and all that is in it, and the sea and all that is in it, and said, "There will be no more delay! ⁷But in the days when the seventh angel is about to sound his trumpet, the mystery of God will be accomplished, just as he announced to his servants the prophets" (Rev. 10:5–7, NIV).**

THE MYSTERY OF GOD

Jesus Christ lifted his right hand and swore by the Almighty Creator that there would be no more delay. God swore by himself because there is no one greater. God made a promise to Abraham and swore an oath by himself to confirm it (Gen. 22:15–18). The oath was true because God cannot lie (Heb. 6:13–18).

Our Savior standing over the earth and the sea raises…*his right hand to heaven. And he swore*. This gives us an image of the God Jehovah who raised his hand with Mighty Power to deliver Israel from bondage in Egypt (Exod. 6:6–8, Ezek. 20:6). This points to the mystery of God when Jesus delivers us from the bondage of sin and death.

The angel Jesus Christ swears that…*the mystery of God will be accomplished*. The mystery brings the message of Jesus Christ as the Savior to all people even to the Gentiles (Rom 16:25; Eph. 3:3–6). This again shows us that each trumpet blows throughout the Gospel Age. The end will come after Jesus finishes the job of bringing all his children to salvation. Jesus spoke to his disciples about the mystery of God just before his ascension into Heaven. (Luke 24:45–47)

The prophets of the Bible gave many revelations about the mystery of God. In the OT, God chose the Israelite people for his promise of salvation. In the NT, God expanded his promise of salvation to the Gentile nations. Our God of grace made the Gentile people heirs together with Israel into one body through the promise of Jesus Christ (Rom. 11:25).

THE ANGUISH OF THE CROSS

Jesus Christ gave us a statement of his unending love by the mystery of the cross. God could have used other ways to give us salvation, but he chose the cross. Crucifixion was a symbol of shame and humiliation (Heb. 12:2). The Romans used the cross as an instrument of punishment to execute the worst and lowest of criminals. Death on the cross was the most cruel and degrading form of execution. The crucifixion of our Savior turned into an obstacle for the Jews because of its humiliation (1 Cor. 1:23).

As True God and true man, Jesus Christ knew what he would endure in the future. Just a few hours before his crucifixion, Jesus asked the Father if they could change the plan of salvation so he wouldn't die on the cross.

> [42]Saying, Father, if thou be willing, remove this cup from me: nevertheless not my will, but thine, be done. [43]And there appeared an angel unto him from heaven, strengthening him. [44]And being in an agony he prayed more earnestly: and his sweat was as it were great drops of blood falling down to the ground (Luke 22:42–44, KJV).

It was extremely difficult for Jesus to volunteer his body, mind, and spirit to the intense suffering of the cross. As he prayed, his sweat turned into blood because of the agony and the knowledge of his future suffering. Some people only consider the physical side when they think or talk about the cross.

During a crucifixion, the physical torment increases on a person until the body reacts by shutting down. Then the person passes out and dies. Jesus went through terrible physical pain, but it was probable less than the other agony. Something else happened on that first pre-Easter Friday. The Father withdrew from his Son!

> [46]And about the ninth hour Jesus cried with a loud voice, saying, Eli, Eli, lama sabachthani? that is to say, My God, my God, why hast thou forsaken me (Matt. 27:46, KJV)?

Jesus felt the horrible weight of our sins when he hung on the cross. We need to remember that Jesus Christ never committed a sin when he lived as a man on earth. Because God is Holy, it's an abhorrence for him to come into the presence of sin. Still, the Father permitted all of our sin and evil to rest upon his Son. It was more than any normal person could endure. The Father withdrew from his Son for the first time. Jesus was alone!

THE MYSTERY OF THE CROSS

Something happened on the cross that we cannot understand. Jesus endured a high level of pain in the physical, spiritual, and mental realms. The pain touched his whole being. The Father allowed Jesus to endure the consequences of our sins. Our Savior took our place when he felt the agony and the distress of the cross.

The cross indicated the mystery of salvation that man had sought since Adam's fall into sin. The grace of the cross gave the opportunity for all people to gain eternal life. The mystery of God points to the salvation of man through the cross (Col. 2:2–14).

Jesus Christ promises us that he will fulfill the mystery of God. After the last trumpet finishes, the Almighty will pass the final judgment on all people. Some will receive a glorious inheritance; others will receive what they don't want. The Lord swears this by himself: he cannot lie. The Creator guarantees us that his promises in the Bible are true.

"**Father,** we thank you for the gift of salvation that you offer us. Lord, we thank you that you reach down and draw us. Holy Spirit, we thank you for directing our walk on earth. We praise you for your everlasting love and kindness. Praise your Holy Name. Alleluia. Amen!"

> **8And the voice which I heard from heaven spake unto me again, and said, Go *and* take the little book which is open in the hand of the angel which standeth upon the sea and upon the earth. 9And I went unto the angel, and said unto him, Give me the little book. And he said unto me, Take *it*, and eat it up; and it shall make thy belly bitter, but it shall be in thy mouth sweet as honey. 10And I took the little book out of the angel's hand, and ate it up; and it was in my mouth sweet as honey: and as soon as I had eaten it, my belly was bitter (Rev. 10:8–10, KJV).**

The voice from Heaven told John to take the open book from Jesus. The Lord then told John to…*Take it and eat it*. He told his servant John that when he ate the book, it would taste sweet like honey, but it would seem bitter.

EAT GOD'S WORD

John revealed a picture of OT prophets who ate the Word of God. The Almighty told Ezekiel to eat a scroll and then go speak to the house of Israel. The scroll was full of lamentation, mourning, and woe (Ezek. 2:9–3:3). Ezekiel took the scroll from God and filled his stomach with it. He didn't just nibble on the scroll or Word of God: he consumed it completely. Like

John's scroll, Ezekiel's scroll tasted as sweet as honey in his mouth. Later the Spirit sent Ezekiel to speak the Word to the people of Israel. He went in bitterness and with anger in his spirit. (Ezek. 3:14).

The Word of God tastes sweet when people hear it. The Bible says that the Word tastes sweeter than honey (Ps. 119:103). When Jesus rides the white horse and proclaims the Gospel to his church, it tastes sweet like honey. Then the red and the black horses follow the Word of God. For some, persecution turns their stomach bitter.

Jesus says that when persecution comes, many will turn away from the faith (Matt. 24:10). A Christian should fill his mind, body, and spirit with the Word and not nibble on it. The Gospel helps to hold men and women near their faith when troubles come. Our Lord uses many women in his Church to help carry the faith and pray for their families.

WOMEN IN THE CHURCH

The history of women in the Bible reveals several contrasts. Men considered women their property in the OT. Even the Ten Commandments suggested this. The tenth commandment listed wives as property, which men should not covet (Exod. 20:17). Of course, men enjoyed their superior position, and they left women in a subordinate class.

God created man and woman together in the first creation example. The Almighty created man and woman in his image. The Creator created male and female in the image of God (Gen. 1:27). Because the Almighty created the man and the woman in his image, this makes them equal in God's eyes. Jesus Christ said that there are no sex differences in Heaven. We will appear like the angels (Matt. 22:30).

God created the woman from man in the second creation example (Gen. 2:22). However, the Creator said that man united with his wife and the two became one flesh (Gen. 2:24). It appeared that God created men and women equal before the fall of man. Mankind went into a long period of decline after Adam and Eve sinned. The Devil corrupted man's perfect nature that God had given them in the garden.

The Devil wants to keep people submissive to him and to each other. Because males were stronger than females, men began to dominate women. The Devil helped men control their wives and treat them as property. This attitude continued through the time of the flood, the OT, and until now. Some men of the world still want to control women.

JESUS LIFTED WOMEN

Jesus helped the status of women when he walked on earth. The Lord treated women with respect and not as a sub-male. Jesus talked to women, healed them, and responded to their needs. He also let them help him in his ministry. Martha complained because her sister, Mary, was listening to the teaching of Jesus rather than helping in the kitchen. Most men would have said, "Mary go to the kitchen." Our Lord and Savior said, "Mary has chosen the better things of life, and it won't be taken away from her" (Luke 10:38–42).

Jesus didn't lower the status of females: he only raised them up to a higher plane. Paul told us that there was no difference between Jews and Greeks, slaves and free people, and males and females for we are all one in Jesus (Gal. 3:28). Paul also used many women in his ministry to help support him. He considered them partners in the spreading of the Gospel (Rom. 16:1–5).

GOD USES AND LOVES WOMEN

The Bible used the word *prophetess* eight times for women, including Miriam, Deborah, and Anna. Philip, one of the seven, had four virgin daughters who prophesied (Acts 21:8, 9). The Bible listed many other women whom God gave gifts to. Paul listed prophets second in importance right below apostles (1 Cor. 12:28). From this, we understand that our Father used women in high positions in his Church.

The Lord used women in both the Old and the New testaments to help spread the Gospel even in the man-dominated society. God began the human race with men and women in separate but equal roles. As time passed, men forced women into a lower status than themselves. I suspect that wives of overbearing Christian husbands will receive many rewards in Heaven (Luke 9:48; Matt. 18:1–7).

Our Savior desires to use women in the ministry of his Gospel. Men and women still have different roles in most churches. Many of our families consist of one parent. When a mother and the head of a family needs counseling, she probably doesn't want to go to a married male pasture. Many need to talk to a female who can understand them.

We have many different opinions on this subject today. Our Lord calls both men and women into ministry. The Lord and the Church needs both. To understand the heart of our Father on this subject, we should look at the entire Bible. We shouldn't just read the few verses that men repeat to prove their point. Our Wise God stands ready to lead our thinking as we listen to the Spirit and pray for guidance.

> [11]**And he said unto me, Thou must prophesy again before many peoples, and nations, and tongues, and kings (Rev. 10:11, KJV).**

The Lord tells John that he must prophesy to and before every ethnic group and country on earth. In this verse, Jesus reinforces his command to proclaim the Gospel to all people (Matt. 28:19).

> It is not merely John who will continue to sound out the Word through the ages, but all of the apostles, and by extension the whole church of God throughout the dispensation, who will continue to prophesy, or proclaim God's truth.[1]

PROPHECY IN THE CHURCH TODAY

Some Christians don't understand the gift of prophecy that Jesus gives in the church today. The Lord gave many different spiritual gifts to the early NT Christian Church. God makes these same spiritual gifts available to equip and edify today's saints in his Church (Rom. 12:6).

Prophesy (*propheteuo*) means "to speak forth by divine inspirations and to break forth in praise to God."[2] It means to predict or to declare something that only God can know. The Lord uses prophecy to strengthen, comfort, and encourage men and women in the church (1 Cor. 14:3). Paul says we should eagerly desire the gift of prophecy so that we can use it to edify the church (1 Cor. 14:1, 4).

Prophets spoke in all the services of the early Christian Church, but the spirits of the prophets were subject to control by other prophets (1 Cor. 14:29–33). When a person speaks words of prophecy, his words must agree with the Bible. Christians sometimes misuse the gift of prophecy in Bible studies and pray meetings. It's a wonderful gift from God, but forgiven sinners should use it with care and with tender love.

God gives many gifts to his church today, but we should treasure the gift of love for our brothers and sisters in Christ. Love never fails, and love will follow us into that perfect place with the Rose of Sharon. In love, we seek truth, and this gives us hope and faith for a better life beyond this one. The love that God gives each of us for our family in Christ should also reach out to our natural families.

THE FAMILY REUNION

Last year, I went to a family reunion in the community where I lived the first twenty years of my life. People told me things I didn't think were true. Some of my relatives said I was a wild kid when I went to high school. Other family members had the nerve to tell me about things they imagined I did, and yet I don't remember these incidents!

One of my first cousins said I teased her when our families came together. She was four years younger than me and claimed I picked on her, even though I don't remember it that way. Life is strange, people view situations in different ways. What's fun and adventuresome for one person may cause harm to others.

Beginning in high school, some of the other boys picked on me. I clearly remember those times and places, but I doubt if the boys responsible remember them. In my young working career, some of the other men I worked with harassed me, but they probably don't remember the occasions.

Life has a way of leveling out people and situations. I sometimes teased my younger cousins and brothers. Later in life, other men harassed me. Men don't bother me anymore because I know that Jesus Christ loves me.

Whenever anyone starts to annoy me, I just tell them that Jesus loves them. After I tell them that Jesus loves them most tend to shut up and leave me alone.

REUNION IN HEAVEN

I pray for the people I work with. God then helps the situations at work to go better for me. Praying for our friends and people we work with will help break down problems. God gives us the gift of prayer to help us travel the road of life and come out winners.

Someday we will gather with our brothers and sisters in the Lord for a family reunion in Heaven. No one on earth really knows what awaits us in our true home. Whether we will walk on golden streets I don't know. Perhaps the description of heaven indicates a beautiful and joyful place. When God created Adam and Eve, he put them in a peaceful garden where everything was perfect. The Bible suggests that all our home in Heaven will be perfect. Amen!

NOTES

1. Coffman, *Revelation*, p. 222.
2. Prophecy, *propheteuo*, G4395. To foretell events, speak under divine inspiration.

The Two Witnesses

MEASURING THE TEMPLE

Chapter 11 continues the interlude that started in chapter 10. John ate the little book, and then the Lord told him to prophesy to all people on earth. The Lord told John to measure the Temple of God and the worshipers in it. The Lord wanted to know the size of his Temple and the exact number of his children.

We see two witnesses from the Christian Church. The beast ascends out of the Abyss and kills the two witnesses, and yet the witnesses rise again! The Devil can't keep a child of God from going to the Father.

> **[1]I was given a reed like a measuring rod and was told, "Go and measure the temple of God and the altar, and count the worshippers there. [2]But exclude the outer court; do not measure it, because it has been given to the Gentiles. They will trample on the holy city for 42 months" (Rev. 11:1, 2, NIV).**

THE NEW TEMPLE

John painted a word picture of the NT Church in chapter 11. Jesus sent John to...*measure the temple of God and the altar*. The *Temple* (*naos*) referred to the Sanctuary of the Temple used by the Israelites.[1] The Sanctuary included the Holy Place and the Holy of Holies.

This vision may have reminded John of the Temple that Herod built in Jerusalem. John was an Israelite who had visited that Temple since his childhood. The Romans had destroyed the Jerusalem Temple in A.D. 70, twenty years before John saw this vision. This stopped the OT system of worship for the Israelite people. The Jewish nation never reinstated their Temple worship.

God revealed a new and better covenant for his people that made the first covenant obsolete (Heb. 8:10–13). The moment Jesus died on the cross, the thick curtain to the Holy of Holies in the Jerusalem Temple was ripped in two from top to bottom (Matt. 27:51).

HEAVEN'S OPEN DOOR

The risen Christ entered the Sanctuary of Heaven itself and appeared for us before God (Heb. 9:24–28). He suffered and shed his blood once for our sin. We receive forgiveness of sin through the death and resurrection of Jesus Christ. Because Jesus takes our place before God, the Holy Creator sees us as holy and perfect (Heb. 10:9).

Jesus opened the way for us through the curtain of his body. His body replaced the ripped OT curtain to the Holy of Holies. He's our living high priest today. Therefore, we can go into the Holy of Holies and draw near to God (Heb. 10:19–23). Each of us in the Christian Church forms a part of God's Temple in the new covenant (2 Cor. 6:16; Eph. 2:19–22).

> [16]Don't you know that you yourselves are God's temple and that God's Spirit lives in you (1 Cor. 3:16, NIV)?

The Almighty gave us a picture of John counting his children who have a living relationship with his Son. Measuring the Temple was similar to the sealing of the 144,000 (Rev. 7:4). Our Father put a special protection around each of his children when he measured the Temple and counted the worshipers.

GENTILES TRAMPLE JERUSALEM

Someone gave John a...*reed like a measuring rod* to help illustrate the Christian Church in this view. The Lord told John not to measure the outer court because the Gentiles controlled it.

> The inner Temple, the Temple proper, then, is the true Church, the holy Christian Church, the communion of saints; while the outer Temple seems to represent the so-called visible Church, which has often been torn apart and trampled upon by heretics and antichrists.[2]

The Gentiles trampled...*on the holy city for 42 months.* Jesus brought this into perspective when he spoke of the Gospel Age. He said that armies would surround Jerusalem and that the Gentiles would trample on Jerusalem until the times of the Gentiles were fulfilled (Luke 21:20–24). Armies surrounded Jerusalem in 70 A.D., and the Gentiles still trample on Jerusalem today. Paul said that Israel would harden her heart until the full number of Gentiles have come into God's kingdom (Rom. 11:25).

The forty-two months or three and one-half years point to this time of fulfillment for the Gentile people. This age of grace covers the time span from the Ascension of Jesus until just before his return at the end of the Gospel Age.

This time of forty-two months covers the same time as the 1,260 days that the two witnesses give prophecy in verse three. The time also equals the time, times, and one-half time that the dragon persecutes the woman or the church in chapter 12. The picture of forty-two months shows us the length of the Gospel Age except for a brief period at the end of the Age.

> **"³And I will give power to my two witnesses, and they will prophesy for 1,260 days, clothed in sackcloth." ⁴These are the two olive trees and the two lampstands that stand before the Lord of the earth (Rev. 11:3, 4, NIV).**

TWO WITNESSES—TWO ANOINTED ONES

John describes the two witnesses as...*the two olive trees, and the two lampstands* that stand by the Lord of the Earth. Jesus calls the lampstands churches in Revelation 1:20. This indicates that the witnesses or lampstands represent the Christian Church.

The two prophesied for 1,260 days...*clothed in sackcloth.* The sackcloth symbolized forgiven people who lived their life in repentance. Today we might say that they were sold out for Jesus Christ.

The prophet Zechariah saw a vision of two olive trees standing on each side of a golden lampstand. Zechariah asked the angel what the golden lampstand was. The Lord told him, "It was not by might, nor by power, but by his spirit" (Zech. 4:6).

Zechariah asked what the two olive trees with the two golden pipes were. The angel told him that they were the two anointed ones that serve the Lord of all the earth (Zech. 4:11–14). These verses gave us an OT picture of the oil of the Holy Spirit that lives in each of us.

John writes that Jesus gives...*power to my two witnesses.* The Almighty God promises each of his children power to witness. We see a picture of the anointed sons of fresh oil standing beside the Lord of limitless power. The Almighty said that we do not witness by our might, nor by our power, but by his Spirit.

KEEP PLENTY OF PURE OIL

Jesus told a parable about ten virgins waiting for the bridegroom (Matt. 25:1–13). Five of the virgins carried extra oil for their lamps, while the other five did not. When the bridegroom came, only five had enough oil to light their lamps. The five virgins with sufficient oil went with the bridegroom to the marriage.

Jesus promises fresh oil from the Holy Spirit to all who seek him (Luke 23:49). With the oil of the Holy Spirit, our lamps will never run dry and our light will shine for the entire world to see.

WITNESS BY TESTIMONY

Christians witness by testifying about God's love and forgiveness in their life. A personal testimony about the power of God working in a life gives a strong witness for God. When a person quotes the Bible, people may say, "I don't believe the Bible."

If a Christian says to someone, "God did this or that for me in my life," then they confront him or her with personal evidence. It's difficult to discount a Christian's personal testimony about how the Lord changed their life.

Prayer used in combination with personal testimony will reach many individuals for Jesus. Prayer and love break down the resistance to the Word of God. The Lord uses personal testimony in private and in church services to help people understand his love for them. A testimony that focuses on the love of Christ helps others to recognize his tender forgiveness and mercy.

> **⁵And if any man will hurt them, fire proceedeth out of their mouth, and devoureth their enemies: and if any man will hurt them, he must in this manner be killed. ⁶These have power to shut heaven, that it rain not in the days of their prophecy: and have power over waters to turn them to blood, and to smite the earth with all plagues, as often as they will (Rev. 11:5, 6, KJV).**

TWO WITNESSES

The two witnesses speak words of fire from their mouths. The fire represents the Word of God (Jer. 5:14; 23:29). The fire devours their enemies and the enemies of the Church. What does this mean?

John describes two witnesses that do the acts of Moses and Elijah. Elijah has...*power to shut heaven, that it rain not* for three and one half years (1 Kings 17:1; 18:41–45). Moses turns the waters...*to blood* (Exod. 7:14–21). What do these prophets mean to the Church today?

Many Christians understand Moses as the giver of the Law and the deliverer of God's people from slavery. Moses did this, but he also revealed love, mercy, and compassion. Moses symbolized the Law and our Father's love and mercy toward his children.

Moses went on Mount Sinai for forty days. The people of Israel made a golden calf and worshiped it (Exod. 32). God's angry burned against his people; he wanted to destroy the Israelite nation. Moses pleaded with the Almighty God for mercy toward his people. He reminded God of his promises to Abraham, Isaac, and Jacob until God relented (Exod. 32:9–14).

Later the Israelites sinned and spoke against God and Moses. God then sent venomous snakes to bite and kill the people. In compassion, Moses prayed for the people until the Lord withdrew the serpents (Num. 21:4–9).

ELIJAH CALLED FOR FIRE

Ahaziah, king of Israel, wanted to see the prophet Elijah. The king sent a captain and a company of fifty men to bring him in. Elijah sat on a hill as the captain said, "Man of God, the king said come down."

> And Elijah answered and said to the captain of fifty, If I be a man of God, then let fire come down from heaven, and consume thee and thy fifty. And there came down fire from heaven, and consumed him and his fifty (2 Kings 1:10, KJV)

King Ahaziah then sent another captain and fifty more men to get Elijah. The captain told Elijah to come down at once. The fire of God fell from Heaven and also destroyed them. The king, who didn't seem too smart, sent a third captain and his fifty men. The third captain humbled himself on his knees and begged Elijah not to call fire down from Heaven (2 Kings 1:11:15). The third captain recognized a greater power than king Ahaziah.

The two witnesses give us picture of our power from God today. The OT uses physical examples for the enemies of Israel. The NT has spiritual enemies that come against God's children today (Eph. 6:12, Acts 26:18).

PRAY LIKE MOSES AND ELIJAH

Moses and Elijah gave us an example of how to intercede for results. Moses prayed out of love and mercy for his brothers and sisters. Elijah represents the power of intercessory prayer to destroy the works of the Devil. He used the power and faith that God gave him to remove the prophets of Baal. Elijah had no mercy on the evil prophets but destroyed them all (1 Kings 18:40).

Our Lord Jesus Christ invites his children to pray with mercy and compassion for our brothers and sisters. Jesus also wants us to use all the power we have from the Mighty God to pray against evil. We don't pray against the people: we pray against the evil they represent.

We should show no mercy toward Satan's kingdom in this world. The Devil embodies every mean, sinister, degenerate, and demonic force. He does things that we cannot begin to imagine. Many people do not have a concept of Satan's true intention for them.

When persecution rains on the Christian Church, the Christians may wonder where the fire is? Verse 5 says that all persecutors of God's children will die. The Greek word for *die* (*apokteino*) means "to kill or destroy."[3] The metaphor means "to take spiritual life and bring eternal misery in hell." At the last judgment, unbelievers won't mock the Bible or the Lord because the Word will stand Supreme.

> [7]Now when they have finished their testimony, the beast that comes up from the Abyss will attack them, and overpower and kill them. [8]Their bodies will lie in the street of the great city, which is figuratively called Sodom and Egypt, where also their Lord was crucified. [9]For three and a half days men from every people, tribe, language and nation will gaze on their bodies and refuse them burial. [10]The inhabitants of the earth will gloat over them and will celebrate by sending each other gifts, because these two prophets had tormented those who live on earth (Rev. 11:7–10, NIV).

Satan Attacks Witness

After the witnesses finish...*their testimony*, the beast from the Abyss overpowers and kills them. This symbolizes the attack on the witness of the Christian Church. The beast can't stop the true Church of Christ, but he can silence the public witness.

Forces from the kingdom of darkness have attacked the Christian Church and the message of the Gospel throughout the Age. The rise of Communism in this century gives us an example of how the beast works. The anti-Christian forces in Russia and China silenced the public witness of the Church, and yet the underground Christian Church increased in numbers.

The invisible Church began to show itself after the fall of Communism. The Lord raised the silent witness of the Church to life. The

Christian Church once thought dead by the communist leaders continued alive and well.

The bodies of the silent witnesses lie in the great city, which is spiritually or...*figuratively called Sodom.* The word for *great* points to an exceedingly wide and large place for a long period. The term for *figuratively* (*pneumatikos*) shows a "non-physical or divine place."[4] The city of Sodom pictured here indicates a spiritual place that covers the earth.

The beast from the Abyss symbolizes the powers in the world that agree with the works of the Devil. The beast kills the two witnesses in...*Sodom and Egypt, where also their Lord was crucified.* The power of the beast comes from: Sodom, representing sexual perversion and lust, Egypt representing greed and world government power, and Jerusalem, representing the religion that crucified Christ.

THE WORLD RESENTS CHRIST

Christian values always torment the people of the world. Their values put a damper on a good party where the wine flows and the men and women don't say no. People of the world want to live their life to the fullness and not consider the results.

The people of Christ bother their conscience by calling them to accountability. The world hates that. They want to have it their way with no interference. That's why the people...*of the earth will gloat over them and will celebrate* when the witness dies to public openness.

We need to protect ourselves from forces of evil in the world. The Bible gives many types of prayers that we can use. In this section, we will cover some that help keep the Devil and his powers at a distance.

IN THE NAME OF JESUS CHRIST

I had limited knowledge of different types of prayers in my early Christian years. I studied the Bible and read specific books that the Lord led me to read. One day Barbara, an older lady whom I knew from a Bible study, asked me to pray for her.

After I went to bed that night, I began to pray. I thought about the prayer promises God gives to each of us. I asked the Lord to give me the wisdom and the authority to pray. I said, "Satan in the name of Jesus Christ, I bind your power over Barbara."

Suddenly, a heavy weight covered me, and I could not move! Fear began to build in me. This was a difficult moment. I had never experienced anything like it before or since. The weight pressed so strong that I could only cry in my mind, "Jesus." As I slowly thought the name, "Jesus, Jesus,

Jesus," he came and eased the demon away. The Devil and his spirits are strong, but Jesus and his angles are stronger (Phil. 2:9–11)!

INTO THE HEAVENS

The Lord lifted the veil after he removed the spirit: I caught a glimpse of the supernatural. Astonishing power and energy passed between the opposing forces. With spiritual eyes, I saw a different form of power than we have on earth. It was more intense than lightning storms and large explosions. I was impressed!

The view into the heavens only lasted a moment, and God has never shown me anything like this since. Nevertheless, I know something happens when you say, "Satan, I bind your power in the name of Jesus."

After I prayed for Barbara, the resistance she had encountered for witnessing went away. Barbara then had freedom to study the Bible and talk to her friends and relatives about Jesus.

God increases his influence in a person's life after someone prays to bind Satan's power in him or her. The person then has more freedom to follow God's leading.

Since that first time, I have not had a problem praying for anyone. When I intercede for people and situations, I often feel a spiritual resistance. The resistance causes a pressure on my chest and neck.

PRAYER EXPERIENCES DIFFERENT RESISTANCE

Every Christian who prays experiences different forms of spiritual resistance. God reveals and displays the Holy Spirit through his children in many different manifestations. Jesus says in John 7:38 that out of our belly or innermost being shall flow rivers of living water. This living water is the Holy Spirit flowing out of our innermost being, when we speak the Word of God in faith.

I have talked to two different people who tried to pray like this and didn't follow through. When Satan attacked them, they backed off because of fear (1 Pet. 5:8). Neither of them had tried to bind any spirits again at that time.

If they had studied the Word and learned their authority in the Lord, Satan could not stop them. I also believe that the Lord allowed Satan to jump on me so that I would understand the Devil's mighty power and the Lord's Almighty Power.

The Devil's far ahead if he can bluff someone from binding the spirits of his kingdom. Satan hates it when someone learns how to intercede for others. The Devil will roar like a lion and try to deceive Christians from praying, but God is faithful. He helps us through the hard places when we fix our eyes on Jesus (Heb. 12:1, 2).

KEYS OF THE KINGDOM

Jesus Christ came to destroy the works of the Devil (1 John 3:8). When the Father raised his Son to life, they destroyed the Devil's power. However, for some reason, God continued to permit the Devil to roam around and influence people.

> [18]And I say also unto thee, That thou art Peter, and upon this rock I will build my church; and the gates of hell shall not prevail against it. [19]And I will give unto thee the keys of the kingdom of heaven: and whatsoever thou shalt bind on earth shall be bound in heaven: and whatsoever thou shalt loose on earth shall be loosed in heaven (Matt. 16:18, 19, KJV)

Jesus told Peter that...*the gates of hell* would not *prevail against* (*katischuo*), meaning "to overcome or overpower" the church.[5] Jesus gave Peter the keys to the Kingdom of Heaven. Peter passed the keys down through the ages until now. What do the keys mean?

Peter led the new Christian Church. He then passed the keys of leadership down to the next generation of bishops, priests, and pastures. Each generation of leaders transferred their authority to minister the Gospel to each new generation throughout the history of the Christian Church. This has been the understood meaning of the keys for many. When we look at the Scriptures, the Holy Spirit gives us another meaning for the keys.

KEYS UNLOCK THE GATES OF HELL

The holder of the *keys* (*kleis*) has power to open and shut.[6] The metaphor for (*kleis*) gives power and authority. The authority comes through the name of Jesus Christ and by the power of the Holy Spirit. The plural of keys (*kleis*) gives Christians many forms of prayer power and authority in the Kingdom of Heaven. We have authority because of the shed blood.

The Bible says that the Almighty put the key to the house of David on the shoulder of Jesus. Whatever he opens no one can shut; whatever he shuts no one can open (Isa. 22:22; Rev. 3:7). In the spiritual domain then, Jesus Christ becomes the key that opens the gates of hell.

Jesus gave Peter...*the keys of the kingdom of heaven*. Our Lord wanted Peter to bind the spirits and loosen the spiritual gates that hold back the spread of the Christian Church.

The Lord told Peter, "Whatever you shall *bind* (*deo*) on earth shall be bound in Heaven." (*Deo*) means "to fasten with chains or to tie up."[7] Satan *bound* (*deo*) the crippled woman with a spirit for eighteen years (Luke 13:10–16). Jesus also told Peter that whatever he shall *loose* (*lou*) on earth shall be loosed in Heaven.[8] (*Lou*) means "to loosen, break the chains of a person, or to set a person free from prison." When Christians pray for people, Jesus breaks the chains of darkness and sets the person free for a relationship with his or her Savior.

REMOVE THE STRONG MAN

The Risen Savior told Peter that if he bound spiritual powers on earth, then the influence from the binding would last into Heaven. Christ the Power of God also told Peter that when he loosed a gate of hell for an individual person, then the influence from opening the gate would remain on into Heaven.

Jesus taught his disciples about Satan. He told them that he cast out devils with the finger of God. The Lord said that when you do this, the Kingdom of God has come upon you. He said that only someone stronger could remove the strong man from a house (Luke 11:17–22). The strong man in a house represented the Devil's influence in a person.

The risen Christ has full authority to remove the strong man because of the cross. Jesus gave his disciples and us, the Church, his authority over evil spirits and demonic influences (Mark 16:15–18; John 15:7, 8; John 16:23).

God commissions the Church to extend his power by speaking in the name of Jesus Christ. Because we belong to the Christian Church that forms the Lord's body on earth, it's also our job to pray and help destroy the works of the Devil (Eph. 1:15–19; Col. 1:9–14; 4:12). Every child of God in the Christian Church has a copy of the keys that our Savior gave to Peter. Nevertheless, for the keys to work, we must apply their power in the name of Christ.

FAITH TURNS THE KEY

It takes God given faith to bind the powers of darkness. The Lord gives us faith as a gift when we ask for it (Eph. 2:8). Faith also increases by reading and studying the Word of God (Rom. 10:17).

We turn the key in the name of Jesus Christ with our God-given faith (John 14:12). God then sends the power of the Holy Spirit to push aside the evil spiritual forces. It's not our power: it's the Lord's power. We should remember that Jesus said, "I will be with you always" (Matt. 28:20).

I didn't understand the true authority that we have in the name of Jesus Christ when I began binding the Devil's power. God in his abundant grace honored my prayers, and the prayers have continued until today.

FREEDOM FROM BINDING

The power in the keys of binding and loosing works for our families and each of us. I command every spirit or influence from Satan to leave me every day in the name of Jesus Christ and by his blood. I don't want the influences of Satan around me or around my family. Satan tries extra hard to deceive committed Christians. All the Devil desires to do is to tear down and destroy. He does not bring good to anyone. His influence will never help people; it only hinders.

Jesus Christ desires to love and touch people through us. Jesus came to give freedom—freedom to love our brothers and sisters in the world and in the Church. Jesus wants to give us freedom by breaking the chains that keep us from understanding and using the power that we have within us. He breaks the chains of darkness by our prayers of authority and our obedience to him.

What Christians do on earth shall modify what happens in Heaven. When we bind the powers of darkness, this changes lives. Many longtime Christians don't understand the depth of the Word, the height of the Gospel, and how wide the Father's authority in us goes.

Jesus emphasizes prayer in the Gospels. God considers prayer one of his highest calls to Christians. Prayer moves the Kingdom of God. The prayers of the saints help control the world and causes nations to rise and fall.

WORTHY IS THE DELIVERER (ISA. 61)

Our Savior sees the tears of the broken hearted.
He hears the rattle of the chains and shackles.
The Lamb waits—He waits for the key to turn.
Worthy is the Lamb who shatters the shackles.
Our Deliverer hears the cries from the darkness.
He sees and hears the pain of the oppressed.
The Lamb waits—He waits for the key to turn.
Worthy is the Lamb who lights the new day.

[11]**And after three days and an half the Spirit of life from God entered into them, and they stood upon their feet; and great fear fell upon them which saw them.** [12]**And they heard a great voice from heaven saying unto them, Come up hither. And they ascended up to heaven in a cloud; and their enemies beheld them**

[13]And the same hour was there a great earthquake, and the tenth part of the city fell, and in the earthquake were slain of men seven thousand: and the remnant were affrighted, and gave glory to the God of heaven. [14]The second woe is past; *and,* behold, the third woe cometh quickly (Rev. 11:11–14, KJV).

WE SHALL MEET JESUS

The influence of the Christian Church has risen and fallen through the centuries. Since the Resurrection of our Lord, many governments and groups of people have tried to destroy the message of the Gospel. God has always left a remnant to carry the massage of Jesus Christ to the next generation. Suddenly the witnesses stood…*upon their feet, and great fear* fell on the people who killed them!

John painted a word picture of Christians going to the Father after their physical death on earth. It reminded us of the three days that the body of Jesus stayed in the tomb. After three days the Almighty Creator came down and gave the…*Spirit of life from God.* Just as the Father gave Jesus life after death, he will give life to each of his children after their death on earth.

The two witnesses rise in a cloud to Heaven after the mighty voice says…*Come up hither.* They go to meet the Lord in the sky the same way that Jesus did at his Ascension (Acts 1:9). Some would call this a type of rapture for the two witnesses. Scripture points to the Lord coming for his children at their death (1 Thess. 4:14–16; John 14:1–3). We will meet God the Father, God the Son, and God the Holy Spirit after our last sunset on earth.

CINDERELLA

Jesus has given us good news. They killed the body, but they didn't kill the spirit. Seeing the two witnesses ascend into Heaven reminded me of the old fairy tale about Cinderella. She was a beautiful young lady oppressed by an evil stepmother. Cinderella didn't have much hope in life, because she labored without end for the wicked stepmother.

Then something wonderful happened, her fairy godmother intervened. Cinderella won the prize. She married the prince and became a princess. The prize was larger than she could have hoped for.

As children of the Father, we also have the hope of winning the prize. We shall become princes and princesses because the King considers us his sons and daughters. Cinderella marries the prince, but her prize was only temporary. We have a better prize because it's the gift that keeps on giving. We shall marry the King and live in the King's castle forever and ever.

THE END OF THE AGE

*The second woe is past...*gives us a picture of the end of the Gospel Age. The God of mercy protects the spiritual life of his children and his Church from the attack of the beast that rises out of the Abyss.

Satan loses the war, but until he skips across the lake of fire, he won't admit it. Satan shall understand his loss when he slips into the hot brimstone and begins to fry.

"We thank you, Lord, for the power of prayer that you offer us. I pray, Lord, that when forgiven sinners read these words, the Holy Spirit will give them revelation and understanding. I ask you, Father, that each of your children could comprehend the height and the depth of their prayers. Amen!"

> [15]**And the seventh angel sounded; and there were great voices in heaven, saying, The kingdoms of this world are become *the kingdoms* of our Lord, and of his Christ; and he shall reign for ever and ever.** [16]**And the four and twenty elders, which sat before God on their seats, fell upon their faces, and worshipped God,** [17]**Saying, We give thee thanks, O Lord God Almighty, which art, and wast, and art to come; because thou hast taken to thee thy great power, and hast reigned (Rev. 11:15–17, KJV).**

The Lord shows us another interlude between the third and forth visions. The seventh angel blows his trumpet. It appears that the seven trumpets blow throughout the Gospel Age, and this interlude covers it from beginning to end.

OUR GOD REIGNS

The kingdoms of our world...*become the kingdoms of our Lord*. This indicates the reign of Christ for the complete Age. The Lord has...*taken to thee thy great power, and hast reigned* through his Church on earth from his Resurrection until today (Eph. 1:19–23; Col. 2:9–15).

The angel Jesus in Revelation 10:7 spoke of the blowing of the trumpet by the seventh angel. Jesus declared that the mystery of God would see completion as the angel prepared to blow the seventh trumpet. The mystery of God, the salvation of all his chosen, nears completion as the trumpet blows.

The 24 elders leave their seats and fall on their faces before the Lord to worship him. They give God glory and praise because of his Mighty Power. He's the...*Lord God Almighty* who reigns today, who reigned yesterday, and who will reign for all time.

> ¹⁸And the nations were angry, and thy wrath is come, and the time of the dead, that they should be judged, and that thou shouldest give reward unto thy servants the prophets, and to the saints, and them that fear thy name, small and great; and shouldest destroy them which destroy the earth. ¹⁹And the temple of God was opened in heaven, and there was seen in his temple the ark of his testament: and there were lightnings, and voices, and thunderings, and an earthquake, and great hail (Rev. 11:18–19, KJV).

The elders say…*the nations were angry, and thy wrath is come*. The kings and the rulers of earth stand against the Almighty and his Anointed One (Ps. 2:1–4). The Creator sits in Heaven and laughs at the feeble efforts of man to overthrow him. God has crowned his King to rule over all the earth. The Almighty has crowned his Son King, and no power on this earth or in the spiritual world can change that (Ps. 2:6–12).

John writes…*thy wrath is come*, and the time has come to judge the dead. The *dead* (*nekros*) means "a deceased person whose soul is in Hades."[9] The metaphor for (*nekros*) points to a spiritually dead person who doesn't recognize God.

At the same time, our Wonderful God begins to hand out rewards to his…*servants the prophets, and to the saints, and them that fear thy name*. Then the Holy Creator begins to…*destroy them which destroy the earth*. John paints a perfect word picture of the end of the Gospel Age and the final judgment.

THE ARK OF HIS TESTAMENT

They opened God's Temple and saw the…*ark of his testament*. The Bible always referred to the ark that Moses made as the Ark of the Testimony (Exod. 25:10–21). The Bible never called it the Ark of his Testament. God did not make any mistakes in the Bible. If this were the true OT ark of the testimony, Jesus would not have called it the ark of his testament.

People approached the God of the OT in the Temple as he hovered over the ark of the testimony. In this interlude, the…*temple of God was opened in heaven*. Our Lord died on the cross, came to life, and began a new covenant with his people. Jesus Christ stopped the old covenant at the cross. I believe verse 19 points to the time of the cross.

Jesus appeared before his Father in the Temple of Heaven after his Resurrection (Heb. 9:24). Jesus opened the way for us through the Vail that covered the Ark of the Testimony in the OT covenant (Heb. 10:20–25).

People could not go into the Holy of Holies where God dwelt except for the high priest.

Because Jesus opens the way by his shed blood, we have confidence to enter the Holy of Holies (Heb. 10:19–23). We can go right into the presence of our Father. They couldn't do that in the OT. God lives in us in the new covenant. Therefore, we see...*in his temple the ark of his testament.* This symbolizes the new covenant that God gave to us. We have a view of the Lord's new covenant with us as he begins the next vision.

"**Thank you,** Holy Savior, for the new covenant that you developed for us. Thank you Lord for giving us the opportunity to live in you and you in us. All praise to you for your compassion, mercy, and Love. Amen!"

Notes

1. Temple, *naos*, G3485. The Temple at Jerusalem, but only the Sanctuary of the Holy Place and the Holy of Holies.
2. Paul E. Kretzmann, *Popular Commentary of the Bible*, (St. Louis: Concordia Publishing House, 1923), p. 622.
3. Killed, *apokteino*, G615. To kill or destroy. Metaphor means to deprive of spiritual life and give eternal misery in hell.
4. Figuratively, *pneumatikos*, G4153. Non-physically, divinely, spiritually.
5. Prevail, *katischuo*, G2729. To overcome, overpower, or to use force.
6. Keys, *kleis*, G2807. A key. Metaphor means the keeper of the keys has power to open and shut. Gives power and authority.
7. Bind, *deo*, G1210. Tie, fasten with chains.
8. Loose, *lou*, G3089. Break, unloose, destroy. To unloose a person chained or tied.
9. Dead, *nekros*, G3498. Lifeless, one whose soul is in Hades. Metaphor, spiritually dead without God.

CHAPTER 12

The Woman, Child, and Dragon

POWER NEEDED TO REMOVE

In 1985, Linda and I moved twenty-five miles west of Portland to a home located in the forest. We wanted to erect a building and began to clear an area forty feet by ninety feet. Three old growth Douglas fir stumps hindered us from clearing the area. Their size ranged from four feet to six feet in diameter.

I had a neighbor come over with his medium size bulldozer to push them out of the way. He worked several hours on the smallest but could not move it. They were tough! We then waited six weeks until a professional operator came through the area with his large bulldozer.

Tom used the bulldozer, equipped with a stump splitter and a brush rake, to clear and level the area in one hour and ten minutes. He would back into each stump two or three times with the stump splitter and then push them out of the way with his blade. After Tom cleared the stumps, he then used the brush rake on his crawler tractor to take out the roots from the stumps. If you use the right piece of equipment with lots of power, you can get rid of even the most stubborn problems.

The Almighty God desired to restore a personal relationship with his children. The OT covenant of obedience didn't do what the Creator wanted. Our Father wanted to remove the Devil's authority from the world. Our Father prepared to send the power of his own Son to remove

Satan's power from the earth. In a spiritual sense, Jesus Christ worked like the bulldozer when he removed the hindrances to our salvation.

In our walk through the Revelation of Jesus Christ, we begin the fourth vision. Jesus shows us Satan's kingdom attacking the church in this vision. John describes the satanic trinity that imitates the Trinity of God. The Lord reveals his divine protection that keeps the evil one from destroying his Church. This vision begins with an unusual sight.

> **¹And there appeared a great wonder in heaven; a woman clothed with the sun, and the moon under her feet, and upon her head a crown of twelve stars: ²And she being with child cried, travailing in birth, and pained to be delivered (Rev. 12:1, 2, KJV).**

The Radiant Woman

John looks into Heaven and sees a woman...*clothed with the sun*. She radiates the Light of the World. The Sun of Righteousness rises from her presence (Mal. 4:2). This woman contains the Living Word of God.

The...*moon stays under her feet*, which indicates her dominion over the light of darkness. The woman wears...*twelve stars* on her head placed in a wreath of victory. The twelve stars in the crown indicate God's people. The woman represents the people of God on earth.

The woman symbolized Israel before the birth of Christ. The woman also symbolized the Christian Church after the birth of Christ. The description of the woman identified her as the people of God from Adam to the Second Coming of Christ.

God called his people a woman in several passages of the OT (Isa. 54:1–6). The prophet Micah described a woman waiting to deliver a King.

> ⁹Why do you now cry aloud—have you no king? Has your counselor perished, that pain seizes you like that of a woman in labor? ¹⁰Writhe in agony, O Daughter of Zion, like a woman in labor, for now you must leave the city to camp in the open field. You will go to Babylon; there you will be rescued. There the LORD will redeem you out of the hand of your enemies (Mic. 4:9, 10, NIV).

Mary

Out of love, the Almighty used the woman Israel to bring forth his King, Christ Jesus our Lord. Some Christians believe that the woman represents Mary, the mother of our Lord. Although Mary is a special saint of God, the description of the woman does not indicate that it's her.

God required the Christ child to be true man and True God to complete his role as Savior of the World, (Heb. 2:14–18). Mary gave Jesus all the traits of man, and his Father gave Jesus all the traits of God. The Savior of the World needed all the traits of man, and yet live a life without sin. If Jesus was only True God and not also true man, then Satan could not have tempted him, because no one can tempt God with evil (James 1:13).

Mary conceived her son, baby Jesus, in the flesh of man as true man (Heb. 2:11–18). The Holy Spirit conceived his Son, baby Jesus, as True God (Heb. 1:1–5). Our Creator used the combination man-God for the perfect sacrifice. Christ was sacrificed once to take away all the sins of mankind (Heb. 10–10).

MARY IN THE CHURCH TODAY

God chose Mary in the beginning to bring forth our Redeemer (Gen. 3:15). Mary gave us a picture of holiness in her obedience to the Lord. Mary was the first Christian to say yes to Jesus. Our Savior loved Mary as his mother and as one of his special children.

Mary, a beautiful humble child of God, bore the perfect gift to mankind. She was the mother of our Lord and Savior Jesus Christ. She was a humble servant whom God gave a special task. Our Father, Jehovah, trusted Mary enough to bring his only Son into the world and to raise him. Mary nurtured our Lord from birth and had a worthy influence on him.

Mary held a unique place in the Christian Church. God came into Mary not once, but twice. God came into Mary the first time when the Holy Spirit created Jesus Christ in her (Luke 1:35). God came into Mary the second time at Pentecost. The Holy Spirit filled her with the Spirit along with her Christian brothers and sisters (Acts 2:1–4).

The Lord loves his mother, Mary, with a special love, and she's our sister in Christ. The Scriptures say that she's blessed. I am sure that she holds a high place in the Kingdom of Heaven, because she is the King's mother. Moses and the prophets gave us the Word in the OT. The disciples wrote the Word in the NT. Mary gave us Jesus, the True Word of God.

> **³Then another sign appeared in heaven: an enormous red dragon with seven heads and ten horns and seven crowns on his heads. ⁴His tail swept a third of the stars out of the sky and flung them to the earth. The dragon stood in front of the woman who was about to give birth, so that he might devour her child the moment it was born (Rev. 12:3, 4, NIV).**

THE FIRE RED DRAGON

John looks into heaven and sees…*another sign*. The *sign* (*semeion*) indicates a wonder that's set apart from others.[1] John sees a monstrous seven headed…*red dragon* that appears on *fire* (*Purrhos*.)[2] The Bible only uses the word (*Purrhos*), meaning "fire red," twice in the NT. John uses it here and in Revelation 6:4 to describe the color of the red horseman. The red dragon and the red horseman must represent the same nature. Verse 9 tells us that Satan is the red dragon.

Dictionaries describe dragons as fierce and violent monsters They have fearful claws and teeth and often spout fire. John shows us a picture of something we should stay away from. The…*ten horns* characterize the dragon as a beast with fullness of power. The…*seven heads* imply perfection and intelligence. The…*seven crowns* do not represent crowns of victory, but normal crowns of world power.

The serpent waited in front of the woman so that he could destroy her child. Throughout history, Satan has tried to kill the Christ Child, beginning in Genesis 4:8. He wanted to stop the line of descendants that would bring forth the Savior.

ABORTION AND A SPIRIT

Satan lost the battle: the Savior came. Yet, Satan did not stop killing the children of the Savior. Today, through state-approved murder with the knife, the demon dragon has killed millions of God's children every year. Jesus gave us good news: the murdered babies will rise again. Jesus came to destroy the Devil's work and defeat death. The Almighty, who created life, has given new spiritual life to the aborted babies.

The Lord puts a spirit or soul within each person born on earth. You cannot touch it, see it, or feel it; nevertheless, it's there. The Creator gives each of us a spirit while still in the womb (Jer. 1:5; Luke 1:14). The Lord looks at us as individuals, even when we only consist of a few cells.

The Creator gives each of us a desire to win in life. Some people strive for money, fame, homes, and nice cars. Others spend their lives in hero worship or chasing elusive dreams. A person may receive the whole world but still lose if he rejects the Deliverer. True happiness only comes from a relationship with Christ the Lord.

Our Father longs to fill our spirit with his Holy Spirit. His Son Jesus desires our close unity with him. He wants to give us a victorious spiritual life. The Son of Mary will give us the greatest victory in·life if we build our life around her Son.

⁵**She gave birth to a son, a male child, who will rule all the nations with an iron scepter. And her child was snatched up to God and to his throne. ⁶The woman fled into the desert to a place prepared for her by God, where she might be taken care of for 1,260 days (Rev. 12:5, 6, NIV).**

THE GENTLE SHEPHERD

The woman representing Israel gives birth to...*a male child.* We understand by the description that he's the Good Shepherd who gives his life for the sheep (John 10:11). The Good Shepherd rules...*all the nations with an iron scepter. Rule (poimaino)* means "to feed, to nourish, or to tend a flock of sheep."[3] The Good Shepherd *rules (poimaino)* his sheep. He feeds them living bread and water by nourishing them with his Word and his Spirit.

The iron scepter can refer to a shepherd's walking staff. The gentle Shepherd uses his staff to lead and protect us as we go through places where deception and evil wait for us. When we walk through the shadow of death, his rod and his staff comfort us (Ps. 23:4).

The Good Shepherd died on the cross and rose to life for our Salvation. Then the Almighty...*snatched* the child up to his Throne in Heaven. This pointed to the Resurrection of our Savior. He sat at the right hand of the Almighty God and rules the earth today (Ps. 2:4–9).

The Father...*prepared a place* for the woman, and he prepares a place for each of his children. God has...*taken care (trepho)* of the woman.[4] The word *(trepho)* means "to feed, nourish, or to support." God prepares a path for each of his children to walk on. If we stay on the path while we walk through this life, he provides for us. When we stray off our road, the gentle Shepherd leads us back with his iron scepter.

TIMES IN THE GOSPEL AGE

In the Bible, the Lord uses different symbols for listing the same time shown in the Gospel Age (Rev. 11:2). The separate visions in the Revelation of Jesus Christ point to the same period in the Gospel Age. We see the time revealed as: 42 months, 1,260 days, 1,000 years, and time, times, and one-half time.

God prepared a place for the woman...*for 1,260 days.* The time given here equals the time, times, and half a time that God supported the woman in verse 14. It's the same woman and the same time from a different viewpoint. The period describes the complete Gospel Age except for a brief time just before the return of Christ. The brief time at the end of the Age points to the three and one-half days in Revelation 11:9.

THE TIMES LISTED IN REVELATION

The Gospel Age length	Period Listed in Verses
42 Months	Rev. 11:2 and 13:5
1,260 Days	Rev. 11:3 and 12:6
Time, times, and one-half time	Rev. 12:14
1000 Years	Rev. 20:2 and 20:4–6
Short Time at End of Age	
Three and one-half days	Rev. 11:9
A brief time	Rev. 20:3
The Judgment or End	
Second Vision	Rev. 6:14–17
Third Vision	Rev. 11:18, 19
Fourth Vision	Rev. 14:7, 17–20
Fifth Vision	Rev. 16:17–21
Sixth Vision	Rev. 18:10 and 19:17–21
Seventh Vision	Rev. 20:10–15

It is clear, therefore, that the period described as "a time and times and half a time" begins at the moment of Christ's *first coming*—birth, ministry, cross, coronation—and extends to a point of time very near to his *second coming unto judgment*.[5]

The prophet Daniel used the term time, times, and one-half time to write prophecy about the coming Gospel Age (Dan. 7:25; 12:7). Daniel spoke about the Antichrist oppressing the saints for a time, times, and one-half time. John said that the antichrist had already come into the world (1 John 4:3). This then indicated that the Antichrist persecuted saints throughout the Gospel Age.

Daniel 12:7 says that the time, times, and one-half time will last until a period of difficult distress breaks the power of the holy people. The time of distress will be worse than any other time on earth (Dan. 12:1).

At the end of the brief period when the Antichrist finally destroys the power of the holy people, the end of the Age will come (Dan. 12:7). Then the children of God will go into eternal bliss: the people of the Devil will go to another place.

> **⁷And there was war in heaven. Michael and his angels fought against the dragon, and the dragon and his angels fought back. ⁸But he was not strong enough, and they lost their place in heaven. ⁹The great dragon was hurled down—that ancient serpent called the devil, or Satan, who leads the whole world astray. He was hurled to the earth, and his angels with him (Rev. 12:7–9, NIV).**

THE FALL OF LUCIFER

Jesus said that...*there was war in heaven.* The angels of God fought against...*the dragon and his angels.* The Almighty and his angels threw Satan and his evil angels onto the earth. I understand that this happened before the creation of man on earth. The Bible doesn't give us many answers as to why Satan and his angels rebelled against God. Several verses in the OT do give us some background.

> ¹²How you have fallen from heaven, O morning star, son of the dawn! You have been cast down to the earth, you who once laid low the nations! ¹³You said in your heart, "I will ascend to heaven; I will raise my throne above the stars of God; I will sit enthroned on the mount of assembly, on the utmost heights of the sacred mountain. ¹⁴I will ascend above the tops of the clouds; I will make myself like the Most High." ¹⁵But you are brought down to the grave, to the depths of the pit (Isa. 14:12–15, NIV).

> ¹²"Son of man, take up a lament concerning the king of Tyre and say to him: 'This is what the Sovereign LORD says: " 'You

were the model of perfection, full of wisdom and perfect in beauty. [13]You were in Eden, the garden of God; every precious stone adorned you: ruby, topaz and emerald, chrysolite, onyx and jasper, sapphire, turquoise and beryl. Your settings and mountings were made of gold; on the day you were created they were prepared. [14]You were anointed as a guardian cherub, for so I ordained you. You were on the holy mount of God; you walked among the fiery stones. [15]You were blameless in your ways from the day you were created till wickedness was found in you. [16]Through your widespread trade you were filled with violence, and you sinned. So I drove you in disgrace from the mount of God, and I expelled you, O guardian cherub, from among the fiery stones. [17]Your heart became proud on account of your beauty, and you corrupted your wisdom because of your splendor. So I threw you to the earth; I made a spectacle of you before kings' " (Ezek. 28:12–17, NIV)

My heart trembled when I read these verses about Lucifer, the bright morning star. I can't believe he was so stupid! Think about an angel who was perfect, blameless, beautiful, and full of wisdom. God created him as an anointed cherub over many other angels. As one of the cherubim, Lucifer was one of the highest created beings. God used them to cover and protect his creation.

The Creator covered Lucifer with the finest gems in the universe. He was next to God in the structure of heaven. Then pride overtook Lucifer: he wanted to ascend...*above the stars of God,* or the other created angels. The sly serpent tried to make himself equal with God. He wasted his position!

FALLEN ANGELS HATE CHRISTIANS

Perhaps we could understand why the fallen angels hate God's children today if we look at the past. For unknown millenniums of time, the created angels stood in the very presence of God. They felt his love, peace, joy, and power without end. Everything in their existence was perfect.

Suddenly, their leader swelled with pride. Lucifer's defective mind led him to think that he was better then his Creator. He rebelled against God and carried one third of the angels with him. They fell from God's grace: there was no forgiveness!

The party was over. Their relationship with their Maker was finished never to return. Did Satan and his fallen angels think that the Eternal God would do nothing? Did the Devil think that he could make a fool out of his Holy Creator? The Alpha and Omega condemned Lucifer and his fallen angels to this earth.

The Absolute Judge cast Satan and his fallen angels into the Abyss after the cross (Eph. 4:8; Heb. 2:14). They tied the Devil and his angels with a great chain and only gave the demons limited freedom to harass people—see Revelation 9:1. Why didn't God just give the fallen angels their sentence when they rebelled? The Christians on earth would have a much easier life without the kingdom of darkness on earth.

I stand in awe when I think about this. I do not understand why all the events took place. Unlike the angels, I live at the foot of the cross. When I make a mistake and sin, I know that my Redeemer will forgive me because of his unending love and grace. Yet, our Savior didn't forgive the fallen angels.

WE HAVE—THEY HAVE NOT

The fallen angels had no hope for the future; their attitude deteriorated. Bitterness, anger, and jealously consumed the thoughts of the angels. The fallen angels began to vent their evil thoughts at the Savior and his Church. The children of God have what the angels can never have.

Satan falls from the top of the mountain in Heaven down to the lowest place. He will go where the worm does not die and the fire never goes out (Mark 9:48). Because the Devil's kingdom has no hope for pleasure in eternal life, they try to destroy their Creator's children. Satan has no mercy on any Christian. He will hurt them as much as God permits.

The fallen angels lost much. We might feel compassion for them until we consider the hurt and the deception they cause for God's children. The evil serpent gives distress and problems to millions of people who don't know how to defend themselves.

MEMORIES OF RATTLESNAKES

The Devil is who he is: he will not change. Thank God that we have authority, in the name of Jesus, to put him under our feet (Luke 10:19). I detest the actions of Satan toward people. I never make fun of the Devil. Satan has dreadful authority and power here on earth. If a person makes fun of Satan, they set themselves up for a fall. If you're looking for trouble, just call on the Devil!

I loathe Satan, but I have much respect for him. When I was a child in South Dakota, we sometimes found rattlesnakes in the fields and around the house. I was not stupid enough to pick up a rattlesnake and play with him. If you play with the Devil, he will turn and bite you. God tells us this in his Word (1 Pet. 5:8; 2 Cor. 11:13–15).

We always gave the rattlesnakes plenty of room so that they could not strike us or give us trouble. We then used a weapon and killed the rattlesnake!·

I remember one incident when I was about eight years old. My brothers and I found a rattlesnake about 150 foot from our house. We watched the snake until our dad came home. He drove up, and we showed him the snake. He took a round point shovel and quickly severed the head from the rattlesnake. Good-bye serpent! He didn't show any mercy toward that rattlesnake. Our Heavenly Father doesn't want any of us to show any mercy toward the old serpent and his kingdom of evil.

> [10]And I heard a loud voice saying in heaven, Now is come salvation, and strength, and the kingdom of our God, and the power of his Christ: for the accuser of our brethren is cast down, which accused them before our God day and night. [11]And they overcame him by the blood of the Lamb, and by the word of their testimony; and they loved not their lives unto the death. [12a]Therefore rejoice, ye heavens, and ye that dwell in them (Rev. 12:10–12a, KJV).

Verse 10 pointed to the cross of Christ. Jesus Christ destroyed the Devil's power when he rose from death to life in victory over evil. He stripped him of all authority (Col. 2:15; 1 John 3:8). Satan lost his place in Heaven, but the All-Powerful God still gives him some authority to harass people on earth.

CONTEST BETWEEN GOOD AND EVIL

Christians have many unanswered questions in the power struggle between light and darkness. If God has all power and authority, why does he permit evil (Matt. 28:18)?

The Lord sits on his Throne and watches us here on earth. In a sense, it's a gigantic contest between good and evil. The Creator permits Satan and his fallen angels a limited amount of power (Rev. 9:11). The Devil uses this power to try to keep people away from God. The Lord uses our testing to draw us toward him (James 1:2–4).

The Lord could come to each of us and overwhelm us with his love and glory. Almost every person on earth would then follow him. God could control people just as a puppeteer controls his puppets.

Thank God, he didn't use this method to give us salvation. Instead, the Lord uses prayers from his children and sweet nudges by the Holy

Spirit. Through this process, people pass from future life in the fires of hell to future eternal bliss with Jesus Christ.

Christians win the victory over Satan...*by the blood of the Lamb*. God allows the Devil to harass us, but Jesus gives us a weapon to overcome him (2 Cor. 10:3, 4; Rom. 16:20). We use the word of our testimony and the blood of the Lamb. Sometimes Christians pay the price of physical death here on earth because of their testimony.

The voice in Heaven said...*now is come salvation*. This meant deliverance and safety. Many of the saints...*loved not their lives unto the death*. If a Christian has given his life for Jesus, we may wonder where's the deliverance and safety? The verse, after the Christians gave their lives, said...*rejoice, ye heavens, and ye that dwell in them*. Why has Heaven rejoiced over the physical deaths of God's children?

AN IMAGE OF HEAVEN

The Bible doesn't talk much about Heaven, but it must be something. The saints in Heaven rejoice because one of their brothers or sisters comes home after their death. They must be delighted, because the person will experience jubilation and pleasure that's unlimited. Our Father loves to surprise his children with good gifts here on earth (Luke 11:11). How much more will he surprise us in Heaven?

WORTHY IS THE LAMB (REV. 7)

They stand with the angels holding palm branches.
They fall on their faces before the Throne and say,
  "Worthy, Worthy is the Lamb who was slain."
The Lamb gives them living water with love.
The Lamb gives joy and wipes away their tears.
  "Praise and glory to the Lamb—Praise him."
They hold their crowns and look into his face.
"Worthy, Worthy is the Lamb who was slain."

PRAYER HELPS

That sly old serpent, the Devil, has a tremendous amount of power. We need to remember that Satan can only do one thing at a time. Satan's the commander of his kingdom. He sends fallen angels or evil spirits to do his work. When I refer to Satan, I refer to his whole kingdom. Yet, I may write about one specific occurrence that's caused by one demon or one spirit.

It's not the big things that annoy me: it's the small things. The Devil knows which buttons to push to irritate me. He grinds day after day until I grow uptight and angry. When I reach the end, I sometimes get angry with God for allowing Satan to harass me. God then takes care of it if the time's right, but sometimes the Almighty holds back.

I pray against Satan in the name of Jesus Christ during this time. I also use the blood of Jesus, which has more effect than his name alone. Since I wrote these words, the Holy Spirit revealed a new level of prayer that seems to keep his kingdom at a distance. I will cover it later in the book.

I remember when I first accepted Jesus as my Savior over twenty years ago. How beautiful those first years were. Then the trials and difficulties came until I began to use the binding types of prayer every day. Our lives then settled down with the peace and joy from the Lord.

I began this book six years ago. The first two years went well. Then the resistance to writing began to increase. I added the Lord's prayer and put on the armor of God every day. This helped keep Satan at bay.

"Holy Father, we thank you for the prayers that you offer us in your Word. We praise you because the prayers help resist darkness and demons. We give you glory and praise your Holy name. Amen!"

WE WIN

Christian people triumph over Satan by faith and the shed blood of Jesus Christ. The cost of victory sometimes means physical death here on earth. The true victory comes from remaining loyal to our Savior until our end here on earth. We will then go stand at the Throne after we overcome all conflict.

The situation doesn't always change immediately when Christians pray. Our Father may not answer our prayers right away. He may want us to spend more time reading the Bible and learning to trust him. The Devil is no respecter of people. He will attack anyone that the Father permits (Job 2:1–9). If God lets the evil serpent harass you or your family, you stand in good company. Satan has always attacked men and women of God.

God gives us more faith to believe when we study the Bible and pray (Rom. 10:17). God gives us faith beyond our hope when we pray every day and ask the Father in the Son's name (John 15:7). The process may take longer than we like; nevertheless, the answers will come. We will win that sweet victory and overcome the deceiving one by faith and by the shed blood of the Lamb.

Jesus will push that evil serpent away from us in his timing. The Devil may harass us, but we know that when the day of judgment comes, our Lord Jesus will harass him in return. Someday, we shall watch the Devil take a long swim in the lake filled with fire. Our Father will give us a good seat to watch him jumping and skipping across the burning brimstone. After a while, he will slip and take a dive. Hallelujah to the Lamb! He reigns forever, and ever! Amen! Amen!

> [12b]**Woe to the inhabiters of the earth and of the sea! for the devil is come down unto you, having great wrath, because he knoweth that he hath but a short time. [13]And when the dragon saw that he was cast unto the earth, he persecuted the woman which brought forth the man *child*. [14]And to the woman were given two wings of a great eagle, that she might fly into the wilderness, into her place, where she is nourished for a time, and times, and half a time, from the face of the serpent (Rev. 12:12b–14, KJV).**

THE THIRD WOE

The verse says…*Woe to the inhabiters of the earth.* This begins the last of the three Woes. The three Woes consist of three different viewpoints of how Satan attacks earth. The third Woe covers the rest of chapter 12 through chapter 13.

This Woe depicts Satan's kingdom after God casts it to earth. He's filled with wrath because he lost the war in Heaven. The Woe continues into chapter 13 where Satan calls for help.

The beast from the sea and the beast from the earth come to help. They form the satanic trinity, which mimics the True Trinity of God. The third Woe concludes with the mark of the beast that he offers to everyone. Satan doesn't care. He wants to destroy everyone, whether good or bad.

The Devil knows that his time is short. He's had nineteen hundred years since John wrote this. In the spiritual realms, that's a short time. We will see an increase in spiritual activity in the final years just before the return of Jesus Christ.

THE HARVEST WILL COME

Jesus said, "The harvest is ready, but we need more workers. Ask the Lord of the harvest to send more workers" (Luke 10:2). The Holy Spirit has increased his activity among the workers for the last few years. God has raised an army around the world to pray for the harvest.

The Holy Spirit called many individual intercessors to seek the Lord's direction and pray. Many of the Christians that God called to pray didn't know that others were praying for the same harvest. Jesus said, "The harvest will come at the end of the Age" (Matt. 13:39).

The Lord wants billions of people brought into his kingdom before he returns. It will only happen by the power of the Holy Spirit (Zech. 4:6). I believe the Almighty God will bring in a mighty harvest in the next ten to twenty years. Billions of people around the world will come into God's Kingdom.

LIGHT AND DARKNESS INCREASE

On the other side, darkness and evil will increase. Satan's activity will expand, just as certain as God's activity will. God will permit the Devil to use more of his power to keep people in darkness who refuse to repent and turn to God. The difference between evil and good will increase. Everyone will have to choose the Lord's way or the Devil's way. The time for fence-sitting in churches will stop.

The mystery—why does the Lord permit Satan to persecute and kill Christians? The verse says the...*devil is come down unto you, having great wrath.* Woe to the people on earth because he will torment them. The Almighty protects his children's spiritual relationship with him. Yet, he sometimes allows the Devil to destroy the body.

PROTECTED BY EAGLE'S WINGS

God used the symbol of...*two wings of a great eagle* to protect his Church in the OT. The wings of eagles gave us a picture of God's divine protection and grace (Deut. 32:11). The eagle represented freedom to the Israelites (Exod. 19:4). God told Moses on Mount Sinai that he brought Israel out of Egypt on eagle's wings. God carried...*the woman* on wings of an eagle to her place of refuge in the wilderness where he nourished and supported her.

Jesus gives us a picture of his people living in the wilderness of the world. The Father calls each of his children to a special walk through this wilderness. He also takes care of us in the place where he wants us to live and work in the world.

The Bible says that if we wait upon the Lord, we will renew our strength. We will ride on wings as eagles, and we will run and not grow tried or faint (Isa. 40:31). The eagle's wings represent strength and endurance from the Lord. The Lord protects us and helps us through all our struggles against evil when we wait on him. All praise to the Savior for his care and grace.

¹⁵**Then from his mouth the serpent spewed water like a river, to overtake the woman and sweep her away with the torrent. ¹⁶But the earth helped the woman by opening its mouth and swallowing the river that the dragon had spewed out of his mouth. ¹⁷Then the dragon was enraged at the woman and went off to make war against the rest of her offspring—those who obey God's commandments and hold to the testimony of Jesus (Rev. 12:15–17, NIV).**

The Devil is angry with the woman who represents the people of God and tries to destroy her in a different way. Out of his mouth,…*the serpent spewed water like a river*. The water symbolizes lies and delusions. Jesus gives water that leads to spiritual life. Satan gives water that leads to spiritual death.

I understand that Revelation looks at life from a spiritual viewpoint rather than a physical viewpoint. The persecution of the Church by Satan starts with spiritual persecution. Nevertheless, the spiritual oppression may spill over into the physical lives of believers.

SATAN'S LIES AND DELUSIONS

Satan spewed or cast water from his mouth at the Christian Church. Jesus said that by our fruit he would recognize us. Good trees give good fruit, and bad trees give bad fruit (Matt. 12:33; Luke 6:44).

Satan spews out lies and delusions toward people on the earth. This contrasts with the living water of Truth that Jesus gives to us. Christians who follow the teaching of Jesus Christ recognize the Devil's lies. The lies pollute God's creation and his values and then lead to delusions. The people of the world open their mouth wide and swallow the lies because they seem logical (Prov. 16:25).

The theory of evolution began with a lie and then gained acceptance throughout the world. The lie of evolution led people to believe that there's no life after death. When people have not believed in a Creator, then they do not need to explain actions to a higher power. People of the world could then do their own thing without answering to the Almighty God.

Perversion and evil come when people do not consider the effects of their actions. Of course, the Devil's always ready to give a helping hand in this area. Out of perversion and evil comes hatred toward the Christian Church, because the Church calls people to accountability. The world turns on the Church and blames it for its problems, because Satan leads the thoughts of people in the world.

Evolution is only one lie that comes from Satan. He has hundreds that he spreads through his followers. The Lord sealed each of his children from spiritual loss. Yet, we need to sort out truth from deception. God gives us the Holy Spirit to help us discern the truth. By following the principals of the Bible and asking God to lead us, we should not accept the lies that...*the serpent spewed out of his mouth.* "Lord, help each of us to understand your Truth, because the Truth will set us free. Thank you for revealing the two kingdoms of Light and darkness."

Notes

1. Sign, *Semeion*, G4592. Indication, supernatural, miracle.
2. Red, *purrhos*, G4450. Fire like, flame colored, red.
3. Rule, *poimaino*, G4165. Feed, To tend as a shepherd, to nourish.
4. Care, *trepho*, G5142. Feed, nourish, pamper.
5. Hendriksen, *More Than Conquerors*, p. 173.

CHAPTER 13

Beast of the Sea—Earth

THE GAME OF LIFE

When a person first accepts Jesus as his personal Savior, the Lord pours out grace and mercy in abundance. The Christian life reflects a game played on credit. The game begins with much grace and mercy from the Lord. Everything's wonderful as you play and win at the contest of life.

Unlimited backing comes from the Almighty. Nothing's too hard for the Lord. There's a learning manual called the Bible on the game of life. You don't read it, because, after all, you have the Almighty on your side.

As you live and play the game of life, small problems begin to appear. You continue thinking, *I'm okay: the Almighty's backing me.* A friend tells you that you should study the learning manual, and learn the rules to understand the game of life.

Finally, the Almighty God begins to call in his markers. You say, "Not today, Lord, I'm to busy." The struggles get harder. Friends encourage you to read the manual because you seem to be losing. Yet, you continue until one day the game of life ends.

Jesus gives the final ruling for each life on earth. He gives us all we need when we play the game on his side. Jesus wrote the rules to the game of life. If we don't play by his rules, we may lose at the final judgement.

Chapter 13 reveals that we need to study the learning manual, or Bible, to survive the challenges of the two beasts. That sly old serpent continues to show us that he's the master deceiver. Unless we ask the Lord for wisdom and study his Bible, we could join the millions of people who accept Satan's lies and delusions.

> ¹And I stood upon the sand of the sea, and saw a beast rise up out of the sea, having seven heads and ten horns, and upon his horns ten crowns, and upon his heads the name of blasphemy. ²And the beast which I saw was like unto a leopard, and his feet were as *the feet* of a bear, and his mouth as the mouth of a lion: and the dragon gave him his power, and his seat, and great authority (Rev. 13:1, 2, KJV).

THE BEAST OF AUTHORITY

The forth vision continues into chapter 13 as John describes a savage creature. John stands...*upon the sand of the sea.* A repulsive beast rises out of the sea with seven heads and ten horns. John sees an ugly brute. Do you suppose that John wanted to run?

Our first look at the beast reminds us of the dragon in chapter 12. The beast has...*seven heads and ten horns* like the dragon. The number seven, for the heads, symbolizes fullness and perfection. The *heads* (*kephale*) indicate "supreme, chief, or a master lord."[1] The *horns* (*keras*) give us a symbol of "strength, courage, and power."[2] The number ten, for the horns, symbolizes "completeness of power." These attributes give Satan and the beast power and authority over their people of the world.

The beast had...*ten crowns* (*diadema*) on his ten horns. The (*diadema*), unlike the victory crowns that the saints wore, were simple crowns or headbands that Persian kings wore.[3] The kingly crowns sat on the beast's horns, which his representing power and authority on earth. In chapter 12, Satan had seven crowns (*diadema*) on his seven heads. The crowns on the Devil's seven heads indicated that he was the perfect and supreme head over the other two beasts.

THE BEAST OF HORROR

The satanic beast came...*up out of the sea.* The prophet Daniel also saw a vision of four beasts that came out of the sea. Each of the four beasts was different from the others. The four beasts had among them all the qualities that John's beast had. Daniel's vision revealed to us in graphic terms the character of the Revelation Beast (Dan. 7).

The first beast from Daniel was like a lion that had eagle wings. Someone ripped his wings off and stood him on two feet like a man. They gave a man's heart to the lion beast (Dan. 7:2–8). The second beast looked like a bear holding three ribs in its mouth. They told the bear beast to eat its fill of flesh. The third beast looked like a leopard with four wings and four heads. They gave the leopard beast authority to rule.

Daniel saw a terrifying and powerful fourth beast. The beast had iron teeth and bronze claws that crushed and devoured its victims. The beast trampled on everyone in its way. The four beasts represented four different kingdoms of the earth. After the forth beast, the Almighty God gave his saints a kingdom that they would possess forever and ever (Dan. 7:7, 17–23).

Many theologians understand that the four beasts or kingdoms represent Babylon, Medo-Persia, Greece, and Rome. The ten horns of the forth kingdom symbolize ten future kingdoms on the earth during the Gospel Age. The number ten for horns symbolize the full or complete number of rulers and countries on earth for the Age (Dan. 7:24). The time of each empire seams short when compared to the Lord's everlasting dominion.

THE BEAST FROM SATAN

The beast out of the sea in Revelation forms a composite of the four beasts in Daniel. The beast out of the sea symbolizes all the governments and countries for the entire Gospel Age. The description of Daniel's four beasts shows us the personality of Satan. Like the eagle, Satan works through the heart of man to molest and deceive the world.

Satan, like the bear, delights in destroying the flesh of man. Satan like the leopard hopes to rule the world. Satan, like the fourth beast, crushes and devours his victims and then tries to trample people who stand in his way.

Satan covets authority in the world. He uses the beast out of the sea of people and the beast of the earth to entice people to submit through pride, lust, and greed. The dragon gave the beast out of the sea...*his power, and his seat, and great authority.* The Devil gave the beast his *power* (*dunamis*), meaning "power, strength, and ability to do miracles."[4] The power came from armies and large numbers of forces. He gave the beast his seat, which represented thrones for kings or heads of a state.

LARGE IN SIZE

Satan gave the beast...*great authority.* The word great indicates large in size or space. Great also symbolizes a living being full of arrogance who oversteps the Creator's boundaries. Satan gave the beast *authority* (*exousia*), meaning "power of choice or the ability to do as one pleases."[5]

This description indicates that Satan, through the beast of government, possesses much power and authority. Satan spiritually devours millions of people in the world every year that don't have the protection of Jesus Christ. We should praise and thank the Lord for his grace, his mercy, and his protection. Praise his Holy Name!

> ³**And I saw one of his heads as it were wounded to death; and his deadly wound was healed: and all the world wondered after the beast. ⁴And they worshipped the dragon which gave power unto the beast: and they worshipped the beast, saying, Who *is* like unto the beast? who is able to make war with him? ⁵And there was given unto him a mouth speaking great things and blasphemies; and power was given unto him to continue forty *and* two months (Rev. 13:3–5, KJV).**

JESUS SLAYS THE BEAST

Daniel gave us a picture of the termination and the return of the four beasts. His prophecy pointed to the destruction of Satan's power by the Resurrection of Jesus Christ. The Ancient of Days sat on his throne and opened the court. The court sentenced the fourth beast to death and destroyed his body. The Almighty stripped the other beasts of their authority, but allowed them to live (Dan. 7:9–14).

The prophecy of Daniel revealed the future Kingdom of our Savior (Dan. 7:9–14). Our Redeemer destroyed the fourth beast of Daniel. The Son of Man came and stood before the Ancient of Days.

> ¹⁴And there was given him dominion, and glory, and a kingdom, that all people, nations, and languages, should serve him: his dominion is an everlasting dominion, which shall not pass away, and his kingdom that which shall not be destroyed (Dan. 7:14, KJV)

The Son of Man, Jesus Christ, received an everlasting Kingdom when he rose to life from death on the cross (Eph. 1:20–22; Phil. 2:9–11). The Lord has always ruled his Kingdom and will always rule it sitting at the right hand of the Father.

The Crucifixion and Resurrection of Christ destroyed the power of Satan and the beasts. The fourth beast of Daniel was slain. This pictures the head on the beast of the sea that was…*wounded to death; and his deadly wound was healed.* Jesus came to destroy the works of the Devil, and yet God let the Devil live and have limited power in the Gospel Age (1 John 3:8–10; Luke 10:17–20).

THE SLAIN BEAST LIVES

John used the Greek word (*sphazo*) for the killing of the beast. He used the same word to show slain Christians and our slain (*sphazo*) Savior.[6] The Devil has always tried to imitate God. John revealed this by showing the beast's imitation of our Savior's death and Resurrection. Why did the Lord let Satan and his beasts come back into limited power after their defeat? The Bible doesn't say; it's a mystery.

> The wild beast = the whole antichristian power set in motion by Satan as the prince of this world. This antichristian power received its death stroke from Christ when he was glorified and enthroned. Christ has the keys of the death and the Hades.[7]

The visions of Daniel and the Book of Revelation give us symbols that point to a higher truth. The images of the beasts symbolize the actions of Satan's kingdom. God interpreted Daniel's vision, and Daniel's vision helps us interpret John's vision (Dan. 7:1–28).

The four beasts of Daniel rose out of the sea like the beast in Revelation. The four beasts represent four kingdoms or nations on earth (Dan. 7:17). This then indicates that the beast of the sea represents government, business, and people (Rev. 17:15). The number of the beasts implies four points of a compass, which indicates that the beasts cover the whole world.

God told Daniel that the beast with ten horns would harass the saints for a time, times, and one-half time. This points to the same time as the time in which the beast was given power...*to continue forty and two months.*

Satan calls the beast, out of the sea of people, to help him persecute God's children. The beast represents government throughout the world. The kingdoms rise and fall, but the power of the Devil stays active from empire to empire.

The woman Babylon rides a beast with the same description in chapter 17. The beast supports Babylon, which represents the evil powers of Satan. God grants him limited power for the Gospel Age until a brief time at the end when he's released with much power. The beast was alive, is not alive, and shall ascend out of the bottomless pit (Rev. 17:8). The beast that the woman rides was alive, he was slain by God, and now he's alive and under the control of Jesus in the Abyss.

BEAST INFLUENCES GOVERNMENT

Unseen forces control the governments of the world. The spiritual forces of darkness work in the shadows behind government workers and politicians. Most government workers and elected leaders don't understand the spiritual powers that manipulate their thoughts and actions. Politicians drift through life changing their opinions when driven by the winds of political correctness.

The prayers of God's people also control the government actions. When the prayers of the Christian Church increase, this pushes back the forces of darkness. If Christians let up in their prayers, then the dark forces take more control.

Satan, through the beast of government, changes the forces of power throughout the world. The Devil wants to control the minds and bodies of all people. He doesn't care about anyone's money, pleasure, or addictions; but he uses these things to control people.

The actions of government agencies and courts around the world may lean toward the side of darkness. The forces of darkness work to entrench themselves in the power centers of government. Satan's on the move in the control centers of the world. If Christians don't pray and push him back, his powers and demons will continue to gain more control. Satan then uses his authority to take away the rights of God's children.

Worship the Beast

The people of the world…*worshiped the beast*, and they…*worshiped the dragon* through the beast. When people honor anti-Christian works and policies of their government, they give honor to the Devil. Jesus said that if people do the things of the Devil, than the Devil is their father (John 8:44).

Some worship the country they live in. The Bible says that we should support and pray for our leaders and country (Heb. 13:7). Many countries offer us a marvelous homeland, but we should not entangle ourselves in nationalism. Our first love, as Christians, has to go to Jesus Christ.

Governments blaspheme God by taking away prayer in school. Governments blaspheme God every time they let a greedy and unwise doctor kill a baby. Governments blaspheme God when they take away the right to worship the One True Lord.

> **⁶And he opened his mouth in blasphemy against God, to blaspheme his name, and his tabernacle, and them that dwell in heaven. ⁷And it was given unto him to make war with the saints, and to overcome them: and power was given him over all kindreds, and tongues, and nations. ⁸And all that dwell upon the earth shall worship him, whose names are not written in the book of life of**

the Lamb slain from the foundation of the world. ⁹If any man have an ear, let him hear. 10 He that leadeth into captivity shall go into captivity: he that killeth with the sword must be killed with the sword. Here is the patience and the faith of the saints (Rev. 13:6–10, KJV).

THE BEAST WAITS

The forgiven sinners study their Bibles and learn that God is Holy, Eternal, Mighty in power, and Faithful to his children. In contrast, the beast of the sea speaks...*blasphemy against* God. He curses God's name, God's Church, and God's saints in Heaven. Then Satan, through the beast, attacks the children of God on earth.

The beast doesn't always have the power to attack saints with deadly harm. Prayer helps God's spiritual forces control the beast. He has to abide by the opinion of the people and the leaders in government. Some governments reflect the values of the Lord.

The beast knows that if he waits a generation or two the winds of politics will change. The beast, like Satan, has time to wait. Two thousand years have passed since the birth of Christ. In that time, the beast has slain millions and millions of holy saints around the world.

THE MASTICATION PROCESS

We use a juicer to make fresh juice from fruits and vegetables. We enjoy drinking the delicious juice. The juicer operates on the mastication process, which separates the pulp from the juice by crushing and chewing. When the Devil assaults Christians, they may feel like fruit going through the mastication process.

The Lord may empower the Devil to put us through a juicer experience. God uses the process to separate the good from the worthless. God allows trials in our lives to strengthen our faith and help us develop a larger trust in him (Rom 5:2–5, Matt. 3:12).

Our Father receives our thoughts and actions, from testing, as a pleasing offering. (James 1:12). Jesus desires to reach out and put the pieces back together. In these situations, he reveals grace, love, and mercy to each of us.

ANGELS AND SPIRITUAL BLOODLINES

In my limited experience as a Christian, I have found two things that help protect us from the beast. I learned in my early Christian years to station angels around our home and property. I also put a spiritual line from the blood of Jesus Christ around our property and us. The shed blood of the Lamb gives us protection against the evil one.

On the first Passover, the Israelites put the blood from slain lambs on the sides and the tops of their doors. The blood kept the destroyer from coming in and killing the firstborn. The Bible says the blood of our Savior has more power than the blood of animal sacrifices (Heb. 9:11–14). The OT saints used the blood of animal sacrifices to protect themselves against evil. For this reason, how much more should we use the blood of Jesus to protect us from evil.

We as Christians may not understand all the reasons for using the shed blood of Jesus Christ. This should not keep us from putting a spiritual line of shed blood around our families. I didn't understand it when I first used God's protection over twenty years ago. Yet, God in his grace sheltered us. We live in the inner city of Portland. We have never had a break-in or a car stolen in twenty-eight years. God's so good; there's power in the blood.

THE BLOOD TAKES CARE OF US

We walked around our home and properties to put angels and a spiritual bloodline around them. As Linda and I walked around, we asked the Lord to circle the property with his blood so that no spiritual or physical enemy could cross it. We asked God in the name of Jesus Christ to put a spiritual line of his shed blood around each member of our family.

We apply the blood and angels to each individual and property. In our prayers, we also ask for protection from the blood each day. Once a year or more, we walk around our home to remind God and to reinforce the angels and the blood of Jesus (Luke 18:2–8).

We use a moving protection line around each of our vehicles, which we reinforce a few times a year. I lived in a motor home while I wrote this book. I reinforced the angel protection and the bloodline around it every time I park it. Some Christians might consider this paying too much attention to the enemy. Yet, I believe that helps to keep the evil one away. The angels from God and the shed blood help keep the deceiver from leading me where the Holy Spirit doesn't want me to go.

USE EFFECTIVE TOOLS

Christians whom God leads into effective spiritual ministry find this true. They experience spiritual battles and learn the...*patience and the faith of the saints*. Some find that without protective prayer their spiritual ministry goes flat.

The Almighty gives his children many tools in the Bible. All we need to do is choose the ones that work for us and use them. Each child of God needs to experiment and find what works best for him or her. We speak the Word, and the power of the Holy Spirit does the rest. "Thank you, Lord, for your Word and tools of protection. Thank you, Father, for your grace and authority that covers the darkness with your Light.

POWER OVER THE COURTS

The Devil gives the beast power...*over all kindreds, and tongues, and nations.* The beast has power or freedom of choice to do as he pleases. His power gives him authority to rule governments and make judicial decisions. Many court decisions stir Christians to anger. We should understand that the court are not at fault. We should direct our anger at the beast and the dragon: they influence the court systems.

Nothing but the power of prayer will change the direction of the court systems in a nation. When the people of God sleep, the beast entrenches himself in their government. The Christian Church needs to remain diligent in prayer for their leaders (1 Tim. 2:1–3).

Many God-fearing people have not learned how to storm the gates of hell. They forgot to pick up their keys to unlock the gates of hell when they committed their life to Jesus Christ (Rev. 11:7). Many pastors and church leaders don't teach on prayer. Some followers of Christ try to live a victorious Christian life, but they don't understand the truth of prayer.

LAMB'S BOOK OF LIFE

The Lord desires to write all names...*in the book of life of the Lamb.* Before the creation of the world, the slain Lamb and the Father knew every name in the book of life. That doesn't mean that we can sit back and watch the world go by.

The Lord puts each of us in places where we can witness Jesus by our lives. What happens when we don't let our light shine? Suppose we do not reveal Jesus to someone whom we should, and the Lord doesn't write his name in the book of life. How would we feel if we went to Heaven and he or she wasn't there?

SPIRIT GIVES WISDOM

Jesus said...*If any man have an ear, let him hear* what the Spirit says to each of the seven churches. The Lord wanted us to listen to what the Spirit said to each church in chapters 2 and 3. In his Revelation, Jesus only used this phrase for the churches and here in chapter 13. Jesus also wanted us to listen to the Spirit for the meaning of the two beasts.

We need to do more than just read the words. The true meaning will only come by revelation from the Holy Spirit. Our Father wants us to live in his Light, and he desires to give us wisdom. In contrast, the Devil and the two beasts treat their followers like a mushroom farmer. They keep mushrooms in the dark and feed them manure.

> [11]Then I saw another beast, coming out of the earth. He had two horns like a lamb, but he spoke like a dragon. [12]He exercised all the authority of the first beast on his behalf, and made the earth and its inhabitants worship the first beast, whose fatal wound had been healed (Rev. 13:11, 12, NIV).

Beast Imitates Jesus

John watches…*another beast, coming out of the earth.* The beast with two horns mimics the slain Lamb shown in Revelation 5. John says the lamb…*spoke like a dragon.* The beast rises out of the earth and holds hidden danger for the Christian Church.

The image of the beast seams similar to a *lamb* (*arnion*).[8] The Bible uses the word (*arnion*), meaning "little lamb," for the beast and the Lamb of God or Christ. Satan gives the world an alternative to Christ. The Devil says, "If you need someone to worship, come and worship my little lamb."

That cunning serpent always tries to help his followers. The Devil knows that people resist submitting to God. Therefore, he offers them an impostor that is similar to Christ. Satan deceives people into worshiping a form of divinity rather than the True God.

John watches the beast come…*out of the earth.* This may symbolize the beast coming out of the bottomless pit. In the fifth trumpet, the Devil lets smoke, darkness, and locusts out of the Abyss. The darkness that comes from the smoke and the locusts brings deception to the people of the world and the Church.

That little lamb with the deadly spikes looks cute and harmless—but don't let him pull his wool over your eyes. He will spiritually knock you down and trample on your head—unless you're smart enough to call on Jesus.

Little Lamb Hides Truth

The beast out of the earth causes Christians to stray from Jesus. God keeps Christians sealed to him unless they turn their back on the Father and blaspheme the Holy Spirit (Heb. 6:4). I believe that it's rare for a Christian to fall away from the grace of salvation (Jude 24; John 10:29). Although, some may loose their effectiveness in God's Kingdom.

The seducing lamb corrupts the Lord's values. He changes beliefs in small stages. From generation to generation, he tries to erode our trust in God's Holy Word. He often succeeds in leading some away from a strong conviction in the whole Truth of the Bible. When Christians water down the stories in the Bible, they loose confidence in the Almighty God.

The little pretender misguides Christians and draws them into areas not of God. The false Christ leads them on paths that lead from shadow to shadow. They seek truth but look in the wrong places. The little lamb leads people on false paths away from the True Savior. People who follow the lamb with bloody spikes live in a spiritual place of grayness, emptiness, and pitfalls.

LAMB WITH HORNS—ANTICHRIST

The deceiving lamb portrays a picture of the Antichrist. John said that many Antichrists have already come (1 John 2:18). The little lamb takes the part of the Antichrist when he speaks through a church. The two-horned lamb never speaks about the blood of Jesus Christ. He always has a better way to salvation.

Many fast-growing churches in the world today claim to have the true answers. A cult church always leaves out the Trinity and the blood of our Savior. The Redeemer sacrificed his blood for our salvation and holiness before God. The little lamb from Satan always skips the grace of salvation by the shed blood.

Cults talk about Jesus as a mediator or as a good person. They always stop short of calling him the real Creator God. The false lamb creates many counterfeit churches. Most of the cults have a form of working their way into Heaven. The cults have many different ways to reach Heaven. Their way may seem right, but it's not the way of God and leads to spiritual death (Prov. 16:25).

FINDING FAULT WITH CHURCHES

Some authors of commentaries feel called to criticize the Roman Catholic Church and the Pope. Some suggest the Pope as a type of Antichrist. Some Christians of today feel the same calling. Perhaps the Catholics of the past fit their description, but the Roman Catholic Church has changed much in the last few hundred years. The past has expired; let the past die.

Our Savior uses the Roman Catholic Church to bring millions to salvation as he does in Protestant churches. Many Catholics have a close relationship with Jesus Christ. The Lord tells us that the wind or Spirit blows where he wants it to go. We can hear it, but we don't know where it comes from or where it is goes. The Spirit raises some to life and only he knows why (John 3:8).

God does not honor some denominations more than others. He loves the Roman Catholic people, just as surely as he loves the Protestant people. Our Faithful God will use all Christian denominations for his purposes.

On the other side, many Catholics believe that they have the true church of God. Jesus Christ has news for all Christian congregations. No Church, or body of believers, follows the Gospel of Christ with perfection. Man made rules and errors always creep into worship and practices. Not one church appears 100 percent right in God's eyes, and yet he loves all of his children.

The call to criticize churches of other Christian groups doesn't come from the Lamb of God. The need to find fault with other Christian beliefs comes from the imperfect lamb that utters dragon sounds. The slain Lamb gives us peace and love toward our brothers and sisters in Christ. The little lamb with spikes gives discord and a critical spirit toward others who aren't exactly like themselves.

DON'T JUDGE SAINTS

Paul said that we should not judge our brothers or sisters in Christ. Each of us will stand before the judgment seat of God (Rom. 14:4–10). He said that we should not put obstacles in the way of others. He writes about different things that Christians did and distinct ways to serve God. Paul said that the Kingdom of God is righteousness, joy, and peace through the Holy Spirit. He said that everyone who serves Christ by the Spirit pleases God (Rom. 14:9–18).

Any attitude of judgment toward other Christian bodies should not happen. The lamb, speaking like a dragon, moves among the Christian churches. Evangelicals judge Pentecostals, and Pentecostals judge evangelicals. Pentecostals and evangelicals judge Catholics, and Catholics judge evangelicals and Pentecostals. When we all get to Heaven, who's right? Only the Lord knows!

WORTHY IS THE LAMB

They stand shoulder to shoulder with
brothers and sisters from all churches.
They stand with wonder praising him.
Praise him—Praise him—Praise him.
Worthy, Worthy, Worthy is the Lamb.

Who forgives their sins of judgment.
Worthy, Worthy, Worthy is the Lamb.
Who gives lasting love for the others.

[13]**And he performed great and miraculous signs, even causing fire to come down from heaven to earth in full view of men. [14]Because of the signs he was given power to do on behalf of the first beast, he deceived the inhabitants of the earth. He ordered them to set up an image in honour of the beast who was wounded by the sword and yet lived. [15]He was given power to give breath to the image of the first beast, so that it could speak and cause all who refused to worship the image to be killed (Rev. 13:13–15, NIV).**

ANTICHRIST TYPES

The Bible says that there will be many imitators of Christ and false prophets. They will do signs and miracles that deceive people (Luke 21:8). The Devil has monstrous power to use when God grants him authority. Satan can use supernatural power to work through and control people on earth. The miracles of the little lamb cause people to take their eyes off Jesus and look toward our government and false churches.

Every nation has examples of the Antichrist. Some appear well known when they lead hundreds of unwise followers to destruction or death. Most people recognize these spiritual leaders as not normal. Christian people need to study the Word of God and follow the teachings of Jesus. This will keep Antichrists from deceiving them (Matt. 24:24).

Some use sports as their religion. People spend many hours of the week with their eyes glued to the TV watching their favorite sport. In the spring, it's soccer. In the summer, it's baseball. In the fall, it's football. In the winter, it's basketball. The avid sports nut can take his or her choice of many other sports all year long. The little lamb speaks, and the TV goes on. They watch another game similar to the last one they saw.

THE TELEVISION GOD

The little lamb causes many to...*worship the image* of television. Some people spend most of their free hours watching the idol of TV. The broadcast media assaults Christians with worldly values day after day. If a Christian turned off the TV for twenty percent of the time and read the Bible, this would change his or her life.

The influence from TV causes many Christians to take their eyes and thoughts away from Jesus. Most of the content of programs point away from the Truth of God. The television idol lets people live their lives in the make-believe of TV land.

A few times a year, the news media grabs people's attention with some tragic drama. Men and women immerse themselves in the unfolding story. They sometimes forget about the world around them and concentrate on the emotions of the media event.

The false lamb uses his influence to honor the first beast or the people of the world. Humanism honors people and rejects religious authority. On the surface humanism seems good because of high principles and values. Many people worship the god of humanism or self. The false lamb leads people to worship any philosophy or religion that doesn't have the True Savior in it.

People suffer from the same beast under different names through the centuries. The Devil uses his tried and effective tricks over and over and over. He still uses them today and will use them until Jesus returns.

IN THE CLOUDS

I remember a flight from Seattle Washington to Montana. Over the Cascade Mountains we approached a beautiful white cloud about five miles wide. We flew from sunshine into dense fog. Suddenly we hit moderate turbulence for a minute.

I didn't consider it a problem because the Cessna 177 handled the turbulence. I kept it in a semi level attitude on a straight course. It was a rough ride, but experience and the Lord helped keep the plane upright. We broke out of the clouds into the sunshine and could see 300 miles into Idaho. I saw the beauty, and Linda said, "Praise the Lord."

My sister-in-law said, "Praise him—I thought we were going to meet him."

A person riding in a small airplane through a cloud has a different perspective than the pilot flying the airplane. When in the clouds, you can't tell up from down because you can't see the horizon. All you can sense from moderate turbulence is the violent action. The pilot has gyroscope gages to indicate the horizon and the airplane's attitude position. If the pilot focuses his attention on the gages and flies the airplane, the plane will carry him through. In the same way, when we focus our eyes on Jesus, he will carry us through.

"But you are a shield around me, O LORD; you bestow glory on me and lift up my head" (Ps. 3:3, NIV).

Satan offers many beautiful white clouds in this world to entice the unaware. They look good on the outside, but sometimes the centers hold surprises. The little lamb, with spikes that pierce, loves to put Christians in perilous positions. If the child of God focus his eyes on Jesus, this will help keep their wings level. "Thank you, Lord, for helping us to keep our eyes on you.

> [16]He also forced everyone, small and great, rich and poor, free and slave, to receive a mark on his right hand or on his forehead, [17]so that no one could buy or sell unless he had the mark, which is the name of the beast or the number of his name. [18]This calls for wisdom. If anyone has insight, let him calculate the number of the beast, for it is man's number. His number is 666 (Rev. 13:16–18, NIV).

THE DEVIL'S MARK

Almost everyone has heard about the number 666. Why shouldn't the Devil have his own mark for his followers? God sealed and marked his people in chapter 7, and he measured them for his Temple in chapter 11. Satan wants everything that the Lord has. If the old serpent couldn't have a mark for his followers, he might creep away and pout.

Jesus Christ gave the readers of Revelation two warnings in chapter 13. In verse 9, he said that we needed to listen with our spiritual ears to hear the meaning of the two beasts. Verse 18...*calls for wisdom* so we can calculate the number. We need to use wisdom and insight from the Holy Spirit to understand the meaning of the mark of the beast. If we just read the words, we won't comprehend the true spiritual meaning.

John wrote the Revelation of Jesus Christ for the entire Gospel Age. The early church probably would have put it aside if they had believed it was only for the end days. The early church didn't put Revelation aside because Jesus had John write it for their time and for our time. The principles in Revelation have applied to every age; therefore, the 666 mark was for every Age.

CALCULATE WITH WISDOM

We look at the number six...*for it is man's number.* Seven gives us the symbol for perfection and the creation of God. God created man on the sixth day, or one day less than perfection. John says we need wisdom to understand how to...*calculate the number of the beast.* The word *count* (*psephizo*) means "to compute or to calculate."[9] We calculate the number 666 by multiplying 10 x 10 x 6 + 10 x 6 + 6 = six hundred plus sixty plus six, or 666.

The Lord gives wisdom to understand the symbols of the Bible. Six gives us the number of man. Six times ten times ten tells us that the number of man is complete or squared. The number 666 simply points to a symbolic mark given to men, women, and children of the world who don't follow Christ.

Jesus indicates in Revelation that we have either the seal of God or the mark of the beast. The seal and the mark symbolize what people serve while on earth. The mark of the beast and or the seal of God point to the loyalty of each person to Satan or to God.

CHOOSE THE SEAL OR MARK

The beast puts the mark on...*his right hand or on his forehead.* The right hand symbolizes what people do with their hands and their actions in life. The mark on the forehead symbolizes the way people think.

If a person does the deeds of the world and thinks evil, then the beast gives him a mark. The Lord looks at our hearts and knows our thoughts (Ps. 139:23). Our Lord tells us that out of our hearts come thoughts of evil, which do not come from God (Matt. 15:19).

> [7]Do not be deceived: God cannot be mocked. A man reaps what he sows. [8]The one who sows to please his sinful nature, from that nature will reap destruction; the one who sows to please the Spirit, from the Spirit will reap eternal life (Gal. 6:7, 8, NIV)

So then, a person's mind, heart, and spirit control his thoughts and actions. If a man's heart leads him toward God, then God's spirit will control his life. If a man's heart leads him toward the world, then the Devil's spirit will control his life.

A person who dies with the Devil's mark will go to judgment. If a person living for the world repents and begins to follow Jesus, then God removes the 666 mark and seals the person for eternal life. Hallelujah! Glory to God who wants all to repent and come to him.

THE LITERAL MARK—666

The black horse of the third seal leads the charge to deny economic trading to Christians. The black horse persecutes Christians in monetary ways. If a Christian lives in a country where the government is anti-Christian, then the government persecutes him. Under government oppression Christians cannot buy or sell when they confess that Jesus is Lord.

Because of Satan's bitterness and his twisted humor, the Antichrist will bring out a literal number in the years ahead. Revelation speaks to the entire Church Age, but it also speaks truths for that brief time at the end. The Devil will do this to fulfill God's Word in the final years just before the return of Jesus Christ. The Antichrist and the governments will use a mark to identify the people in the world. This will put fearful pressure on Christians and cause much suffering.

Churches and people use the world economic system more than they realize. Banks and businesses use numbers to buy and sell. We have social security cards, bank charge cards, and debit cards. The experts say that sometime in the future the world will go to a banking system without cash. People will buy and sell with debit cards.

BANKS LOSE MONEY

Banks that lose money from card thefts and fraud will look for ways to stop the losses. Someone will read Revelation 13, and the banks will see the light. The banks will use an ingenious solution of putting a number on your hand and forehead. This number could be a microprocessor injected under the skin. People already use this technology to identify animals.

The first beast will control the banking system. The Antichrist will then require anyone using the mark to give allegiance to the world system of government. Satan, who controls the world system, will demand that people reject their relationship with Jesus Christ. This will help set the stage for persecution of the Christian Church.

When and if it gets to this point, I don't have any easy answers. Every child of God will need to pray and listen to the Holy Spirit for direction.

Sometimes when I am praying and thinking about the Lord, I can sense the presence of the Lord around me. His presence is refreshing like the smell of the air after a summer rain shower. The summer showers sweeten and freshen the air while they renew the land. Coming into the peaceful presence of Jesus refreshes and renews me. When I'm in the arms of the Lord, there is no better place. The world gives nothing: in the end, only Jesus matters.

NOTES

1. Heads, *kephale*, G2776. A head. Metaphor, anything supreme, chief, or prominent.
2. Horns, *keras*, G2768. A horn. A symbol of strength and courage.
3. Crowns, *diadema*, G1238. A crown. A blue and white headband that Persian kings wore.
4. Power, *dunamis*, G1411. Miraculous power, mighty, strength.
5. Authority, *exousia*, G1849. Ability, privilege, force, jurisdiction.
6. Wounded, *sphazo*, G4969. To slaughter, butcher, slay, or wound.
7. R. C. H. Lenski, *The Interpretation of St. John's Revelation* (Minneapolis: Augsburg Publishing House, 1943) p. 394.
8. Lamb, *arnion*, G721. Lamb, meaning Christ, a little lamb.
9. Calculate, *psephizo*, G5585. To count, compute, or calculate.

CHAPTER 14

144,000 Saints—The Harvest

GOD'S GRACE FOR DAD

I experienced God's amazing grace from the power of prayer in 1997. My dad went to stand on Mount Zion instead of the other place. He had never wanted to discuss God or salvation for the last thirty years. Dad always seemed indifferent to the Lord. Several people in our family prayed for him through the years.

Dan fell into hard times the last five years of his life. He developed emphysema and needed one hundred percent oxygen. Dad sat in his chair and watched television for five years.

My brother Jerry, a Roman Catholic, enjoyed watching the Catholic TV network. However, Dad hated it. When he slept, Jerry sometimes changed the station, but if dad woke up, it never stayed on the Christian station.

Linda and I saw him four weeks before he won the victory. Because of God's grace, Dad was open to prayer and discussing God. During the last four weeks of his life on earth, he only watched the Catholic TV network.

Dad slept much, but he wanted it on that station. If my brother put it on the news, this disturbed him. Dad heard the message of the Gospel over and over. Praise the Lord for his grace and mercy. Praise him because he hears our prayers and then draws our loved ones into eternal life.

Chapter 14 reveals the results of our prayers. It closes the fourth vision of the Revelation of Jesus Christ. The chapter contains three separate parts. Verses 1, 6, and 14 begin with and I looked, or I saw. John starts a new theme each time he looks or senses something new. Chapter 14 shows us a short view of the full Gospel Age.

Chapters 12 and 13 symbolize the power of Satan and the two beasts by their attack on the Christian Church. Chapter 14 gives Christians hope. The Lord previews the result of our hope with the picture of saints singing a new song on Mount Zion.

> **¹Then I looked, and there before me was the Lamb, standing on Mount Zion, and with him 144,000 who had his name and his Father's name written on their foreheads. ²And I heard a sound from heaven like the roar of rushing waters and like a loud peal of thunder. The sound I heard was like that of harpists playing their harps. ³And they sang a new song before the throne and before the four living creatures and the elders. No one could learn the song except the 144,000 who had been redeemed from the earth (Rev. 14:1–3, NIV).**

144,000 ON MOUNT ZION

John looks and sees the Lamb. The Lamb, Jesus Christ, stands on Mount Zion with 144,000 redeemed saints. Whom do these saints represent? The prophet Joel says that whoever calls on the name of the Lord shall be delivered. The deliverance shall come out of Mount Zion and Jerusalem (Joel 2:32). The writer of Hebrews gives us hope with his words.

> ²²But you have come to Mount Zion, to the heavenly Jerusalem, the city of the living God. You have come to thousands upon thousands of angels in joyful assembly, ²³to the church of the firstborn, whose names are written in heaven. You have come to God, the judge of all men, to the spirits of righteous men made perfect, ²⁴to Jesus the mediator of a new covenant, and to the sprinkled blood that speaks a better word than the blood of Abel (Heb. 12:22–24, NIV)

The scene of the Lamb on Mount Zion describes for us two types of hope. Jesus shows us our future hope with a view of Heaven. He also shows us the Christian Church today symbolized by the spiritual Mount Zion.

MOUNT ZION OF TODAY

We have come to Mount Zion and to the Lamb of our salvation. The Lamb stands on Mount Zion, which represents the Christian Church (Ps. 48:2). He stands with and lives in the saints that he has...*redeemed from the earth*. Even while we still live on the earth, in the spiritual sense, we have already come to Mount Zion. Revelation shows us a picture of the Christian Church today from God's spiritual point of view.

This scene also reveals our future hope of life in Heaven with the Almighty God. The victorious Lamb stands with 144,000 saints of God. The 144,000 forgiven sinners appear as the same 144,000 saints that God sealed on their foreheads in chapter 7. In this picture, we see the saints with...*his Father's name written on their foreheads*. In contrast, Satan puts his mark, 666, of ownership on his people.

Chapter 7 specifies the Lord's people as his servants. The Father writes his name on their foreheads in this chapter, which indicates a sense of ownership by God for his people on earth.

THE EUCHARIST ALTAR CALL

I sometimes hear Christians criticize liturgical churches because they don't have altar calls. The Bible says that we should publicly confess with our mouth that Jesus Christ is Lord (Rom. 10:8–10).

I have good news. Liturgical churches have altar calls. Every time they celebrate Holy Communion, the people proclaim Jesus Christ as Lord and publicly ask forgiveness for sin. They confess their faith in the Father, the Son, and the Holy Spirit by speaking the Apostles Creed or another creed. Then the forgiven sinners walk up to the altar and boldly accept the body and blood of Jesus Christ.

Christians repeat their belief in the Savior each time they partake of the Lord's Supper. These are not dead spoken words. In God's eyes, the church and the people live.

So next time you hear or perhaps say that someone goes to a dead church, don't believe it. Our Father has redeemed children in all Christian Churches. God-fearing people in liturgical churches confess with their mouth that Jesus Christ is Lord. They do this often, and the Holy Spirit quickens their spirit and gives them life.

Some Protestants have not understood the liturgical worship services. The words spoken in each liturgy came from the Holy Bible. Our God gave the format for liturgical worship early in the history of the NT Church.

"Father, I thank you for working in the many different types of churches. Father, I thank you for your grace and salvation that you give to each of us. Father, I thank you for your love, mercy, and compassion that you lavishly pour out in all settings. Lord Jesus, we thank you for the gift of life that you give in all churches. Lord Jesus, I praise and glorify your Holy Name. Amen! Amen!"

THE NEW SONG

John hears a sound from Heaven...*like the roar of rushing waters.* Heaven must have many sounds. The redeemed saints play harps and sing a new song. The saints, whom Jesus purchased with his shed blood, sing the same song in Revelation 5:9 and 15:3. Only Christians, redeemed by the shed blood of the Lamb, can sing the new song.

Christians singing the new song also have the name of the Lamb and the Father written on their foreheads. Our Father seals and puts his name on each of his children when they come into his Kingdom. When the parents baptize their child, God places a seal or a mark on him or her.

MY SIGN—THE CROSS

The Lord put his mark on me as a baby in Holy Baptism. Because of the Lord's mark and seal, I have never had any interest in horoscopes even before I was a Christian. Many people, even Christians, read their horoscope every day. Satan uses this to lead people away from God.

On occasion people ask me what my sign is. I say, "I was born under the cross of Jesus Christ."

Most people don't ask for my sign again. If a person does ask me why I have this sign, this gives a golden opportunity to tell them about the Savior.

> **⁴These are those who did not defile themselves with women, for they kept themselves pure. They follow the Lamb wherever he goes. They were purchased from among men and offered as firstfruits to God and the Lamb. ⁵No lie was found in their mouths; they are blameless (Rev. 14:4, 5, NIV).**

CHRISTIANS—FIRSTFRUITS

The Israelites celebrated the Feast of the Harvest by bringing the first part of the harvest, or firstfruits, to God as an offering (Exod. 23:16–20). They also called this the Feast of Weeks when they offered their firstfruits (Exod. 34:22). The Feast of Weeks, known as Pentecost, was celebrated fifty days from the beginning of Passover (Lev. 23:9–16). The Israelites celebrated the harvest by offering their firstfruits to God at Pentecost each year.

Firstfruits of the OT gave us a picture of the harvest that men dedicated to the Lord. In the NT, the Lord changed the spiritual importance of Pentecost. He changed the harvest of produce into the harvest of people for salvation. On that first Pentecost after the ascension of Jesus, God began bringing in his firstfruits or harvest of people. God poured out his Holy Spirit and added 3,000 people as firstfruits to the Kingdom of God (Acts 2:1–4, 41).

Our Sovereign God considers every Christian as a type of firstfruits. Our Savior gave us a new birth through his Word and our faith so that we could be a kind of firstfruits (James 1:18).

144,000 men, women, and children stand with Jesus Christ on Mount Zion. They do not represent super saints who haven't had physical sex with a man or a woman. They represent the full and complete Christian Church throughout the Gospel Age. Our Father considers every Christian as a type of spiritual virgin when they accept Christ as Savior.

> ²I am jealous for you with a godly jealousy. I promised you to one husband, to Christ, so that I might present you as a pure virgin to him (2 Cor. 11:2, NIV)

The Bible calls each of us firstfruits and spiritual virgins for two reasons. God purifies each of us with the shed blood of Jesus Christ. When we ask forgiveness for our sins in the name of Jesus, God forgets all of our sins. The blood cleanses us and purifies us (Isa. 43:25; 1 John 1:9). God doesn't remember our sins: in his eyes, we stand perfect and holy (Titus 2:14).

FAITHFUL TO GOD—VIRGINS

He calls us virgins because we remain faithful to Jesus Christ in our lives. We don't wander away and worship other gods after we begin a relationship with Jesus as his bride. We worship the Lord the remaining days of our life. We do not defile ourselves and serve other gods. We keep his name on our foreheads and refuse the mark of Satan.

The virgins symbolize spiritual faithfulness to God. The Bible calls Israel a virgin bride (Lam. 2:13; Amos 5:2). Only when Israel strayed from the True God and worshiped idols did the Bible call her a prostitute (Jer. 3:6–11; Hos. 2:4, 5). These verses in Revelation picture a redeemed Church faithful to the Almighty God.

The verses above said…*they kept themselves pure*, and…*No lie was found in their mouths; they are blameless*. Even super-saints, who never touched the opposite sex, could never fulfill these conditions. It's impossible because we are all sinners who have no hope except in the grace and love of our Father. God purchased them from among men; therefore,…*They follow the Lamb wherever he goes.*

OUR LAMB ON MOUNT ZION

The Lord our Lamb gives us all we need.
Our Lamb gives us grace and righteousness.
Even when death advances, we shall not fear.
Our Lamb calls us by name and gives us oil.
Our Lamb writes his name on our foreheads.
Our Holy Lamb prepares Mount Zion for us.
We shall live on Mount Zion with the Lamb
for all of our days, and then for all eternity.

⁶And I saw another angel fly in the midst of heaven, having the everlasting gospel to preach unto them that dwell on the earth, and to every nation, and kindred, and tongue, and people, ⁷Saying with a loud voice, Fear God, and give glory to him; for the hour of his judgment is come: and worship him that made heaven, and earth, and the sea, and the fountains of waters. ⁸And there followed another angel, saying, Babylon is fallen, is fallen, that great city, because she made all nations drink of the wine of the wrath of her fornication (Rev. 14:6–8, KJV).

THREE ANGELS—JUDGMENT

John begins the second part of chapter 14. He sees the first of three angels flying through Heaven. The first angle brings an invitation to the Gospel of salvation for all people. The second angel brings a message that Babylon has fallen. The third angel brings a warning from our Creator. He states that a terrible fate follows to those who worship the beast and carry the mark. The picture in verses 6–13 shows us a short view of the Gospel Age.

The first angel carries...*the everlasting gospel* that our Savior offers to all people who live on the earth. The angel mixes a warning with the Gospel. He cries...*Fear God, and give glory to him* because judgment will come. The angel brings a message of hope for Christians and doom for heathens.

Chapter 14 pictures the fearful judgment of our Holy God. Many Christians do not like to speak of God's judgment at the end of the Age. Nevertheless, the Bible shows more images of hell than of Heaven. Because the Bible only speaks truth and God does not lie, judgment will come for unbelievers.

I do not care to write or talk of judgment, yet it will come. We serve a Holy and Righteous God who cannot coexist with sin (Lev. 19:2). The Lord hates sin and must punish it because of his Holiness.

The second angel follows the first angel and gives us a preview of the fall of Babylon. The woman Babylon corrupts all nations and leads them into immoral perversion. The city of Babylon meaning confusion draws many away from the True God for the entire Gospel Age. The Lord guarantees us that judgment will come to Babylon.

> [9]A third angel followed them and said in a loud voice: "If anyone worships the beast and his image and receives his mark on the forehead or on the hand, [10]he, too, will drink of the wine of God's fury, which has been poured full strength into the cup of his wrath. He will be tormented with burning sulfur in the presence of the holy angels and of the Lamb. [11]And the smoke of their torment rises for ever and ever. There is no rest day or night for those who worship the beast and his image, or for anyone who receives the mark of his name" (Rev. 14:9–11, NIV).

Do Not Worship the Beast

The third angel follows with a warning to God's children. Do not go the way of the world. Worship of the beast causes a person to...*drink of the wine of God's fury*. These sound like hard words from our Father, the God of Love.

Jesus writes chapter 14 to Christians to give us hope and joy, and to show us where we shall go. He writes to tell us that judgment will come to our persecutors. Jesus also writes to each of us with a warning. Do not play with the grace and mercy of God! The Lord speaks of deadly consequences to people who disobey him.

The three angels of God begin with the grace of salvation. They then encourage all people to praise and worship our Lord God Almighty. They warn of the coming judgment, and the certainty of Babylon's destruction. The last angel warns of God's fury and wrath if we accept the mark of the beast.

Remove 666

Can a person get rid of the mark of the beast? Christians have debated this question throughout the ages. Some would say no because once the Devil stamps on his mark, the person's lost forever. What does God's Word say?

The mark symbolized the rejection of God and his principals. The apostle Paul gave us a good example of someone with the mark of the beast. When Paul persecuted the Christians, they thought he represented evil. Our merciful God forgave Paul for killing his children, and then the Father removed the mark out of love (Acts 9).

REPENT—TURN TO GOD

People who belong to the Devil can repent, turn to God, and change. God then removes the Devil's mark and seals them with his grace of salvation. The symbolism of the mark reveals where a person's heart rests at the point of physical death on earth. If the person serves the Devil, he has eternal punishment. If the person serves God, he has eternal salvation.

No one can serve two masters. You either serve God, or you serve the world (Luke 16:13). Jesus told this parable. If your hand causes sin, then cut it off (Mark 9:43). If the mark on your hand stops you from serving Jesus, then cut it off. In other words, cling to Jesus and get rid of all worldly things that interfere with the relationship. Jesus wants each of us to lean on him for all.

The Devil can lead people away from God, but the Almighty has awesome power to draw a sinner back through prayer. Our prayers give God the key to removing the mark from the lost.

A man or woman has a good opportunity to throw off the marks of the dragon if someone prays for them. It may take years of prayer before the Lord draws the person. They will then ask Jesus to give them eternal life and to write the Father's name on their forehead. All Heaven will rejoice and praise the Lord because another sinner saw the Light. The Devil lost again. Glory and praise to the Father, to the Son, and to the Holy Spirit. Amen!

MY DISOBEDIENCE—GOD'S WRATH

A few years ago while working for a plumbing company, I went to another job to help them for one day. I worked with Bob, another plumber. I felt that I should tell him about the love of Jesus Christ, but I did not.

That evening as I prayed, I felt the presence of an angry God. It was as if the Spirit said, "You did not tell him." For an instant, I felt absolute terror. Then the horror left, and the Lord loved me!

I realized that the Holy Spirit had prompted me to witness to Bob. God let me know that I should always follow his leading. I also learned that I did not want to fall into the hands of an angry God. I felt helpless in that instant of terror. I understood that without God's grace, mercy, and forgiveness, we have no chance. Our end is set. We are gone, gone, gone!

The next week I went to help on that job again. You can be certain that I told Bob about Jesus that day.

¹²**This calls for patient endurance on the part of the saints who obey God's commandments and remain faithful to Jesus. ¹³Then I heard a voice from heaven say, "Write: Blessed are the dead who die in the Lord from now on." "Yes," says the Spirit, "they will rest from their labor, for their deeds will follow them" (Rev. 14:12, 13, NIV).**

The Lord encourages his children after he gives the warning of eternal torment. The Lord confirms the identity of his children by pointing out their patience and their loyalty to Jesus. *Patience* (*hupomone*) means "endurance and perseverance through trials and suffering."[1] Patience points to someone who waits with loyalty and faith.

The Lord says that his people...*obey God's commandments and remain faithful to Jesus.* Their *faith* (*pistis*) means "a conviction of the Truth of God."[2] Their God-given faith helps them endure the trials of Christian life as they follow Jesus Christ.

BLESSED ARE GOD'S CHILDREN

John hears...*a voice from heaven* that tells him to write. John writes...*Blessed are the dead who die in the Lord from now on.* Happiness follows the saints who die in Jesus. *Dead* (*nekros*) points to "the death of the body." The metaphor means one who died to the world and devotes himself to God. Paul says that we should count ourselves dead to sin but alive to God because of Christ (Rom. 6:11). If Christ is in us, then our bodies are dead because of sin, but our spirits have life because of righteousness (Rom 8:10).

The Spirit says...*they will rest from their labor, for their deeds will follow them.* The term *labor* (*kopos*) indicates "trouble, grief, and sorrow."[3] It describes hard labor united with trouble and toil. In these two verses, our Lord encourages us to persevere in our faith and remain loyal to him throughout our lives.

Jesus paints a picture of the life of Christians who endure hardships. Our Prince of Peace comforts us in times of distress. He gives us hope and joy. At our last sunset, we will go to sleep in the arms of Jesus. We will wake up in our Savior's arms where we will rest forever.

I HAVE A DREAM

Recently in one of Portland's primary schools, I was walking down the hall when I noticed some papers written by the children. The children used the saying, "I have a dream," for writing their themes on the birthday of Martin Luther King Jr.

This school was located in a neighborhood that had a mix of upscale young families and low-income people. These samples show the children's writing.

I have a dream: "That dads wouldn't leave their children before they are born."

I have a dream: "That there were no more drugs, violence, and child abuse."

I have a dream: "I'd like it if grown-ups would stop fighting and hitting each other, because it's scary for me."

I have a dream: "I wish that people would stop pollution because animals will die. We want to save the earth."

By their dreams, we can read what's on the hearts of the children. The first three children want a better home life. They each live with different types of pain and suffering. They just want the pain to stop. As I read the statements, I could here the cries of the children.

In contrast, the children writing about pollution may live in happy homes. Our own neighborhoods have many needs. Most communities have a mission field next to each of us. We can help them in spiritual ways, mental ways, and physical ways. The families of the children above seem to lack love.

Jesus Loves Us

A person loves himself and others when he understands that Jesus loves him. Most people who love Jesus don't leave their children. They fulfill the responsibilities in life. Most who love Jesus stop drinking and using drugs. The Holy Spirit helps them to shake the habits. Most people who love Jesus don't abuse their children or fight with other people. God gives peace not strife.

Then the question arises: how do you minister to people in these situations? There are no simple answers. Prayer should come first for their salvation. Support this with prayer asking for guidance. Then follow the leading of the Holy Spirit. No one person can change large numbers of people (James 1:22–27; 2:14–18).

Pick a family or a few families and follow them until the Lord releases you from them. This may require years of dedication. Sometimes God is not in a hurry to change situations. It takes prayer, work, and commitment.

> [14]I looked, and there before me was a white cloud, and seated on the cloud was one "like a son of man" with a crown of gold on his head and a sharp sickle in his hand. [15]Then another angel came out

of the temple and called in a loud voice to him who was sitting on the cloud, "Take your sickle and reap, because the time to reap has come, for the harvest of the earth is ripe." [16]So he who was seated on the cloud swung his sickle over the earth, and the earth was harvested (Rev. 14:14–16, NIV).

REAPING THE HARVEST

John looks and sees another short view of the Gospel Age. He sees the Son of Man or Jesus sitting on a white cloud. The white indicates brilliant light, and the golden crown of victory points to our Lord. Jesus refers to himself as the Son of Man over eighty times in the Gospels. The Lord has a...*sharp sickle in his hand.* The *sickle* (*drepanon*) comes from (*drepo*) and means "to pluck."[4]

An angel came from the Temple and called to the Lord sitting on the cloud. The angel told Jesus to send in his...*sickle and reap, because the time to reap has come.* What picture was Jesus showing us here?

To understand the meaning of the harvest of the earth, we look at the symbols. Revelation uses many pictures and symbols that point to spiritual truths. We see two separate images in these final verses of chapter 14.

Some Christians describe these verses as the rapture of the Church and the judgment by Jesus Christ. Yet, like so many other illustrations in the Book of Revelation, this picture has more than one meaning. Paul touched on it when he said that he preferred to die and leave his body on earth so that he could go home with the Lord (2 Cor. 5:8).

GOING TO JESUS

The angel told the Son of Man to reap with his sickle...*for the harvest of the earth is ripe.* Jesus also told his disciples to reap because the harvest was ripe (John 4:35–38). Jesus explained the Kingdom of God to his disciples. He said that when the grain was ripe, he used the *sickle* (*drepanon*) to harvest (Mark 4:29). Therefore, God reaps his harvest of saints as firstfruits throughout the Gospel age.

Just before he died on the cross, Jesus told the criminal beside him that he would be with him today in Paradise (Luke 23:43). This means that the God who cannot lie guarantees us that we will also go to Jesus on the same day as we die.

[2]In my Father's house are many rooms; if it were not so, I would have told you. I am going there to prepare a place for you. [3]And if I go and prepare a place for you, I will come back

and take you to be with me that you also may be where I am
(John 14:2, 3, NIV)

Jesus gives a beautiful reflection of the harvest of his children. This harvest, or plucking with the sickle, continues throughout the Gospel Age. Yes, the picture above shows the rapture at the end of the Gospel Age. It also shows the personal rapture of every believer in Christ.

When we die, our Savior who cannot lie will come and take us by the hand and lead us across the river into the Promised Land. There we will see our Lord face-to-face. We see him in his full Glory, which he does not show on earth. We shall stand and bow with saints from other churches and ethnic groups to praise and glorify his Holy name. We will understand that he is worthy of our honor and our songs of praise as we dance before him. Holy is the Lord. Amen!

Jesus tells us in John above that he's going ahead of us to prepare a place for us in Heaven. Every time a Christian dies on earth, Jesus comes and escorts them into Paradise. Jesus swings...*his sickle over the earth* and harvests the saints for the entire Gospel Age. Each of us should look forward to our personal rapture when our Savior plucks us out of here. "Thank you, Lord, for your unfailing Love, your salvation, and for our future home in Heaven.

GOD'S LOVE, GRACE, AND MERCY

Many Christians go through life trying to do the best they can, but they are uncomfortable because they always fall short. God understands our weakness, and he will help us to overcome when we ask him. The Lord loves each of us just the way we are. Only the Holy Spirit can give us the power to change our thoughts and actions.

God looks at Christian men, women, and children without finding fault in their lives. It doesn't matter what they did in the past when they repent and turn to God. The Father wipes away all their sins when they believe in his Son. The gift of our Holy Father seems remarkable.

A saint may work all of his or her life trying to be good, and then God lets some unworthy sinner come in and stand beside them in Heaven (Matt. 20:1–16). The sinner probably lived a terrible life, and then just before he died, he accepted Jesus as Lord. Some righteous Christians may believe that it's just not right for our God of mercy to put a sinner on their same level in Heaven! Most Christians would never say this, but because of our sinful nature and work ethics, some may think that it's not right.

THE LOVE OF GOD

The love of God reaches deep and wide.
Who can measure his everlasting love?
His truth gives us knowledge and hope.
His pure love redeems us from sorrow.
God gives us white robes and pardons all.
For escaping, we will bow before our Savior.
Praise and glory for his gift of life and mercy.
All praise to the Father, Son, and Holy Spirit.

[17]Another angel came out of the temple in heaven, and he too had a sharp sickle. [18]Still another angel, who had charge of the. fire, came from the altar and called in a loud voice to him who had the sharp sickle, "Take your sharp sickle and gather the clusters of grapes from the earth's vine, because its grapes are ripe." [19]The angel swung his sickle on the earth, gathered its grapes and threw them into the great winepress of God's wrath. [20]They were trampled in the winepress outside the city, and blood flowed out of the press, rising as high as the horses' bridles for a distance of 1,600 stadia (Rev. 14:17–20, NIV).

JUDGMENT AND GRACE

These verses show us a gruesome picture of the judgment. The...*grapes from the earth's vine* symbolize the people who reject the Lord's grace. An angel comes from God in the Temple with a...*sharp sickle.* Another angel in...*charge of the fire, came from the altar.* He tells the first angel to collect the clusters of ripe grapes.

The angel from the golden altar had charge of the saints' prayers (Rev. 8:3–5). This judgment may symbolize answers to the prayers of the saints. We do not know from Scripture all the truths of Heaven and hell. Our God of Wisdom left much of it shrouded in mystery.

BLOOD REPRESENTS LIFE

Our Lord's description symbolizes several things. The OT says that blood is the life of a creature (Lev. 17:11; Deut. 12:23). The OT points to the physical life of people, while the NT blood points to the spiritual life of people. This scene shows us a picture of the flowing blood, which represents tremendous spiritual death.

They trample the grapes in the...*winepress of God's wrath.* The symbol of flowing blood portrays the destruction of people without God. The blood loss represents spiritual death.

The blood flowing…*1,600 stadia* indicates a complete judgment. Four times four equals sixteen, which indicates all parts of the earth times all parts. Ten represents completeness; complete times complete equals one hundred percent. This shows a full judgment on all parts of the earth.

Our life appears as a mist for a short time, then it's gone (James 4:14). God gives us a few moments on earth to use as we desire. Our earthly glory seems like grass and flowers. The grass dries and the flowers fail, and yet our spirit lives forever (1 Pet. 1:24).

When we look back on our life from the vantage of eternity, what will we think? Will we view it from a different perspective? Our time on earth slips away long before we finish our destiny. God created us to love him and to love our neighbor.

The lie of evolution teaches people the importance of self. You only go around once, and then it's over. When we all get to Heaven and look back, what will we see? Will we only see satisfaction for self, or will we see an effort to give the joy of God to those around us?

NOTES

1. Patience, *hupomone*, G5281. Endurance, patient waiting, loyalty of faith.
2. Faith, *pistis*, G4102. Faith, conviction of truth, belief.
3. Labor, *kopos*, G2873. Trouble, toil, beating of the breast with grief and sorrow.
4. Sickle, *drepanon*, G1407. From *drepo*, meaning to pluck. A hooked knife for harvesting.

CHAPTER 15

Saints and the Bowls of Wrath

THE DRY PRAYER MEETING

Linda began to go to church about four years after we married. She attended a Bible Community Church a few blocks from our home. Linda encouraged me to go with her, so I visited and enjoyed it.

A man from the church invited me to a prayer meeting. I took my Bible because I expected a Bible study before the prayers. To my surprise, they didn't have a Bible study. When I arrived, the men were already praying. They prayed for two hours one after another. Some of them prayed on and on and on. The prayers lasted a long time! I know because I looked at my watch at least ten times. I didn't go to that church again, nor any other church for five years.

Men and women of God need to let the Holy Spirit lead them in their invitations to people. Some Christians consider it a numbers game. They put on blinders and try to bring people to where they are without praying about each individual case.

If we reach out in sensitivity to others, then Jesus smiles on us. In my situation, the prayer meeting drove me away from the Lord for five years. The Lord drew me back to him a few years later because of his wonderful grace.

Today I would enjoy a prayer meeting. Even twenty years ago after I accepted Jesus, prayers would have interested me. I was not ready for prayer meetings before I was born again. Bible studies and church were good, but dry prayer meetings were terrible.

> [1]I saw in heaven another great and marvelous sign: seven angels with the seven last plagues—last, because with them God's wrath is completed. [2a]And I saw what looked like a sea of glass mixed with fire and, standing beside the sea, those who had been victorious over the beast and his image and over the number of his name (Rev. 15:1, 2a, NIV).

THE SIGN IN HEAVEN

Vision 5 begins in a similar way as chapter 12. Jesus begins both chapters by showing John a...*great and marvelous sign* in Heaven. Great points to large and mighty: an event that covers the whole earth. Marvelous indicates surprise or a wonder passing human wisdom. The sigh indicates an unusual occurrence beyond nature.

John looks into Heaven and sees seven angels holding...*the seven last plagues*. When the seventh plague closes the Gospel Age, then God's anger and indignation toward man's sin will also see fulfillment. The seven plagues spread over the Gospel Age like the seals and the trumpets.

John saw the victorious saints standing on or beside the sea. The sea at the Throne of our Almighty God indicated a barrier between man and God. Our Redeemer shattered the barrier when he rose from death. He opened the barricade between man and God.

Jesus pictures our union with the Father as forgiven and victorious saints. Because of the cross, the Lord doesn't see any sin in our lives as long as we live in repentance and walk in his grace. Therefore, the triumphant saints stand in fellowship with God on the sea. They proclaim their victory with the song of Moses and the song of the Lamb.

THE CREATOR'S CHILDREN

I have wondered what the Lord will do with all his created children who do not know Jesus Christ? Millions, perhaps billions, of them live around the world. These people have never heard the Gospel, or had the freedom to commit their lives to Christ. What will God do with them at the last judgment?

I understand that our Father, Jesus Christ, and the Holy Spirit will have the final word when the judgment comes. It's not our place to take the position as judge over others. We can't measure the loving heart of our Lord. He alone knows what each person thinks and does on earth.

Some wonder how a person can live today and not hear the Gospel of our Lord. Satan, the god of this world, blinds the minds and hearts of people. They cannot perceive the supernatural light and glory of Jesus Christ (2 Cor. 4:4-6). The Redeemer waits to shine his Light of salvation into the hearts of unbelievers.

PICK TWO OR THREE AND PRAY

Five years ago, I felt the Lord wanted me to pray for and speak the names of three people every day. These three men all had a dislike for God. I added their names to the prayer list for my family. I believe that someday each of these men will accept Jesus Christ as their Savior. Because God reveals his faithfulness, his Word will not return empty.

I would like to challenge each child of God to pick one, two, or three persons and speak their name in prayer each day. Ask the Lord to lead your selection of people? God will then bring the persons to your mind. The form of prayer that you use isn't as important as reminding our Redeemer of his children (Luke 18:1–8).

This commitment could last many years before the person accepts free salvation. A woman in our church prayed forty years for the salvation of her husband. He committed his life to Jesus several months before he left the earth. When his wife meets him in Heaven, what do you think her husband and the Lord will say to her?

> [2b]**They held harps given them by God [3]and sang the song of Moses the servant of God and the song of the Lamb: "Great and marvelous are your deeds, Lord God Almighty. Just and true are your ways, King of the ages. [4]Who will not fear you, O Lord, and bring glory to your name? For you alone are holy. All nations will come and worship before you, for your righteous acts have been revealed" (Rev. 15:2b–4, NIV).**

SING TO THE LORD

The servants of God gave him praise and exalted his Holy name. The holy saints stood in the presence of the Majestic Sovereign Lord and worshiped him. They proclaimed his Mighty name and praised his...*Great and marvelous* deeds. The saints honored the...*King of the ages* and gave glory to his name above all names.

They sang the song of salvation from Moses and the song of salvation by the Lamb. Moses sang the song after God delivered Israel from death by the army of Egypt (Exod. 15:1–21). The saints sang the song of salvation after the Lamb redeemed them from spiritual death by the power of the cross (Rev. 5:9–13).

Because they sing both OT and NT songs, it appears that the saints come from both ages. These verses give us a peek at a Holy Everlasting God who rules the ages. Nations worship before the Lord. They bring glory and honor to his name for he is Holy! Holy! Holy!

SAINTS MAY WEEP IN HEAVEN

Our God of Truth and grace affirms the saints in this scene. Yet, some saints of God may weep when they get to Heaven. Because of God's everlasting love and mercy, they will fellowship with him, and yet, they will understand that they missed the mark.

Suppose that you knew a person, or worked with him for five, ten, or twenty years. The Almighty had you scheduled to share your faith with the person. However, you never shared your faith in Jesus Christ. Even worse, you didn't pray for him or her. Because of your prayers, the Savior would have sent someone else to bring the good news of salvation.

I DIDN'T TELL HIM

When I was young, I accepted Jesus.
I went to church, and even worked there.
But, I always left my Savior in the church.
I socialized with many people in my life.
Yet, I never sent a prayer to God for them.
I arrived in Heaven seeking my friend.
God said, "You didn't tell him.
Therefore, is he is not here."

"Father, be merciful to us and bless each of us. Shine your understanding and wisdom our way. Lead us each day, and let our mouths speak of your Love. Let all of our friends experience your salvation. Lord, we praise you for your flowing grace and thank you for your everlasting compassion. Amen (Ps. 67:1–3)."

WOMEN OF GOD

Many men and women held harps and sang before our Savior. Our God created men and women equal (Gen. 1:27). He later placed man over women because Eve gave the forbidden fruit to Adam (Gen. 3:16). Men then ruled over women throughout the OT covenant.

Jesus Christ made all things new when he began the new and better covenant of the NT. All children of God put on the righteousness of Christ through faith. There's no difference between men and women in God's eyes (Gal. 3:26–29; 1 Cor. 12:12–14).

Our Lord died on the cross for his men, women, and children. He prayed with passion, as he asked the Father, that all of us would come together in spiritual oneness (John 17:21). The Creator has viewed each man, woman, and child in a unique way that points to oneness with him.

No Sex Differences in Heaven

Someday each of us will go to Heaven, and the Creator will give us new bodies like the angels (Matt. 22:30). The Creator made the angels one sex. So then, what will happen to our sex differences in Heaven? Somehow, I believe our God of mercy shall equalize all things in the coming kingdom (Luke 13:24–30).

Our Creator instituted a divine order of authority in marriage. He put the husband over the wife as Christ is over the Church (Eph. 5:20–33). Our Savior loves and cares for his Church, the bride of Christ. A man and a woman in a godly marriage should lean on each other for support and care.

Husbands and wives should make decisions in unity, which involve each other. God created men and women equal and separate, and yet he created different thinking processes. Because they think different, women have wisdom in areas that men lack. Men also have wisdom in other areas that women lack. The Almighty created men and women as one; therefore, they should pray, live, and plan their life and marriage in oneness.

We accept that God created ethnic groups and classes of people equal. Why then don't some accept the fact that Jesus restored women and men to perfection in Christ?

Men have always kept women in lower positions because of their hardness of heart and spiritual resistance. When men follow Christ and listen to the Holy Spirit, they understand the heart of Jesus Christ. The Lord always lifted up women to higher rank when he walked on earth.

Our Lord yearns for the equality of all people in his Church. God will help us understand the heart of Jesus when we search the Scriptures and pray without prejudice. I believe our Lord sees men and women as coworkers and coequal in the spirit realms.

> **⁵And after that I looked, and, behold, the temple of the tabernacle of the testimony in heaven was opened: (Rev. 15:5, KJV).**

Again in Revelation, we see the...*temple of the tabernacle of the testimony* opened in Heaven. We saw a similar Arc of his testament in God's

Temple at the end of chapter 11. Jesus opened the Temple in Heaven at the beginning of visions 4 and 5. He changed the OT covenant of obedience to a new and better covenant of grace by the power of the cross.

Moses built a tent or tabernacle to hold the Holy of Holies, where God dwelt in the camp of the Israelite people. The Power of God ripped the curtain to the Holy of Holies when Jesus died on the cross. This closed the OT covenant and opened the way for the new Temple of God (1 Cor. 3:16). The Holy Spirit began living in his church and people, or the temple, in the new covenant.

THE TEMPLE OF THE HOLY SPIRIT

The word for *temple* indicated the Holy of Holies where God dwells. The *tabernacle* (*skene*) means "a tent or a habitation."[1] The word for *testimony* (*marturion*) indicated "a witness or a martyr for Christ."[2]

The verse above indicated that they opened the place where God dwelt in the tent of witnesses for Christ. The opening of the temple of the tabernacle of the testimony appeared to describe the new covenant of God living in his Church. The Bible called us the dwelling place of God, and we witness for Christ by the Holy Spirit living within us (Eph. 2:20–22).

The verse indicates two temples. It shows the Creator's Temple in Heaven. I understand this verse also symbolizes the Church as God's temple of habitation that gives testimony about him. The verse above pictures God's new covenant with his Christian Church as the NT dwelling place of God. This gives us another picture of the Gospel Age and the NT covenant.

> [6]And the seven angels came out of the temple, having the seven plagues, clothed in pure and white linen, and having their breasts girded with golden girdles. [7]And one of the four beasts gave unto the seven angels seven golden vials full of the wrath of God, who liveth for ever and ever. [8]And the temple was filled with smoke from the glory of God, and from his power; and no man was able to enter into the temple, till the seven plagues of the seven angels were fulfilled (Rev. 15:6–8, KJV).

BOWLS OF WRATH

John sees...*seven angels came out of the temple*. The angels wear garments that reveal the Holiness and righteousness of God. The holy beings stand in the presence of our Faithful and True Judge. These agents of the Creator have a message for the world that refuses to repent and glorify God.

One of the cherubim gives the seven angles…*seven golden vials full of the wrath of God.* This sounds serious! Our Sovereign Lord extends much grace and mercy toward the world. He desires that all would recognize who he is because he prepares to allow judgment on those who refuse the gift of salvation.

The Bible says that God reveals his wrath from Heaven against godlessness and wickedness. He gives wrath to men and women who suppress the truth. The Lord says that men do not have an excuse because he has shown his eternal power since Creation (Rom. 1:18–20).

The God of Truth gives up men and women to their sinful desires and lusts. He lets them worship the lie of other gods. Our Holy God allows people to live indecent lives with depraved minds (Rom. 1:21–32). The spiritual consequences, of perversion and unholy values lead to the bowls of wrath.

Judgment on earth comes from unholy lifestyles. The Creator sets up standards to live by. If the created being breaks God's standards, then he suffers terrible consequences. He gives guidelines in his Holy Word on how to live. If we follow them, the bowls will pass over us. Because he loves us, our Father knows best.

THE GLORY OF THE LORD

Smoke filled the Temple…*from the glory of God.* This gave us a picture of God's glory in the OT Temple. When the priests put the Arc into the Most Holy Place in Solomon's Temple, a cloud filled the Temple. The priests could not do their duties because of the cloud of God's power and glory. When Isaiah saw the glory of God, the Temple filled with smoke (1 Kings. 8:6–11; Isa. 6:1–8).

Moses saw the glory when God gave him the Law. The face of Moses shined from God's glory. The people saw his radiant face, and it frightened them. Moses put on a veil until the glory faded away (Exod. 34:29–35).

The Lord also revealed his glory in the NT. An angel of the Lord appeared to shepherds on the night that our Savior was born. The glory of the Lord shined around them (Luke 2:9). When the Sanhedrin stoned Stephen, he looked into Heaven and saw the glory of God (Acts 7:55).

Paul said that the NT ministry of the Spirit is more glorious than the OT glory. The glory of the OT faded away, but the glory of the NT lasts forever (2 Cor. 3:7–11). We have the Spirit of the Lord, and this gives us freedom. Our faces in the Church reflect the Lord's spiritual glory. The Spirit of God transforms us into his likeness and gives us ever-increasing glory (2 Cor. 3:16-18).

Paul saw the Lord's glory in the Spirit domain. He understood that even when we don't see the Lord's glory, it's still here among us. We only see in part. We look through a dark glass at the work and the glory of God (1 Cor. 13:12). God gives us the Good News of salvation, and Christ gives us the Holy Spirit to walk in faith.

THE GLORY OF GOD TODAY

It seems strange that the people appeared to see the glory of God more in the OT than we do today. Peter spoke the words of the prophet Joel. He said that God would give the Spirit to all who called on his name. The young people of God would prophesy and see visions. The old men and women would dream dreams. Then he spoke about the glory of God in the heavens and on earth (Acts. 2:17–21).

God shows his glory today, but Christians need to put on spiritual eyes to see it. The Holy Spirit living in us gives us faith to see God's glory in others. The Church of Jesus Christ remains a spiritual Church today. The God of Truth helps us understand that the Spirit works within the spiritual domain of redeemed children.

Our Father of compassion does many wonderful miracles in the Church today. Every time someone says yes to the call of Jesus Christ, we see the glory of God. When a person decides to follow Jesus through good times and hard times, we see the glory of God. When someone begins to pray for others, we see the glory of God. When a Christian helps another person understand that Jesus loves them, we see the glory of God.

The Spirit works in many mysterious ways. Why does the wind blow on some and not on others? Why do some of our prayers seem neglected? Why does the Lord let us struggle in life? Why doesn't our Father give us more insight into his thoughts and actions?

GOD APPEARS TO HIS CHILDREN

The Spirit of Love appears today in glory to many of his children. The Spirit comes down on churches and prayer groups during worship in glory and power. At times, the glory seems so strong that many saints cannot stand up. Children of the Savior lay prostrate in the presence of the Father, the Son, and the Holy Spirit. The glory we see today is the same that the Spirit has given throughout the OT and NT Ages.

Many children of God change the direction of their life after they feel the glory and love of Jesus. The ways of God become more important than the ways of the world. We see the fruit of the Spirit manifested in their lives. Some appear with a radiance of love and joy from the Spirit.

Saints sit in the presence of the Lord for weeks and years. The Wonderful Physician brings healing to their lives. The Spirit gives them spiritual, physical, and mental healing. We don't perceive all that the Spirit does in our lives. We only know that when we enter the glory and love of Jesus, our values change.

PRAYERS WIN SPIRITUAL BATTLES

Christians gather in small groups to worship and pray together. They may study the Bible, then listen to worship music for thirty minutes to an hour. The music helps each of them focus on the Lord. The Spirit reveals himself in many ways during this time. After the worship time, the group prays for individuals and couples. They use all the gifts of the Spirit as the Lord leads them.

At other times, the group may spend the prayer time interceding for revival as the Lord leads them. They pray for people in their families, churches, cities, and nations. They often bind the dark spiritual powers and spirits as the Lord leads them. Sometimes the group begins in prayer and does not stop to worship with music. God does not have a set format for prayer and worship meetings.

The Almighty begins these groups by prayer, and then He continues them on the power of prayer. They belong to the Almighty's active army against the Devil's army. God fights the battles in the spiritual world through the power of prayer. The large battles between good and evil don't happen in the physical places. They take place in the domain of the good and evil spirits.

The Holy Spirit gives life; the evil spirits give death. Through the power of the Spirit, followers of Christ can help bring life to many children of the world. The next chapter of Revelation speaks much about spiritual death and destruction. As children of the Holy Father, we should always look toward Jesus for his goodness and mercy. We can only pray and do what the Lord leads us to do.

Yes, the Lord shows us his glory today. His peace goes beyond anything that the world gives. His love transcends our emotions. His grace and mercy appears as a twinkling light to our minds of understanding. We know that without him, we have nothing. With him, we have all.

Praise his Holy name. Praise his grace of salvation. Praise him, because he loves us. Praise him, because he lets us see and feel his glory. All praise, honor, and glory to the Father, the Son, and the Holy Spirit. Amen! Amen!

NOTES

1. Tabernacle, *skene*, G4633. A tent or a habitation.
2. Testimony, *marturion*, G3142. Testimony, witness, or martyr for Christ.

CHAPTER 16

Seven Bowls Bring Death

THE PULL OF THE WORLD

A christian friend told me about one of his dreams. He sensed a spiritual truth and related it in this way. I dreamed I was walking along a path next to a deep ravine. A fence with steel rails paralleled the path on the drop-off side.

I strolled along the path enjoying the beauty of the world. As I gazed at the tall evergreen trees, I paused to study the delicate design of the green ferns. The high sun warmed me as I moseyed along. I leaned over the rail and beheld sparkling waters below. I inhaled the freshness of the water gushing over the rocks and thought of God's creation.

Suddenly, up over the edge snaked a long arm with five tentacles on the end! The sucker covered tentacles encircled my bare arm and began to squeeze. The snakelike arm began to pull me over the rail as I grabbed the top rail with my free hand.

I saw and felt the cold slimy appendage stretch my arm. I wondered, "Can I hang on: what can I do?"

I cried, "Jesus help me!" Instantly, I saw a man with long-handled loppers. He reached out and sniped one of the tentacles off. I felt the grip tighten and the pull increase. I cried again, "Jesus help me."

The man cut another tentacle. My grip on the rail began to slip, and I knew that I was about to plunge into deep darkness. With effort, I whispered, "Jesus."

The third tentacle fell when it lost its connection to the arm. I heard sounds of frustration, pain, and anger. The defeated monster recoiled into its hole.

The man reached out and brought me back over the fence. I knew I had almost lost it. As I looked at my arm, I could see welts and traces of blood. The man, loving me with his eyes, reached out and touched my arm; I watched the pain and redness disappear.

I gazed at him with thankfulness in my heart. A smile crossed his lips as he said, "Don't walk too close to the ways of the world!"

> ¹And I heard a great voice out of the temple saying to the seven angels, Go your ways, and pour out the vials of the wrath of God upon the earth. ²And the first went, and poured out his vial upon the earth; and there fell a noisome and grievous sore upon the men which had the mark of the beast, and *upon* them which worshipped his image. ³And the second angel poured out his vial upon the sea; and it became as the blood of a dead *man*; and every living soul died in the sea (Rev. 16:1–3, KJV).

BOWLS OF SPIRITUAL DEATH

The bowls appear similar to the trumpets. The Savior sends trumpets of warning to the people of the world. Some repent and turn to him. He then gives eternal life and healing. The angels pour bowls or vials of wrath on others who refuse to repent and recognize the Sovereign Lord. The trumpets affect people in part: the bowls affect people in completeness.

I attempt to reveal what the bowls imply for today. Throughout the Gospel Age, Christians suggest different meanings for the bowls. Most describe the bowls as touching the physical earth. The bowls destroy in fullness, and yet they do not touch Christians living on the earth. Therefore, the bowls indicate spiritual destruction rather than physical destruction. If they caused physical events, the bowls would also consume the Christians in the world.

GOD WILL NOT DESTROY THE EARTH

The Creator promised Noah and us that he would not physically destroy the earth again. God promised us that although man was evil, he would not kill all living creatures as long as the earth endured. The Word of God has not denied itself. God has guaranteed us that the earth will support life until the end of the Age. Therefore, the bowls have influenced spiritual life rather than physical life on earth.

[21]The LORD smelled the pleasing aroma and said in his heart: "Never again will I curse the ground because of man, even though every inclination of his heart is evil from childhood. And never again will I destroy all living creatures, as I have done. [22]"As long as the earth endures, seedtime and harvest, cold and heat, summer and winter, day and night will never cease" (Gen. 8:21, 22, NIV)

Three of the bowls appeared similar to three of the plagues that God gave to Egypt (Exod. 7–10). God sent blood on the Nile and all the sources of drinking water. The Lord sent a plague of boils on the people and a plague of darkness they could feel. The physical events in the OT pointed to spiritual principles of the NT.

THE RESULT OF DENYING GOD

The bowls show us the spiritual consequences of rejecting God. The bowls do not point to our physical environment. They represent the corruption of the moral values on earth. The bowls indicate that God permits Satan to influence people for the entire Gospel Age. As evil and paganism rises, the Lord permits people to go their own way (Rom. 1:18–32). He lets them worship the creation instead of the Creator. This leads to spiritual destruction and eternal death.

Each succeeding bowl appears to increase the spiritual forces against the life of individuals and nations. The angel pours the first on people with the mark of the beast. This implies that people without the mark lived with them.

The following bowls affect the same people. They seem to increase in harshness as time goes on for a person or a nation. The final bowl brings the end.

THE WICKED SORES

The first angel poured God's wrath over the earth. The Lord's mighty voice spoke...*out of the temple* and sent the angel. This led to...*a noisome and grievous sore* upon people with the mark of the beast.

The Greek for *noisome* (*kakos*) points to the essential character of a person. This indicates "evil, wicked, and harmful qualities."[1] *Grievous* (*poneros*) means "hurtful and evil in effect or influence."[2] The Greek words point to the evil of men and the wickedness of Satan. These words indicate that the bowl permits Satan's kingdom to increase evil and wicked desires on the actions of their people.

Sore (*helkos*) points to an ulcer and means "to drag or draw together."[3] Because this vision symbolizes spiritual attitudes, this must mean that the

Devil draws people of one mind together for his purposes. People of the world then follow and imitate the ways the Devil.

THE BLOOD OF ETERNAL DEATH

The second angel poured his bowl over the sea of people on the earth. The sea turned...*as the blood of a dead man*. The *dead* (*nekros*) indicated "a deceased or a spiritually dead person."[4] Another meaning described a person who had given his or her life over to sin and evil.

The people of the world exchanged the truth of God for the lie of Satan. They worshiped world values instead of the Savior (Rom. 1:25; 1 John 2:15–17). Our Redeemer let them have depraved minds that led to evil, greed, murder, and God-hating. They continued their deeds of sin fed by darkness and self-seeking wills.

The ungodly rejected truth and followed evil. This brought to the sea of people a type of blood like a dead man has. The second bowl of wrath led to the consequence of...*every living soul died in the sea*. The blood from the bowl caused people to *die* (*apothnesko*).[5] This pointed to eternal death and misery in hell for people with the mark of the beast.

The picture symbolizes people or souls who die a spiritual death in the sea of nations. The *soul* (*psuche*) means "soul, life, mind, or the breath of life." The word points to the human spirit, mind, and emotions of life that lives forever with God or away from him.

The Bible says that if we sow evil, we reap the same (Job 4:8). If we sow to the flesh, we harvest our rewards of misery and wasting away. A few hours of pleasure can destroy a physical life on this earth and a spiritual life forever.

THE PRICELESS LIFE

Our Father gives each of us the freedom to live any way we want. If lust, greed, and evil seem more important than serving our Savior, the Divine Judge lets us pursue it. Our Savior does not put a harness on us and then lead us around. He gives us gentle nudges and stronger taps with the Spirit of Love.

Our Father wants us to reflect his glory during our stay here on the earth. He desires that each of us cherish the gift of life. A person sentenced to die for a crime will treasure the last day of life more intensely than others will on that day.

The small details of life count more than the large events. Christians often take the gift of life for granted. I am guilty of that. God reveals how priceless it is when we seek it. I often think of the Majesty of the Lord's creation. Sometimes, we just need to stop and smell the roses of life. The prisoner scheduled to die would give all he has for a few more days of life in a cell.

I often wonder, "Who am I? How could I be so lucky that God created this earth and put me on it? Then he sent his Son to die in exchange for our new life in him." I say again, "How could I be so blessed?"

> **4The third angel poured out his bowl on the rivers and springs of water, and they became blood. 5Then I heard the angel in charge of the waters say: "You are just in these judgments, you who are and who were, the Holy One, because you have so judged; 6for they have shed the blood of your saints and prophets, and you have given them blood to drink as they deserve." 7And I heard the altar respond: "Yes, Lord God Almighty, true and just are your judgments" (Rev. 16:4–7, KJV).**

THE BLOOD OF LIFE—DEATH

The third angel empties his...*bowl on the rivers and springs of water.* The waters turn into blood, which points to death. The angel says that God's judgment on the people of the world seems good because they...*shed the blood of your saints and prophets.* Jesus uses the same word for *shed* (*ekcheo*) that he uses when the seven angels *pour out* (*ekcheo*) the bowls.[6] Because the wicked sheds or pours out the blood of the people of God, our Lord pours the killers a drink of blood in a similar way.

The Bible teaches that if we eat and drink the body and blood of Jesus we have eternal life (John 6:48–58). The Bible also teaches that if we drink spiritual blood from Satan we inherit eternal death. God gives...*them blood to drink as they deserve.* The word *drink* (*pino*) as a metaphor means "to receive into the soul a spiritual refreshment and nourishment for life eternal."[7]

The Bible uses *drink* (*pino*) when it refers to "gaining life by drinking the blood of Jesus Christ." The Lord contrasts this in these verses because he sends the spiritual result from drinking the spiritual waters or blood of Satan. This plague caused an inner filthiness, evil, and spiritual death on the people who reject God.

THE WHITE WASHED SPIRIT

Many people in the world today drink from the rivers and springs that the Devil has polluted. We have a spirit in the world today that Satan has kept alive over the centuries. We shall call it the spirit of prejudice.

The Creator didn't create separate races; he created one race of man from Adam. Different ethnic groups of people came into the world from the one race. The people emerged into different heritages and backgrounds over the earth. Satan has always loved to highlight the differences in people. He did it through Hitler and caused the death of millions of God's children.

The race of man has a history of abusing different people groups. Prejudices exist today throughout the world. Bigotry appears subtle most of the time, and yet the spirit of racism waits to raise its ugly head and do damage. The demons from the abyss control thoughts and actions in this area. The powers of darkness convince people that they have a right to feel superior to others.

Prejudice in the Church

Even within the Christian churches, the same spirit lives. Slavery couldn't happen without the consent of the Christian Church. A passive racism permeates the Church today. It seems strange that our belief in Jesus Christ doesn't overcome prejudice in our society today. Christians often remain as guilty as non-Christians of passive and insensitive bigotry.

Somehow, when salvation made us new creations in Christ, our attitudes didn't change toward different groups of people. As children of the Father, we should always ask ourselves what would Jesus do.

Our Lord always reached out to the untouchables and less favored around him. Jesus lived in a society that scorned anyone that they considered less than themselves. Our Lord ministered in Love to tax collectors, sinners, women, Samaritans, and people with mental and physical handicaps.

Silence of Forgiven Sinners

Our Savior calls each of us to treat all the people around us with love and to help the less desired. Our brothers and sisters in Christ who seem different will stand beside us when we all get to Heaven. If we have racist attitudes on earth, we will need to look the people in the eye in God's Holy presence and explain why. We will need to explain why we stood in silence against their foes.

The prejudice spirit appears as a large issue for the Christian Church today. The demons from hell fuel people's thoughts against others that seem different. There's a mysterious silence from church leaders throughout the world and America. I have heard few words condemning racism from church pulpits. This seems strange because Jesus would address the passive attitude today.

We in the Church need to repent of our lack of obedience to our Savior. He gives us freedom by the cross, and he wants us to help give freedom to others. As children of the Father, we need to take the initial step and ask the Holy Spirit to change our hearts and minds toward other ethnic people. Only by the love of Christ can each of us in the Christian Church begin to love and accept others who appear different.

THE INNOCENT BLOOD

The lies of Satan work on the thinking processes of people. When people believe the lie of evolution and reject the Creator, they loose the understanding of God's principles. Then their own actions and desires become more important than other people's welfare. This leads to the decline in moral values and the sanctity of life.

Many nations drip the blood of sacrificed children. The blood flows when doctors rip a baby from the security of the womb. Abortion appears close to the word *abomination* in the dictionary. *Abomination* means "abhorrence, disgust, or a detestable act." Jesus gives life; then some spurn him when they recommend the act of killing or taking part in it.

Most Christians detest the sin of abortion. Nevertheless, we should pray that the love and grace of Christ work in the lives of the doctors and the victims.

VICTIMS

Mothers and fathers, caught up in abortion, appear as one of the victims. They conceive a child and do not know what to do with it. Friends and family tell them to get an abortion: it is easy. It isn't a real baby: it's just a blob.

Because of many pressures and the lack of good counsel, they go ahead. Yet, killing their baby haunts most people for decades. Even people who seem okay have a nagging sense of guilt and loss of self-worth. It will trouble them until they die, unless they seek healing through the Lord and other people in like circumstances.

Our God of grace and mercy desires to heal and forgive each of his children for past sin. Some men and women, involved in past abortion, stand away from God. In their hearts and minds, they believe that the Creator could not forgive them. They build a hard shell around themselves.

Jesus grieves for the unborn, but he also grieves for the pain of the mothers and fathers. We as reflections of Christ should try to portray his sensitivity to the hurting people around us. Jesus doesn't condemn past errors: he restores them.

THE FATHER'S CREATION (PS. 139:7–16)

My Father created my inner spirit long ago.
He planed my unformed body from beginning.
The Creator designed me in wonderful ways.
He formed my body uniquely in the womb.
God wrote about all my days in his book.
The doctors snatched me from the womb.
My spirit screamed, "not time—not time."
Tears dripped from my Fathers Throne.

⁸The fourth angel poured out his bowl on the sun, and the sun was given power to scorch people with fire. ⁹They were seared by the intense heat and they cursed the name of God, who had control over these plagues, but they refused to repent and glorify him. ¹⁰The fifth angel poured out his bowl on the throne of the beast, and his kingdom was plunged into darkness. Men gnawed their tongues in agony ¹¹and cursed the God of heaven because of their pains and their sores, but they refused to repent of what they had done (Rev. 16:8–11, NIV).

The fourth angel affects the sun. God gives the sun...*power to scorch people with fire*. No one knows what this bowl means. If the sun burned the unbelievers of the world, it would also burn the believers. The burning sun goes on throughout the Gospel Age; so what does it mean?

THE BOWLS OF CONTRAST

The Revelation of Jesus Christ shows us a contrast between good and evil. The bowls reveal the spiritual consequences of living a wicked life without God. Jesus, referring to his followers, says "that the sun will not fall on them, nor any hot heat" (Rev. 7:16).

The fourth bowl and this verse gives us a contrast between the redeemed of chapter 7 and the spiritual lost. The God of Love gives his children all we need. In contrast, the God of judgment gives those who reject and curse him more than they want.

The fifth angel poured his bowl over...*the throne of the beast, and his kingdom was plunged into darkness*. Men and women...*cursed the God of heaven*. They lived in agony because they had no hope, and yet they refused to repent and turn to the Living God. Isaiah painted a word picture that illustrated a life without God.

¹⁹When men tell you to consult mediums and spiritists, who whisper and mutter, should not a people inquire of their God?

Why consult the dead on behalf of the living? [20]To the law and to the testimony! If they do not speak according to this word, they have no light of dawn. [21]Distressed and hungry, they will roam through the land; when they are famished, they will become enraged and, looking upward, will curse their king and their God. [22]Then they will look toward the earth and see only distress and darkness and fearful gloom, and they will be thrust into utter darkness (Isa. 8:19–22, NIV)

Isaiah contrasts the thick darkness when he writes of a Light that comes. He tells us to rise and shine because our Light and the Lord's glory comes. When we look to the Light, God will make us radiant. Our hearts will throb and swell with joy and praise for our God (Isa. 60:1–5).

"Father, I thank you for your Light of Revelation. I thank you for helping us understand the precious gift that you give us. Thank you for your enduring mercy and grace. Amen!"

It Is Finished

My brother Jerry was in church the night my dad moved from his twilight time on earth to the bright land where the Light never dims. After the service, Jerry noticed an old book that he had never seen. He opened the book and saw nothing but white pages. He turned to the front of the book and saw large letters that said, "It is finished."

Jerry told me about the book the next day. That night I spent time in prayer. I asked the Lord, "What does this mean." I felt the presence of the Lord settle around me. I listened intently as I felt the impression of that still small voice.

I sensed in my thoughts, "The white pages mean the record's clean. I remember no sin. When I died on the cross, I died for all people. I give everyone the opportunity to come to me. All anyone needs to do, even in the last moments of life, is to recognize me and say yes."

I felt him say to my spirit, "Your daddy's in Heaven with me. He's loving me, and I'm loving him" (Matt. 20:1–16).

Prayer gives us awesome power in the Kingdom of God. Prayer increases God's abundant grace for people. Our prayers help our Savior to give men, women, and children more moments to say yes to Jesus Christ. God permitted my dad to sit, tied to an oxygen hose, for five years until he could draw him. Our faithful God always answers the pleas of his children. Dad's in Heaven today, and he rejoices with the other saints and members of his family.

Chapter 15 gives us a glimpse of the results of Christian prayers. Chapter 16 of this vision shows us what can happen to people if they don't recognize the Lord. Jesus gives everyone the opportunity to say yes. Nevertheless, a person stands on dangerous ground if he or she waits too long. Sometimes God lets a person go their own way (Rom. 1:20–25).

If a person gambles too long on the grace of God, he or she is a fool. A person should not put off a decision to accept Jesus Christ until near the end of his or her life. We never know when God will require us to account for our life (Luke 12:16–21). We don't know at what point our loving God will quit calling us. For most, Jesus knocks on their door until their death, but not all. If a child of the world pushes it too far, he may go away from the Lord never to return.

> [12]**The sixth angel poured out his bowl on the great river Euphrates, and its water was dried up to prepare the way for the kings from the East.** [13]**Then I saw three evil spirits that looked like frogs; they came out of the mouth of the dragon, out of the mouth of the beast and out of the mouth of the false prophet.** [14]**They are spirits of demons performing miraculous signs, and they go out to the kings of the whole world, to gather them for the battle on the great day of God Almighty.** [15]**"Behold, I come like a thief! Blessed is he who stays awake and keeps his clothes with him, so that he may not go naked and be shamefully exposed."** [16]**Then they gathered the kings together to the place that in Hebrew is called Armageddon (Rev. 16:12–16, NIV).**

EUPHRATES RIVER CHECKPOINT

The sixth angel poured his bowl over…*the great river Euphrates.* Jesus shows us a picture of the Euphrates River drying up to let the kings from the East pass. With today's modern war machines, does it matter if the river is wet or dry? If this were a physical happening, a modern army would build several bridges and roll over the little river in a few days while their planes and helicopters bombed ahead.

Yes, Jesus Christ symbolized spiritual life on earth in his Revelation. It still indicates spiritual life and death today. John saw…*three evil spirits* come out of the mouth of the dragon, the beast, and the false prophet. This refers back to the dragon in chapter 12 and the two beasts in chapter 13. The three evil spirits…*looked like frogs.* The evil or unclean spirits represented demonic images of Satan, governments, and the false prophet of religion.

The demonic frogs...*go out to the kings of the whole world.* The spirits symbolize the fallen angels from the kingdom of darkness. The frogs cover the whole world and try to corrupt all nations. The three frogs show us a picture of Satan's evil spirits roaming over the world (Eph. 6:10–12).

The Euphrates River marked the north and east boundary of the Promised Land (Gen. 15:18). Most of their enemies crossed the Euphrates River when they attacked Israel in the OT (Rev. 8:8). The real opponents of Israel gave us examples of our spiritual enemies in the NT Age.

Babylon rested on the other side of the Euphrates River. Babylon, of OT time, represented the evil from the outside world to God's chosen and set-apart people. John used the NT Babylon as a type of spiritual enemy for Christians. The Bible suggested spiritual and physical boundaries for us to live by. We cross God's boundaries when we cross the spiritual Euphrates into Babylon of the world.

SEPARATE FROM THE WORLD

God has standards and ethical codes to live by, which he gave us in the Bible. We put ourselves in spiritual danger when we disregard God's standards. Our Lord wants us to live in the world, and yet not belong to the world (John 15:19). When we do things not pleasing to the Almighty, we may leave his boundary of protection.

Once an individual or a nation crosses the boundaries, darkness comes in and tears down moral values. As the moral values of a person or a nation decline into the sewage pit, God sometimes dries up the Euphrates River. This allows the Devil's powers and spirits to overrun them with their corrupt value system. Then dense darkness covers the land; men chew...*their tongues in agony* because they have no hope.

The three frogs or...*spirits of demons* performed miracles to deceive the nations of the world. The nations came together at Armageddon. The final battle did not take place until chapter 19. Armageddon simple points to the ongoing spiritual battle between light and darkness. It also symbolizes the brief time at the end of the Gospel Age when Satan roams free.

In the midst of this, Jesus says...*Blessed is he who stays awake and keeps his clothes with him.* The Lord reminds us that we don't know when he will return, or when our last day will come (Luke 12:35–40). He says that we are blessed if we always remain ready to receive him. Our Savior gives us robes of righteousness to cover our naked sins from wondering too near the Euphrates River barrier representing the ways of the world.

Suffering—Seeking God

When we suffer, God draws near to us as we seek him. The Lord already lives in us even when we don't feel his presence. Yet, he waits for us to seek him so he can be found (Acts 17:27).

Our loving Father sometimes permits hard times to touch us when we put other things before him. He knows that most of us will pray more often and ask for relief in times of trouble. Through life's valleys and high points, the Father helps Christians increase their faith and seek him.

Some of God's children only stop their busywork and take time for God when they lie flat on their back. I believe that our God of Wisdom and Love prefers that we seek him without going through anguish.

He just wants us to drink his living water and say, "Yes, Lord. I love you, Lord. I need you, Lord. I yearn for your presence. I seek your leading in my life. I praise you, Father. I praise you, Jesus. I praise you, Holy Spirit. I worship and adore your Holy name. Hallelujah! Hallelujah! Hallelujah!"

It seems so simple; and yet, it is so difficult for some. Our Lord treasures oneness with each of us. He desires a familiar relationship. Our Father wants us to ask him to rest on our hearts as we go to sleep each night.

> [17]The seventh angel poured out his bowl into the air, and out of the temple came a loud voice from the throne, saying, "It is done!" [18]Then there came flashes of lightning, rumblings, peals of thunder and a severe earthquake. No earthquake like it has ever occurred since man has been on earth, so tremendous was the quake. [19]The great city split into three parts, and the cities of the nations collapsed. God remembered Babylon the Great and gave her the cup filled with the wine of the fury of his wrath. [20]Every island fled away and the mountains could not be found. [21]From the sky huge hailstones of about a hundred pounds each fell upon men. And they cursed God on account of the plague of hail, because the plague was so terrible (Rev. 16:17–21, NIV).

The End of the World

The seventh angel releases his...*bowl into the air*. This completes the cycles of the bowls in the world. The angel saturates the air we breathe with the contents of God's verdict. It appears that the seventh bowl finishes the other six bowls. This bowl ushers in the end of the world.

A loud voice from the Temple said...*"It is done!"* This phrase *ginomai* means "come to pass or to happen."[8] The Lord states in Scripture that the end will come when the Son Man comes in power and glory (Luke

21:25–28). Jesus will return at the end of the Gospel Age, and everyone will recognize him.

People of the world cursed...*God on account of the plague.* This contrasts with Christians who sang the song of Moses to the Lamb earlier in this vision (Rev. 15:2–4). Some in the world condemn the Savior while others love him with all their might. Many children of the Father strive to imitate Jesus during their life. They seek a unique oneness with their Lord (John 17:20–24).

ONENESS WITH GOD

Our Savior came to earth as an innocent baby. He was an example of God in human form with all the qualities of each. Jesus lived and worked as a man on earth for thirty years. God then baptized his Son with the Holy Spirit. With the fullness of the Spirit, Jesus could follow his Father's directions with perfection. The Spirit of obedience led our Lord into a oneness with his Father.

The Bible gives us Jesus as an example for us to follow. He requires us to believe and trust him for our eternal destiny. By example, Jesus suggests that we ask him to fill us with the Holy Spirit (Matt. 3:11–17). The power of the flowing Spirit in our lives helps us to obey the leading of God. As we ask God to fill us and refill us with the Holy Spirit, this gives us a spirit of obedience to him.

The spirit of obedience leads us into a oneness with the Father, the Son, and the Holy Spirit. It's an invisible quality contained within the Church of Jesus Christ on earth. Although you can't see it, many Christians sense their oneness with the Godhead. Unlike the people who reject God, these saints strive for a closer relationship with their Lord.

Jesus gives us the fruit of the Spirit in this process. He gives us: his love, his peace, his joy, his patience, his kindness, and his goodness. The Lord does this as we seek him and ask for more of his Holy Spirit. He also gives us: his faithfulness, his gentleness, his knowledge, his self-control, his perseverance, and his godliness (Gal. 5:22, 23; 2 Pet. 1:5–8).

The fruit of the Spirit helps us to imitate Jesus Christ, which he wants us to do (Eph. 5:1). Jesus came to earth out of love for us. We in turn should desire to live our lives out of love for him. The experience of the love of Christ helps us to reach out to others in compassion. People without Jesus have no hope. Their destiny points to eternal separation from the love of God.

The gifts of the Holy Spirit help us accomplish all that our Savior wants us to do. He gives us everything we need to follow him and love others through him. The peace and joy of Jesus comes as we ask him to immerse us in the Holy Spirit. The Lord's fruit and his gifts lead us into a union with his eternal presence.

"Thank you, Holy Spirit, for your gifts, your fruit, and your action in our lives. Thank you, Jesus, for offering each of us the opportunity to imitate your actions. Thank you, Father, for your grace, your mercy, your love, and your compassion. Amen!

NOTES

1. Noisome, *kakos*, G2556. Essential character of a person. Evil, wicked, harmful, or of bad nature.
2. Grievous, *poneros*, G4190. Hurtful and evil in effect or influence
3. Sore, *helkos*, G1668. An ulcer from G1670, meaning to drag or draw together.
4. Dead, *nekros*, G3498. Deceased, lifeless, the spiritual dead. A person living for sin and evil.
5. Died, *apothnesko*, G599. Perish, die, eternal death and misery in hell.
6. Shed, *ekcheo*, G1632. To pour forth, shed, spill.
7. Drink, *pino*, G4095. Drink, Figuratively, to receive into the soul what serves to refresh, strengthen, nourish to life eternal.
8. Done, *ginomai*, G1096. To become, come to pass, happen.

CHAPTER 17

Woman on the Beast

⌒

THORNS ON CACTUS

As a child, I played on the rolling prairie of western South Dakota. Small patches of cactus grew on the grassland. Each of the cactus plants measured one to four inches across, and they had long sharp spines. If a child ran through the grass and fell on a patch of cactus, he instantly recognized his blunder. The hard sharp spines pierced unprotected skin. The cactus plants looked beautiful, but you didn't hug them.

The woman, symbolizing Babylon, adorned in gold and precious gems appears similar to a cactus plant. She looks beautiful and loves to embrace the people of the earth. Nevertheless, when someone hugs her, she may pierce him or her with her deadly thorns.

THE IMPORTANCE OF BABYLON

Our Lord uses more than two chapters to explain the woman Babylon. This indicates that she plays an important part in the Revelation of Jesus Christ. Christians hold several different views of what the woman riding the beast represents.

The different views on Babylon and Revelation should not break fellowship. Salvation demands a relationship with Jesus Christ. It doesn't demand a particular view of the Revelation of Jesus Christ. The Father loves each of his children and their different explanations of Revelation.

I am simply a sinner saved by God's grace. I don't have a theological degree. I only have an official Certificate of Salvation issued by Jesus Christ and signed with his shed blood from the cross. I shall try to explain what I believe Babylon represents as the Lord has led me. The Lord gave us a detailed description of the great prostitute that points to the kingdom of darkness and Satan.

> ¹**One of the seven angels who had the seven bowls came and said to me, "Come, I will show you the punishment of the great prostitute, who sits on many waters. ²With her the kings of the earth committed adultery and the inhabitants of the earth were intoxicated with the wine of her adulteries." ³Then the angel carried me away in the Spirit into a desert. There I saw a woman sitting on a scarlet beast that was covered with blasphemous names and had seven heads and ten horns. ⁴The woman was dressed in purple and scarlet, and was glittering with gold, precious stones and pearls. She held a golden cup in her hand, filled with abominable things and the filth of her adulteries. (Rev. 17:1–4, NIV).**

HEAR THE SPIRIT

An angel carried John...*away in the Spirit.* John used the phrase "in the Spirit" only four times in the Revelation of Jesus Christ. John was in the Spirit when Jesus began his Revelation. John wrote that he was in the Spirit before God revealed his Throne in Heaven, and when an angel disclosed the Holy City, Jerusalem (Rev. 1:10, 4:2, 21:10). Jesus reminds us throughout his Revelation to hear what the Spirit says to us. He says that we should use a mind of wisdom to understand (Rev. 17:9).

The phrase "in the Spirit" always indicates a view into the spiritual realms. Therefore, we must view the woman in the wilderness as a spiritual force and not a physical event or place. The woman Babylon gives us a picture of a type of spiritual evil.

The angel carried John away...*into a desert.* The temptation of Jesus, after his Baptism by John, used similar words to describe the desert or wilderness. The Spirit sent Jesus into the desert, and he was with the wild beasts (Mark 1:13). The Bible used the same Greek words for *desert* and for *beast* in these examples. The Devil has continued to send wild beasts to harass Christians throughout the Gospel Age.

The...*scarlet beast* that the woman sat on pointed to the beast out of the sea in chapter 13. Many Christians believe that the beast out of the sea represented Rome. John probably thought this true. Rome was the major power persecuting the Christian Church. Yet, the Lord said that all who read Revelation would be blessed (Rev. 1:3). The woman and the beast must have symbolized more than just the powers of Rome. What did Babylon represent then and today?

FIVE LEVELS OF DARKNESS

Revelation shows us five levels of Satan's kingdom. The different levels represent: the Dragon, the fallen angels, the beast out of the sea, the beast out of the earth, and the people of the world. Each of these five parts takes an active part throughout the Gospel Age.

The Dragon, the serpent, or the Devil always indicates Satan as the head of the kingdom of darkness.

The fallen angels and the powers that work in the kingdom of darkness take several different forms. The fallen angels persecute the people on earth in spiritual and physical ways. The demons of darkness give us one of the keys to understanding the different visions in Revelation.

The beast out of the sea represents government and business powers in the world.

The beast out of the earth represents the false prophet and the apostate or wayward Christian Church.

The people of the world symbolize people who refuse a relationship with Jesus Christ. They live in darkness and carry the mark of the beast.

THE WOMAN CALLED BABYLON

Jesus introduced us to Babylon in the second trumpet (Rev. 8:8). We saw Babylon as the burning mountain thrown into the sea of people. Babylon caused the spiritual death of billions of people around the world.

OT Babylon represented every form of evil and corruption to the Israelite nation. NT Babylon has represented every form of evil and darkness; only she exercises her duties in the spiritual realm.

Babylon, pictured as the woman, symbolizes the spiritual forces of evil and darkness in Satan's kingdom. She's the reflection of Satan himself. I believe that the principalities, powers, rulers of darkness, and demons make up the spiritual Babylon (Eph. 6:12). The fallen angels that rebelled against God form the ingredients for the powers of evil.

The Spirits of Babylon hate the children of God. Satan uses his system of evil angels to fuel the thoughts and powers of people who control government and business. The woman Babylon rides the beast of the sea and encourages governments to persecute the Christian Church. Powers that control people don't bother other forms of worship such as the eastern religions. Babylon only attacks people who worship our Savior Jesus Christ.

Babylon mimics Satan's thoughts, desires, and attitudes toward God. The forces that make up Babylon seem bigger than any nation, any church, or any time in history. Satan, as the boss, controls the evil spirits. They answer only to him except for the Almighty God. The power of God by our prayers controls Satan, his power Babylon, and his influences in the world.

WORSHIP PLEASURE AND IDOLS

The kings of the earth committed adultery...with the prostitute. What did this mean? The word for *adultery* (*porneuo*) indicated "fornication." The metaphor pointed to one drawn into worship of idols.[1] The people of the earth didn't have physical sex with the spiritual woman. The evil powers seduced them into the worship of lust, money, sports, television, and anything that led away from the Holy God. Every person could make his or her own specific list of idols.

The picture of a woman sat as the queen of darkness. She appeared in...*purple and scarlet, and was glittering with gold, precious stones.* The scarlet pointed to sin, and the purple indicated royalty (Isa. 1:18). The gold and precious gems pointed to the riches of the world. The riches enticed many hopeless and blind people away from faith in God.

Jesus gave us a symbol of a beautiful prostitute holding a gold cup...*filled with abominable things and the filth of her adulteries.* The picture indicated money, pleasure, and lust; and yet if you followed evil and darkness, then you gained bitterness.

"Eternal and Majestic God, we glorify you for your protection from the kingdom of Satan. We thank you for leading us through the minefield of darkness and corruption. Jesus we thank you for your safety net that keeps us from falling into outer darkness. Continue to hold on to us as we finish of time on earth. Amen!"

> [5]And upon her forehead *was* a name written, MYSTERY, BABYLON THE GREAT, THE MOTHER OF HARLOTS AND ABOMINATIONS OF THE EARTH. [6]And I saw the woman drunken with the blood of the saints, and with the blood of the martyrs of Jesus: and when I saw her, I wondered with great admiration. [7]And the angel said unto me, Wherefore didst thou marvel? I will tell thee the mystery of the woman, and of the beast that carrieth her, which hath the seven heads and ten horns. [8]The beast that thou sawest was, and is not; and shall ascend out of the bottomless pit, and go into perdition: and they that dwell on the earth shall wonder, whose names were not written in the book of life

from the foundation of the world, when they behold the beast that
was, and is not, and yet is (Rev. 17:5–8, KJV).

SEDUCTION BY EVIL

Our Lord reveals a description written on her forehead. He calls her a
mystery, meaning "something secret and unknown." The metaphor for
mother (*meter*) in...*MOTHER OF HARLOTS* means the source of something.[2] All of the *abomination* (*bdelugma*) on earth comes from the spirits
of Babylon.[3] This describes the Mother of Harlots giving people detestable
things and idol worship that leads them into idolatry.

John saw an image of a woman...*drunken with the blood of the saints* and
with the blood from the martyrs for Jesus. *Drunken* (*methuo*) indicated "one
who drank to intoxication."[4] The metaphor pointed to someone who shed
blood or murdered much. Her description pointed to the hideous powers of
Satan on earth.

John seemed so amazed at the vision that he...*wondered with great
admiration.* Even John, after sixty years of following Jesus, was surprised at
Satan's enticing ways. The Devil designed his system of ruling powers to
lure people into submission to him. He baited the trap with seven items:
drugs, alcohol, witchcraft, lust for sex, lust for riches, and lust for fame, and
the pride of doing it my way.

The powers of Babylon seduced people into Satan's way of thinking.
Babylon then used authority of leadership in government to persecute and
slay Christians. The beast out of the sea symbolized the physical authority
of the nations.

The scarlet woman sat on the beast with...*seven heads and ten horns.* The
heads and the horns pointed to perfect and complete wisdom and power. The
heads and horns symbolized rulers and nations, which spanned the entire
Gospel Age. Spiritual Babylon, made up of Satan's demons and powers, has
continued as the link between Satan and the people of the world.

BABYLON—THREE WOES

The beast ascended...*out of the bottomless pit,* and the people saw that
he...*was, and is not, and yet is.* Each of the seven visions in Revelation
points to the Gospel Age from a different viewpoint. The images in this
vision refer back to visions 3, 4, and 5. The three Woes come from
Babylon, the kingdom of darkness.

In the first Woe, Satan lets demons, pictured as locusts, out of the bottomless pit. They cover the earth and torture people without the seal of
God (Rev. 9:1–11).

In the second Woe, the same beast shown in this vision crawls out of the bottomless pit to attack the witness of the Church (Rev. 11:7–11). The beast slays the two witnesses, but the King of Glory raises them to life.

In the third Woe, the Almighty hurls the Devil and his fallen angels to the earth. They then attack Christians and the Church (Rev. 12:7–12).

BABYLON IN THE VISIONS

Each of the visions shows us Babylon and Satan in a different form. The different forms of the kingdom of darkness help us to better comprehend the Revelation of Jesus Christ.

Vision 2 portrays Satan and the power of Babylon attacking the Christian Church. The red, black, and pale horses symbolize the different forces of evil from the Devil.

Vision 3 describes Babylon as symbolizing the first and second Woes. Babylon takes the form of locusts with tails like scorpions and the beast. Babylon controls the beast that attacks the Christian witness.

Vision 4 shows us Babylon as the third Woe. The power of Babylon uses the fallen angels that live on earth to attack the Christian Church.

Vision 5 portrays Babylon as the three evil spirits that look like frogs (Rev. 16:12–14). The frogs come out of the mouth of the dragon, the beast, and the false prophet. Verse 14 calls them the spirits of demons. This indicates the principalities, powers, rulers of darkness, and demons that take orders from Satan.

Vision 6 reveals the end of Babylon and the two beasts (Rev. 19:19–21). Revelation introduced them in vision 3.

Vision 7 shows us the end of Satan or the dragon that appeared in vision 2. Jesus uses different images and symbols to show the parts of Satan's kingdom on earth. Each type of image indicates the same force of evil. When we recognize the different models of evil forces, the separate visions in Revelation tie together.

> 9"This calls for a mind with wisdom. The seven heads are seven hills on which the woman sits. 10They are also seven kings. Five have fallen, one is, the other has not yet come; but when he does come, he must remain for a little while. 11The beast who once was, and now is not, is an eighth king. He belongs to the seven and is going to his destruction. 12"The ten horns you saw are ten kings who have not yet received a kingdom, but who for one hour will receive authority as kings along with the beast. 13They have one purpose and will give their power and authority to the beast.

¹⁴**They will make war against the Lamb, but the Lamb will over-come them because he is Lord of lords and King of kings—and with him will be his called, chosen and faithful followers" (Rev. 17:9–14, NIV).**

THE BEAST COMES AND GOES

The spiritual powers that controlled Rome, when John saw the vision, continue to raise their filthy influences throughout the Gospel Age. *The beast who once was, and now is not...and is to come* continues to come and go. The influence from the kingdom of darkness never dies. Darkness flows in and out of each nation opposite the Light of Jesus Christ.

When the Church prays for revival, God answers with his Spirit of Power and grace. This causes more saints to pray against the Devil's influence. The demons run for cover after the Almighty sends the Spirit of repentance, holiness, wisdom, and prayer. Righteousness causes the powers of darkness and deception to withdraw and wait for a better time. The evil spiritual forces wait until the influence of God begins to diminish. Darkness then creeps back into the nation.

The process of the changing spiritual dominion takes generations. Many nations have new governments or kings, and yet the spiritual powers that control remain the same. Babylon leads the beast of the sea or nations with evil influence. Governments change direction when the spiritual forces bring light and darkness. The beast and Babylon comes and goes just as the ocean tide rises and falls.

Babylon encourages the beast to...*make war against the Lamb*. Jesus gives his Revelation to show that he controls the powers of Satan's kingdom. The evil forces cannot overcome the Lamb...*because he is Lord of lords and King of kings*. Jesus also says we will go with him as...*his called, chosen and faithful followers*. The Lamb of God seeks disciples who will love and obey him. The Almighty then gives us all we need to follow him.

HOLY SPIRIT GIVES WISDOM

The Author and Finisher of our Faith...*calls for a mind with wisdom.* Jesus says we need wisdom to understand the relationship between Babylon, the beast, and the Kingdom of God. This doesn't come by just reading words in the Bible. The Spirit of Truth desires that his children comprehend the difference between darkness and Light. The Light of this World gives many gifts. The gifts help us discern how the spiritual and the physical realms interact.

To visualize the Word of Truth, we need to seek more of the Holy Spirit. A fresh filling of the Holy Spirit does much to strengthen our link with the wisdom of God. The Almighty gives us many gifts with the baptism of the Spirit. The gift of speaking in other languages mystifies many in the body of Christ. Nevertheless, speaking, praying, and singing in other languages or tongues seems valid for hundreds of millions around the world.

SEEK THE HOLY SPIRIT

At Ephesus, Paul finds some disciples of the Lord. Paul asks them if they had received the Holy Spirit after they had believed (Acts 19:1–7). The Greek word for *received* (*lambano*) means "to take, to act, or to choose."[5] The word points to taking hold of something for one's self. The Greek does not mean a Christian passively receives the baptism in the Holy Spirit when they are born again. It indicates that Christians need to pursue the release of the Holy Spirit in their lives.

Paul explained the baptism in the Holy Spirit to the disciples at Ephesus. They then baptized the disciples into the name of the Lord Jesus. After that, Paul laid hands on them, and the Holy Spirit came upon them. They spoke in tongues and prophesied (Acts 19:5–7).

The believers in the Lord had to choose to receive the Holy Spirit baptism after they were baptized with water in the name of Jesus Christ. The baptism of the Holy Spirit came after the prayer of asking for it and the laying on of hands.

Many Christians need to surrender to Jesus Christ in a fuller way to receive the Baptism of the Holy Spirit. Our Father gives his children the desires of their hearts. If they seek the baptism of power to do the Lord's will, God gives it. If Christians seek the baptism to fulfill their own desires, God may withhold it.

THE GIFT OF TONGUES

Our Father desires that we ask for an overflowing of his Spirit so that we may flow in his Spirit. The Holy Spirit gives many gifts, including various kinds of tongues or languages (1 Cor. 12:4–11). As I understand the gift of the Holy Spirit, most Christians receive a prayer language as evidence of the baptism in the Holy Spirit.

Paul lists three types of tongues, which are speaking in prophesy, praying, and singing (1 Cor. 14:13–15). Paul said that when a person speaks in tongues publicly, he or she needs an interpretation. Most do not have the gift of speaking in tongues for prophecy. Nevertheless, the gift of praying and singing in tongues seems common among God's children.

When we pray in our prayer language, our spirit prays with the leading from the Spirit of God. The Holy Spirit uses our prayer language to speak the prayers that he wants to say through us. We don't speak to men: we utter mysteries to God with his Spirit (1 Cor. 14:2). Paul recommended that we pray and sing in tongues plus pray and sing with our minds (1 Cor. 14:15).

Paul said tongues was less important than the other gifts, and yet our prayer language seems a good place to start (1 Cor. 12:27–31). The gift opens the door and frees us for an intimate encounter with Jesus Christ. The Holy Spirit edifies us when we pray in this way. (1 Cor. 14:4).

TONGUES BRINGS GOD NEAR

I often pray softly in tongues when God seems distant. This seems to activate the Holy Spirit that lives in my spirit and draws his peace and comfort. The Lord often gives insight into the Bible with his Love. The prayer language helps me identify what comes from God and what comes from the world and the kingdom of darkness.

It's useful to combat evil and darkness in my life. The spirit of Babylon from the Devil roams the earth seeking to devour, and yet if we resist he flees (James 4:7, 8). I pray every day for all influences of Satan's kingdom to stay away from my family and me. At times when the powers of darkness try to defeat my other prayers, I pray in tongues for a time. I pray and praise God until the evil darkness leaves.

The prayer language helps us to intercede for others. When we don't know how to pray, tongues permits the Holy Spirit to pray as he wills through each of us. God releases his power and grace from this exercise. This gives Christians a powerful and effective tool to use in their prayers. We may not understand the reason that God gave his Church the gift of tongues. Nevertheless, it's available if we ask for it and seek it with a sincere heart.

SATAN HATES TONGUES

Although Paul says tongues is the least of the gifts, the Devil resists the gift more than any other gift. We should ask, why does the Devil resist this gift with such dedication? Why do some Christians say that the gift of tongues does not come from God when the Scriptures seem plain?

Satan uses tongues to divide Christian churches and people. Satan uses more persecution against tongues than any other gift from the Holy Spirit. Even Christians who have a prayer language tend to use it on the sly.

I am not ashamed of the Gospel from my Lord (Rom. 1:16). Jesus gave us tongues as part of his Gospel. I use all parts of his Gospel and all of his gifts that the Lord gives me. The spirit of the world and Babylon convince many Christians that the gift is not for today. However, if Jesus gives the other gifts, he also gives tongues because he cannot lie (Heb. 6:18).

Satan reacts against tongues because he knows the power of the gift in the spiritual domain. The Devil lives in the spirit world on earth. He knows what stops his actions against people. The Holy Spirit prays in specific ways through the prayer languages of his children. The gift gives us another effective way to pray and pull down the strongholds of the Devil's kingdom. The gift of tongues helps Jesus hinder the Devil's work on earth.

"Holy Spirit, we thank you for your gracious gifts that you give to each of us as you will. We know that we need your gifts to walk on the center of the road that you designed for us. Thank you, Father, for giving us your wisdom that keeps out of the road ditches of destruction. Amen!"

> ¹⁵Then the angel said to me, "The waters you saw, where the prostitute sits, are peoples, multitudes, nations and languages. ¹⁶The beast and the ten horns you saw will hate the prostitute. They will bring her to ruin and leave her naked; they will eat her flesh and burn her with fire. ¹⁷For God has put it into their hearts to accomplish his purpose by agreeing to give the beast their power to rule, until God's words are fulfilled. ¹⁸The woman you saw is the great city that rules over the kings of the earth" (Rev. 17:15–18, NIV).

PASSION BRINGS REGRET

The angel clarified that the waters and the sea, where the prostitute sat, represented...*peoples, multitudes, nations and languages*. The powers of evil sat on the beast, which was made up of the people and nations in the world. The prostitute intoxicated the people of the earth with her wine of lust and her idols. The people of the world seemed to love her for what they could get. Their love only lasted until she turned on them with her endless evil.

The emotion of love sometimes turns to hate. The world loves the darkness until it overwhelms with sorrow and pain. People of the world desire idols and physical pleasures from Satan's kingdom. The idols, the lust, and the pride take many to places where they don't want to go. When people loose spiritual salvation, they will then...*hate the prostitute*. Where there's no forgiveness, hate often replaces love.

THE BEAUTY OF LUST

I love your beauty.

But, don't do me wrong.
I love what you do for me.
But, don't do me wrong.
I love the lust you give me.
But, don't do me wrong.
I hate your very presence.
Because you did me wrong.

Jesus gives love, kindness, and forgiveness. The mother of abominations gives hate, discord, and vengeance. These verses show us the stark reality between light and darkness. Babylon uses people and throws them away. Jesus seeks people and keeps them forever.

The throwaway people symbolize the bitter loathing of the spurned lover toward the kingdom of sin. They desire to destroy the influence of sin, and yet that will only happen through the prayers of God's children. Prayer gives us the key to the destruction of Babylon in the place and time we live.

Babylon appears as...*the great city that rules* in the nations of the world. Babylon will continue bringing filth and idols until the return of Christ. *City* (*polis*) indicates "a city on earth or a spiritual city." The word also means "warfare, battle, and fighting,"[6]

Jesus calls Babylon the great city. Revelation again shows the contrast in the form of a city. The city of Babylon represents the evil fallen angels of Satan's kingdom. The city of the New Jerusalem represents the redeemed holy saints of the kingdom of God. The city of Babylon brings wars, lust, and worship of false idols. The city of God brings peace, fulfillment, and worship of the True Living God.

SEEK HOLINESS FROM JESUS

God calls each of us to live a holy life. We can't do it on our own. As poor miserable sinners, we have no hope except in the grace and the shed blood of Jesus Christ. By the power of the Holy Spirit living in each of us, God helps us try to live as the Lord desires.

> [1]Since we have these promises, dear friends, let us purify ourselves from everything that contaminates body and spirit, perfecting holiness out of reverence for God (2 Cor. 7:1, NIV)

Our Father wants each of us to strive for personal holiness. We should purify our minds, bodies, and spirits from lust, evil, and idols. Because of original sin, our minds always want to turn away from God. We should seek to follow his ways and live a moral life. We can only do this by asking our

Father to help us get rid of the idols and bad habits in our lives (1 Pet. 2:1–5).

THE LIVING GARBAGE DISPOSAL

The kingdom of Babylon enjoys bringing filth and idols into a Christian's life. Foul spirits begin to smell when they stay to long. We need to clean the Devil's wickedness out of the Lord's house. We are the Lord's house or temple because the Holy Spirit lives in us.

As a plumber, I have installed many garbage disposals. A disposal grinds up garbage and sends it down the drain. A garbage disposal needs three things to work properly: water, electricity, and a drain.

The Lord gives each of us a built-in garbage disposal to help us remove the trash out of our lives. When we find unwanted filth and idols in our lives, just give them to our built-in disposal. Stop and seek God's wisdom, then pray. Ask the Father to send the living water of Jesus and the electric current of the Holy Spirit to activate our personal disposal.

Continue praying for more water from Jesus and more power from the Spirit until the foul spirits disappear from our lives. Always command the evil spirits to go to Jesus in his name. The Lord can then send them down the drain into the Abyss. The Lord's drain pit or abyss has no bottom, so he invites you to clean your house and send all the filthy idols and bad habits to him. The Abyss has sufficient room for all of the Devil's deceptions and idols.

NOTES

1. Adultery, *porneuo*, G4203. Commit fornication. Metaphor means to worship idols.
2. Mother, *meter*, G3384. A mother. Metaphor—the source of something.
3. Abominations, *bdelugma*, G946. A foul thing, a detestable thing, idols and idolatry
4. Drunken, *methuo*, G3148. Drunken, Metaphor—one who has shed blood or murdered abundantly.
5. Received, *lambano*, G2983. To take or act with the hand. To get hold of, to take for oneself, to choose.
6. City, *polis*, G4172. City. From polemos, G4171. Warfare, battle, fighting.

CHAPTER 18

The Fall of Babylon

DEAD TREES IN THE FOREST

Trees, covering millions of acres, live and grow in forests around the world. Snags or dead trees stand watch over the live trees. The trees die for many reasons, and some stand in stark contrast to the living. The large snags seem beautiful from a distance. When we inspect them up close, we find decayed and defective wood.

The dead parts of the wood make old snags hazardous. A dead snag can cause unexpected difficulty for the unaware. Many people approach the beauty of the woman of Babylon and tangle themselves in a dilemma. The Devil offers many seductive pitfalls. Yet, if someone walks too near a snag, the pointed limbs may reach out and rip a hole in the tender skin. Our Lord offers many tools that protect us from the spiritual dangers around Babylon.

> [1]And after these things I saw another angel come down from heaven, having great power; and the earth was lightened with his glory. [2]And he cried mightily with a strong voice, saying, Babylon the great is fallen, is fallen, and is become the habitation of devils, and the hold of every foul spirit, and a cage of every unclean and hateful bird. [3]For all nations have drunk of the wine of the wrath of her fornication, and the kings of the earth have committed fornication with her, and

the merchants of the earth are waxed rich through the abundance of her delicacies (Rev. 18:1–3, KJV).

THE BRIGHT ANGEL

John sees...*another angel come down from heaven.* The angel makes the earth bright with his glory, and he has endless power. *Glory (doxa)* ndicates "the honor, praise, and the majesty of something belonging to Christ."[1] The angel covers the whole earth with the light of his glory. A created angel can't do this; they can only be in one place at a time. The angel seems similar to the angel in chapter 10. Therefore, this angel must represent our risen Lord Jesus Christ.

Jesus Christ suffered agony and death on the cross to defeat the powers of Satan. Therefore, it seems fitting then that our Redeemer should announce the fall of Babylon. Christ defeated the kingdom of darkness, and yet he lets Babylon of sin spread perversion until the end of the Age. For me, this appears as one of the greatest mysteries in the Bible. Why does our loving God allow the Devil to pervert and destroy his children after Satan's defeat by the cross?

WHY GOD PERMITS SATAN'S EVIL

As I learn more about our Creator, I sense that there is much more happening than we can see and know from the Bible. The Holy Spirit gives us the Word of God and principles to live by. When we follow the teachings of Jesus, we do well. Nevertheless, I believe that God didn't give us everything in his Word (2 Cor. 12:1–4) Our Lord doesn't explain why he permits the Devil's kingdom to persecute and kill Christians.

Our time on earth reminds me of a super sports game. God calls us to war against spiritual darkness. We see many battlefield casualties as the Church fights evil. I have a strong sense that our obedience to our Savior will set our place in Heaven. I am not writing here about works righteousness. We obey the Lamb as we follow and obey him because of grace and love.

BABYLON PERVERTS PEOPLE

Babylon holds devils, foul spirits, and...*every unclean and hateful bird.* The *foul (akathartos)* spirits indicate a moral uncleanness in thought and life.[2] This again symbolizes Babylon as the spiritual powers of evil and filth from Satan's kingdom. The evil of darkness leads some politicians, bankers, and business people to worship idols and their own personal lust. The spirits of Babylon causes every immoral perversion on earth today.

This vision shows us the major theme of Christ bringing down the powers of evil at the end of the Age. The angel of glory says Babylon has fallen, and yet the rest of the chapter points to her future sudden end.

GOD CREATED PERFECTION

The Lord says that men and women should live by the Spirit and not by our sinful nature (Gal. 5:16–21). The Bible lists many sins that come from our sinful nature and from the Devil's kingdom. The Bible teaches that our Holy God views all sin with disgust. He considers sin as sin; it's all loathing to him. Without the Father's love and grace, all of us would be doomed because of our sinful nature.

Our Holy Father created the heavens, the earth, and man. The Infinite Spirit created all things perfect without blemish. After Adam and Eve sinned in the garden, then Satan began to pervert God's perfect creation. Early in the history of man, the serpent polluted man's nature. The devil enticed mankind to rebel against God and his moral laws. Satan seduced man's thinking and enticed him into immoral sexual acts and impurity that was contrary to the Holiness of God.

Jesus came to restore people to wholeness. Our Lord healed every form of plague when he walked on earth. He has continued healing the same diseases throughout the Gospel Age. Our God of grace and mercy offers the living waters of healing for all perversion and disease (Matt. 4:23,24; 9:35).

Jesus wants people to repent and desire a change, and then he will send his healing waters of holiness and love. The most efficient way to come away from sin comes when a person asks God to immerse him or her in the Holy Spirit. When the Holy Spirit fills a person, the Spirit begins to deliver people from immorality and desire for sin.

Immoral sin clings to men and women. They need deliverance from the sin and physical healing. This will only happen through prayer using the name and the blood of Jesus Christ. Seeking out a godly Christian prayer group and praying together helps quicken the deliverance. The Christians doing the praying need to understand the power of prayer and how to use their authority in the name of Jesus Christ.

WE STAND BY THE GRACE OF GOD

Each of us, who calls ourselves a Christian, stands at the foot of the cross. It's only by God's grace and mercy that we can have a relationship with Jesus Christ. We as Christians tend to forget the hopeless situations that we came out of before God's grace (Titus 3:3–7).

Our Heavenly Father considers sin as sin. Even our small sins would keep us away from Heaven without his love and mercy. Some Christians stand back like the Pharisee who said, "I thank you God that I am not like that other sinner" (Luke 18:9–14). Except for the grace of God, you and I could be like that. Under different circumstances, you and I could make different choices and live an immoral life style.

"**Lord, we thank you** for your glory and Light of Salvation. We rejoice in you because you extend your peace and comfort like a flowing river. Thank you, Lord, for raising us out of darkness into your marvelous Light. We praise your Holy name. Amen!"

> **⁴Then I heard another voice from heaven say: "Come out of her, my people, so that you will not share in her sins, so that you will not receive any of her plagues; ⁵for her sins are piled up to heaven, and God has remembered her crimes. ⁶Give back to her as she has given; pay her back double for what she has done. Mix her a double portion from her own cup" (18:4–6, NIV).**

COME AWAY FROM SIN

The voice said…"*Come out of her, my people.*" God wants us to stay far away from the influence of Satan's kingdom. To understand God's attitude toward sin, we need to look at the OT enemies of Israel and God's approach to them. The OT physical enemies of Israel represent the spiritual enemies that we have today.

Moses led Israel through the wilderness to the Promised Land. The people of Israel destroyed most tribes that opposed them. Because they feared the Israelites, Balaam the sorcerer told the women of the Moabites and the Midianites to entice the men of Israel (Rev. 2:16).

The tribes of Israel lived next to the Moabites and the Midianites. If we can imagine, the Israelite men worked in the fields when the women came by. The women probably began to talk to them and show themselves to the men. The women enticed the men to have sex with them.

The women then invited the Israelite men to go with them and worship their gods. The men, who followed the women, appeared like goats that crossed a fence into the wrong pasture. Fence jumping goats usually end up at the slaughterhouse.

Many men of Israel began to have sexual relations with the Moabite and Midianite women. The women took them to sacrifice to their gods and eat the sacrifices. The lust for the flesh of the women enticed the men to worship their gods and Baal of Peor (Num. 25:1–3). God's anger burned against them for worshiping other gods!

DESTROY THEM

The Lord told Moses to have the leaders of Israel kill all the men who had worshiped the Baal of Peor. An Israelite man brought a Midianite woman into his home. Phinehas, a grandson of Aaron, drove a spear through both of them as they lay together. This stopped the Lord's plague after 24,000 men of Israel had died. The Lord was pleased with Phinehas because he had pinned the illicit lovers together with a spear. God then honored him with a special covenant (Num. 25).

Moses took vengeance on the Midianites as his last act before he died (Num. 31). He sent 12,000 men from Israel, and they killed Balaam the sorcerer and every Midianite man. The Israelite army took the Midianite women, children, and the livestock back to Moses.

Moses grew angry when he saw the women. He ordered them to kill all the women who had slept with a man, and all the boys including infant males. Moses told them to only save the female babies and the young virgin girls (Num. 31:13–18).

The Israelites then separated the spoils. They divided 675,000 sheep, 72,000 cattle, 61,000 donkeys, and 32,000 young virgin girls (Num. 31:32). Israel wiped out a large tribe of people and gained all their wealth.

WHY DID ISRAEL KILL SO MANY

This story was one occurrence that happened among the Israelites. They destroyed many other tribes of people and cities during their conquest of the Promised Land. Many Christians and non-Christians do not understand why God had them kill so many people, even babies. God did this in the OT to protect his chosen people from the influences of false gods.

God set Israel apart when he called Abraham and his descendants. He told Moses that Israel was his special treasure. God called the people of Israel a kingdom of priests and a holy nation (Exod. 19:5, 6). Nevertheless, the Lord is a Jealous God, and he destroyed his chosen people if they chased after other gods (Deut. 6:13–16).

The Almighty told them to worship One God and him alone. He commanded them not to worship any other gods (Exod. 20:3–5). God didn't want his holy chosen people defiled by other gods and the world. He commanded his people to follow One God.

HAVE NO PITY ON THEM

The Sovereign Lord prepared his people to cross the Jordan River into the Promised Land. He told them that he would help them destroy seven mighty nations stronger then Israel. (Deut. 7:1–7). God told Israel to destroy the nations. He did not want Israel to make a covenant with them or show them any mercy. The Lord told Israel not to intermarry with the other people because that would cause them to serve the people's other gods (Deut. 7:4).

> ¹⁶You must destroy all the peoples the LORD your God gives over to you. Do not look on them with pity and do not serve their gods, for that will be a snare to you. ²⁴He will give their kings into your hand, and you will wipe out their names from under heaven. No-one will be able to stand up against you; you will destroy them. (Deut. 7:16, 24, NIV)

These verses help us understand why Israel had no mercy on their enemies. When the Israelites worshiped other gods, the Lord considered them defiled and cursed. The Holy God didn't want his holy people influenced by the gods of the heathens. The unrighteous people led Israel astray from the worship of the One True God. That's why the Lord blessed his people when they destroyed other kingdoms of people and removed their names from the earth.

OT CONTRASTED WITH NT

I stand in awe as I look at these events. I understand why the God of Love had Israel destroy their enemies; however, I don't condone their actions. Today, people would call this genocide. We live in a different time, and Jesus changed the moral values of the world. These tragic stories contrast the difference between the OT and NT covenants.

In the OT covenant, God dwelt with his people. He gave them rules to stay clean. God expected his people to obey him. When they didn't follow the rules, God considered them unclean and defiled (Lev. 19:31).

In the NT covenant, the Holy Spirit lives in us. The Lord gives us a special grace so that if we sin, we can ask Jesus to forgive us. We don't need to sacrifice an animal.

The Holy Spirit lives in us and protects us from false gods. As long as we fix our eyes on Jesus, the false gods will not harm us. This is far better than the OT covenant, because God doesn't want us to kill our neighbors that influence us. Our Savior doesn't want us to destroy our neighbors; he wants us to pray for and witness to them. Jesus wants to give our neighbors salvation and make new creations out of them (2 Cor. 5:17).

Our Father says that the OT gods would cause a snare to the Israelites. In the same way, the city of Babylon causes a snare to Christians. Jesus tells us to come away from Babylon so that we...*will not share in her sins.* Our Holy God wants us to have no mercy on sin in our lives. He wants us to pray against the spirits and bad habits that cause offenses in our lives. Jesus desires that we try to imitate his ways.

> [7]"Give her as much torture and grief as the glory and luxury she gave herself. In her heart she boasts, 'I sit as queen; I am not a widow, and I will never mourn.' [8]Therefore in one day her plagues will overtake her: death, mourning and famine. She will be consumed by fire, for mighty is the Lord God who judges her. [9]"When the kings of the earth who committed adultery with her and shared her luxury see the smoke of her burning, they will weep and mourn over her. [10]Terrified at her torment, they will stand far off and cry: " 'Woe! Woe, O great city, O Babylon, city of power! In one hour your doom has come' (Rev. 18:7–10, NIV)!

JESUS—KINGDOM OF DARKNESS

*The Lord God who judges...*the woman of Babylon gives her torture and grief in relation to the...*glory and luxury she gave herself.* The woman boasts that she sits like a queen and...*not a widow.* The metaphor for *widow* (*chera*) indicates "a city that's stripped of people and riches."[3] The Lord states that her end will come...*in one day.* Suddenly, the Almighty God will judge Babylon, the kingdom of darkness, and fire will devour the evil.

THE SERVANT

The Lord humbled himself and then obeyed God to his death on a cross (Phil. 2:6–8). Our Lord prayed in anguish to the Father over the coming crucifixion. He was so distressed that he sweat drops of blood, and yet he obeyed the will of his Father (Luke 22:44).

Jesus Christ came to heal, bring deliverance, and give salvation. He used his Mighty Power to heal all that came to him (Luke 9:11). Our Lord felt compassion when he ministered to each of the people. Jesus often asked the people what they wanted him to do for them (Mark 1:41; 10:51). He was always sensitive to their spiritual, mental, and physical needs.

Revelation shows us the Savior's victory and Majesty. However, the Gospels picture our Lord as a servant to all people. In the kingdom of God, values seem backward. What is first shall become last and what is last shall become first (Mark 10:43–45).

Each child of God has a different calling. Our higher calling points to following Christ as his servant. God helps each of us fulfill his calling when we ask each day, "Lord, what do you want me to do today?"

The kingdom of darkness entices people of the world to get all they can from life. The evil spirits encourage them to desire instant pleasure and satisfaction. In contrast, true followers of Jesus Christ desire to please him. They want to imitate the actions of their Savior (Eph. 5:1–3). Followers of Christ desire to love him and his other children. We love him because of his rich love for us.

Prayer on Our Knees

When we pray on our knees, our stature grows higher than the mighty fir and redwood trees. We leap across this vast land; we fly across the ocean waves. The winds of the Spirit carry us to the furthest reaches of the earth.

The Eternal God sees us as a mighty David when on our knees. With the mighty power of the resurrection, we destroy the spiritual Goliaths in the land. Our Savior offers us his unending power to use when on our knees. Because we pray as a servant of Jesus in humility before him, he gives us his Mighty Power when we pray in his name (Eph. 1:18–23).

> [11]**And the merchants of the earth shall weep and mourn over her; for no man buyeth their merchandise any more:** [12]**The merchandise of gold, and silver, and precious stones, and of pearls, and fine linen, and purple, and silk, and scarlet, and all thyine wood, and all manner vessels of ivory, and all manner vessels of most precious wood, and of brass, and iron, and marble,** [13]**And cinnamon, and odours, and ointments, and frankincense, and wine, and oil, and fine flour, and wheat, and beasts, and sheep, and horses, and chariots, and slaves, and souls of men (Rev. 18:11–13, KJV).**

Babylon fuels the business practices in the world. She causes people to gain riches from buying and selling all forms of commodities. These verses list all the types of goods at that time. The…*merchants of the earth* wept over the end of Babylon. They put emphasis on their jobs and riches rather than into the kingdom of God.

Ninety Percent Gives More

God leads many Christians to give a portion of their income to the church. The Bible required people in the OT to pay a tithe of 10 percent (Lev. 27:30–32; Num. 18:26). I began to tithe 10 percent on our income after I committed my life to Jesus over twenty years ago. In 1980, a recession began in Oregon. I was unemployed part of the time and quit tithing when I didn't work.

Our ability to pay bills went downhill after part-time work for several months. Finally, I made a commitment to the Lord and began to tithe on my unemployment checks also. A strange thing happened!

Although, I continued to work part time, we began paying our bills on time. I still don't understand how God took care of the money flow. There wasn't enough money, and yet somehow we caught up. In God's calculation, ninety percent gave us more than one hundred percent. From that point on in my life, the Lord's money always went to him first (1 Cor. 8:1–7; 9:6-11).

> **14"They will say, 'The fruit you longed for is gone from you. All your riches and splendor have vanished, never to be recovered.' 15The merchants who sold these things and gained their wealth from her will stand far off, terrified at her torment. They will weep and mourn 16and cry out: " 'Woe! Woe, O great city, dressed in fine linen, purple and scarlet, and glittering with gold, precious stones and pearls! 17aIn one hour such great wealth has been brought to ruin' (Rev. 18:14–17a, NIV)!**

TRUST OUR FATHER WHO CARES

Jesus said...*All your riches and splendor have vanished*. The people who served themselves and Babylon lost all. Our Lord told a parable about a rich fool (Luke 12:13–21). The man had a good crop, so he built new barns to hold it. Then he said, "I will take life easy because I have ample money. I will eat, drink, and enjoy luxury."

Then the Lord told him, "You fool, today you will die, and you will reap what you sowed."

The man had many riches and material goods, and yet he lacked what was required to gain eternal life with the Lord. What good did all his riches do after he died? While on earth, he should have sought the wisdom of God and then obeyed the Lord in all his actions.

THE FOOL SAYS (PS. 53)

The heart of a fool says, "There is no God."
They live for wickedness and stand corrupt.
None who follows the prostitute does good.
Our God looks down from Heaven at men.
The Savior checks to see if any seek him.
He sees all turning away; they seem foul.
A terror comes on people who hate God.
God scatters their bones giving shame.

17b"Every sea captain, and all who travel by ship, the sailors, and all who earn their living from the sea, will stand far off. 18When they see the smoke of her burning, they will exclaim, 'Was there ever a city like this great city?' 19They will throw dust on their heads, and with weeping and mourning cry out: " 'Woe! Woe, O great city, where all who had ships on the sea became rich through her wealth! In one hour she has been brought to ruin! 20Rejoice over her, O heaven! Rejoice, saints and apostles and prophets! God has judged her for the way she treated you' " (Rev. 18:17b–20, NIV).

WEEP THE GREAT CITY

Three classes of people weep and mourn over the fall of Babylon. They stand far off and cry...*Woe! Woe, O great city*. The kings of the earth, the merchants of the earth, and...*every sea captain* stands far off and mourns for her. All the people on earth who give themselves to the city of evil suffer when she falls. They give all to the kingdom of the world, and they don't plan for life after death.

The people grieve when they understand the truth of spiritual life. They speak out an epitaph for the darkness of Babylon and for their own lives. They express sorrow for the deceased city. The people desire to repent for their wrongs, but it's too late.

THE SNIPE HUNT

I was eleven years old and naive in many ways. Then some of my mean uncles took me snipe hunting. I waited in the night for a long time. I faithfully held the sack waiting for my uncles to herd the little bird to me. But the bird never came!

I went back to the house after I didn't hear any movement for what seemed like a long time. I walked in without a snipe, and they all laughed. That night I grew smarter. I understood the ways of a good snipe hunt.

The god of this world uses deception to entice people to walk through darkness and try to find the elusive snipe. The snipe hunt represents the lust and pride of living. The Devil and his kingdom entice their children to pursue the perfect experience. Many children of the world wonder around in the dark seeking a little bird, but never finding it.

Our Creator gives everyone a spirit. In this spirit lives a desire for fellowship with God. People without God seek fulfillment from the lust of the eyes, the lust of the flesh, and the pride of life. Yet, only God can satisfy the spirit living within each of us. Until a person commits his or her life to

Jesus Christ, he will wonder around chasing elusive dreams of happiness.

"Father, we thank you that we can trust you. We know that you will never deceive us or entice us into wrong choices. We thank you for your unending patience toward our errors in life. Thank you for the pleasure of your abundant Love. Praise you, Lord! Amen!"

> 21And a mighty angel took up a stone like a great millstone, and cast *it* into the sea, saying, Thus with violence shall that great city Babylon be thrown down, and shall be found no more at all. 22And the voice of harpers, and musicians, and of pipers, and trumpeters, shall be heard no more at all in thee; and no craftsman, of whatsoever craft *he be*, shall be found any more in thee; and the sound of a millstone shall be heard no more at all in thee; 23And the light of a candle shall shine no more at all in thee; and the voice of the bridegroom and of the bride shall be heard no more at all in thee: for thy merchants were the great men of the earth; for by thy sorceries were all nations deceived. 24And in her was found the blood of prophets, and of saints, and of all that were slain upon the earth (Rev. 18:21–24, KJV).

THE END OF BABYLON

The...*great city Babylon* lies in ruin. The end has come. No one lives in the city any longer. This points to the end of the Age when Jesus fulfills his promise to destroy the Devil's kingdom represented by Babylon. We know that Jesus broke all the powers of Satan's kingdom on the cross. Nevertheless, until our Lord releases the fullness of his power, the Devil will continue to kill, molest, and deceive.

We live by faith, and by faith the Lord leads us in his ways. The people of the world live by faith in self and in nothing. Their faith in nothing leads them to their ultimate destruction.

The powers of Satan deceive all nations...*by thy sorceries*. The word *sorceries* (*pharmakeia*) means "to use or administer drugs."[4] The metaphor points to deceptions and seduction caused from worshiping idols. The Greek for...*deceived* causes people and nations to go astray from truth. This results in going down the path to ruin. The drugs point to age-old marijuana, heroin, or any substance that causes hallucination.

LEAF OF ENTICEMENT

Marijuana use was common from the sixties on. Many people smoked and never realized the danger from the drug. Marijuana caused people to lessen their duties and responsibilities. I knew several people that marijuana took down a road to nowhere. Some recovered; others did not.

Marijuana holds hidden pitfalls, although some consider it a harmless intoxicant. The drug lowers inhibitions and opens the mind to outside influences. Satan uses drugs and alcohol as a way to gain entrance into the minds of the unaware.

I worked with a man who smoked marijuana often. He told me that he had seen many visions of Jesus Christ alive and in color. I wasn't a Christian at the time, and I found it interesting. I have since believed that this was not the real Christ. The father of lies loves to lead the unwise astray. He uses drugs to help people feel good, to take away their worries, and to give them an idol to worship.

Drugs Make an Easy Mark

It is easy for the Devil to kick down the door of resistance in a drug-soaked mind. Drugs lead the mind to distorted thoughts and delusions from hallucination. The serpent uses his power to enter the mind and then influence and sometimes control it. Then the users tell their friends that drugs won't hurt anyone. They say, "We need to legalize marijuana." Then they reach for another joint and claim they're not addicted, but they just enjoy it.

The demons begin to draw people away from God after the spirits push the resistance out of the way. The Devil keeps them doped up and under his rule. Authorities say that hard drugs do more damage than marijuana. The serpent uses many fiendish ways to destroy people.

I believe that when someone uses drugs, he or she faces spiritual danger. The power of God lives in people from Holy Baptism, or from accepting Jesus as Savior. The Power of the Spirit helps people understand that they should put the drugs aside. If people don't have the Holy Spirit in them, or people don't pray for their salvation, they could smoke themselves over the edge.

Notes

1. Glory, *doxa* G1391. Glory, honor, praise, majesty. A thing belonging to God or Christ.
2. Foul, *akathartos*, G169. In moral sense, unclean in thought and life.
3. Widow, *chera*, G5503. Metaphor, A city stripped of inhabitants and riches.
4. Sorceries, *pharmakeia*, G5331. Medication, drug, magic, witchcraft.

CHAPTER 19

Wedding Supper—White Horse

ALZHEIMER'S IN REMEMBRANCE

The pastor of our church, Pastor Tyrus H. Miles, told us about a visit he made with a shut-in. The woman was in the late stages of Alzheimer's disease. As Pastor Miles spoke with the lady, she appeared restless and couldn't focus on their conversation. Pastor Miles then led her in the Lord's Prayer in preparation for Holy Communion.

The lady settled down and spoke the Lord's Prayer with her pastor. She knew exactly what she was doing as she prayed to the Lord. Even Christians with severe memory loss have not forgotten how to speak the Lord's Prayer and the creeds they used during times of worship.

The Holy Spirit always remains active in the lives of saints until their last sunset here on earth. It's sad to see someone with Alzheimer's disease, and yet the Lord protects their spiritual life until they go to Jesus (Heb. 13:5). Our Lord stays with each of us until he brings us into Heaven to join with the many saints saying glory, honor, and power to our Savior.

> ¹And after these things I heard a great voice of much people in heaven, saying, Alleluia; Salvation, and glory, and honour, and power, unto the Lord our God: ²For true and righteous *are* his judgments: for he hath judged the great whore, which did corrupt the earth with her fornication, and hath avenged the blood of his

servants at her hand. ³And again they said, Alleluia. And her smoke rose up for ever and ever (Rev. 19:1–3, KJV).

GOD JUDGES SIN

These verses show a multitude of…*people in heaven* proclaiming the goodness of God's judgments. Many people around the world don't believe that a kind God would judge with wrath. Yet, the saints in Heaven praise the Lord and say…*true and righteous are his judgments.* Some Christians have a difficult time with the concept of a Holy God who hates sin so much that he must punish sin.

I do not like to talk about a God of judgment either, and yet the Scriptures seem plain. If we believe that our Savior came down as a man and suffered misery for our sins, then God requires us to accept the complete Bible. The people said Alleluia and watched the smoke of Babylon rise…*for ever and ever.*

> ⁴The twenty-four elders and the four living creatures fell down and worshiped God, who was seated on the throne. And they cried: "Amen, Hallelujah!" ⁵Then a voice came from the throne, saying: "Praise our God, all you his servants, you who fear him, both small and great!" ⁶Then I heard what sounded like a great multitude, like the roar of rushing waters and like loud peals of thunder, shouting: "Hallelujah! For our Lord God Almighty reigns" (Rev. 19:4–6, NIV).

HALLELUJAH TO GOD

Jesus shows us the angels and saints dwelling in the Kingdom of Heaven. We see the…*twenty-four elders* representing the Church and the…*four living creatures* representing the host of angels. They cry…*"Amen, Hallelujah"* as they praise God. John then hears a great multitude of saints and angels shouting…*"Hallelujah! For our Lord God Almighty reigns."*

The saints pictured in these verses have served their time on earth. They lived their life and followed Jesus as he led them. Some followed him for a short time in their lives. Others followed him most of their life. The saints came from all the Christian churches on earth. All believed that Jesus gave them salvation by his shed blood on the cross. Yet, they held many different views on doctrine. When we all get to Heaven, then we will know what our Savior considered important.

What Christians Believe

Christians have held different beliefs about Christian doctrines through the centuries. When I began this book, I had personal opinions on how to worship the Lord. Through the years, the Lord softened my convictions on issues of doctrine. He has shown me that he uses different ways and practices to reach his children.

Most Christians hold convictions of baptism, the Lord's Supper, and distinct worship styles close to their hearts. Part of the Church practices adult water baptism. The other part practices infant baptism. What does Jesus believe?

The Bible does not specify whether we should baptize as infants or adults. A good Bible scholar can prove the case for both adult and infant baptism. It depends on your viewpoint of the Word of God and personal beliefs. In these last days, our Redeemer wants his children to stop fighting over unsolvable issues. He wants us to team up to proclaim the Gospel of Salvation to our neighbors and people without a Savior.

Christians sometimes say that other denominations don't have the right beliefs. Perhaps these Christians have a limited view of our Unlimited and Sovereign Creator. Our giant God understands the cries of our hearts. He permits his children to seek him in different ways. Paul said that only God makes the Kingdom grow, and we should not have divisions among churches (1 Cor. 3:1–11).

Our Savior wants to reach into our hard hearts and soften them for his work in the universal Christian Church. I believe the Lord goes beyond man's limited views of the sacraments in the Church. We should respect other Christian beliefs even if we don't agree with them.

The Lord's Supper

Most Protestant churches believe that the elements of the Lord's Super symbolize the body and blood of Jesus Christ. Some liturgical churches believe that the elements of the bread and wine contain the real presence of the Lord's body and blood. The Roman Catholic Church believes that the elements become Christ's body and blood at the point of offering.[1] What does Jesus believe?

Jesus broke the bread and blessed it. He then said to his disciples, "Take it and eat; this is my body."

Jesus gave thanks and gave the cup to them. He said, "Drink from the cup. This is the blood of the new covenant, which is poured out for the forgiveness of sins" (Matt. 26:26–28, Mark 14:24–25).

He told them and us to do this in remembrance of him (Luke 22:19, 20). Paul reinforced the Words of Jesus when he wrote about Holy Communion (1 Cor. 11:23–25).

Our Lord called himself the Bread of Life, which is the true bread from Heaven. He told us that when we ate the living bread, we would live forever. Jesus stated that his flesh was true food and his blood was true drink. Our Lord said that when we do this, he lives in us and we live in him (John 6:32–58). In a spiritual sense, we grow into oneness with him.

WORDS FROM THE HEART OF JESUS

Over the last 15 years, the Lord has led me to worship in different Christian church denominations. I know that the Father, the Son, and the Holy Spirit make their home in each church. By his grace, the Lord has given me the gift of sensing his Spirit in different settings.

Our Savior goes beyond man's thoughts and actions in the Lord's Supper. Jesus acts through the bread and the wine or fruit of the vine to expand our spiritual oneness with him. No matter what an individual believes about the elements of the Eucharist, the Lord is in them.

God honors our belief whether we understand that the elements symbolize Jesus, or that the elements are Jesus. Then the Lord does even more than any of us can comprehend. Jesus works through the body and blood of Holy Communion to draw us into a deeper spiritual unity with him (John 6:56; 17:21). To many, this seems as an elusive goal, but the Lord does what he desires through his food for eternal life because he gave his body for the forgiveness of our sins.

IMPORTANCE OF HOLY COMMUNION

Some churches consider the Lord's Supper less important than other churches. Many celebrate it only a few times a year. The early Church shared the breaking of bread at least on a weekly cycle, and some fellowships shared the breaking of bread each day (Acts 20:7).

Our Savior stated that we should eat his body and drink his blood in all four Gospels. Jesus said to do this in remembrance of him. As I understand the Lord's heart, he desires to celebrate his gift more often. Jesus works deep under the surface even when people can't feel his presence. He supernaturally uses the elements to draw our spirits into his Spirit.

I am not a theologian and don't know all the technical names for the process. Jesus says in the Bible, this is my body; this is my blood (John 6:53–58; Mark 14:22–25). The Words of Jesus seem plain to me! For some Christians, this seems a hard teaching (John 6:60-64). Yet, nothing is too hard for the Lord God Almighty. If we believe that Jesus is risen, why not believe all of his Words?

I don't know when the bread and the fruit of the vine is his body and his blood. However, Jesus sacrificed his body and his blood for us. He will change the elements in his timing and not ours.

JESUS GAVE HIMSELF

Some church denominations believe they have an exclusive handle on how God works in the Eucharist. Our Redeemer gave his body and shed his blood because of his love, grace, and mercy. I have attended churches that said, "You can't commune here because you don't meet our rules, or you don't belong to our church."

Jesus weeps tears of pain over churches that do this. He gave his body and blood on the cross so that all of his children who believe in him could receive that special grace. Jesus desires that all come to him in the Lord's Supper. We should believe that he died for our sins, and God raised him from death to life (1 Cor. 11:23–29). If a person doesn't believe this, he should not take Holy Communion.

Men stand in God's place and decide who may partake of the Lord's Supper. They do it their way and not the Lord's way. One large church denomination says that we consider it a family celebration. Wouldn't you let your brothers and sisters in Christ sit at your table in your home when you eat your meals (Matt. 15:22–28)?

Jesus desires that we follow his command and celebrate the Lord's Supper. Some churches practice open communion. They invite all that believe in Jesus Christ as their Savior. As I understand the teachings of the Bible, Jesus smiles on these churches and encourages them to continue the practice.

Many churches have set the Lord's Supper aside to a few times a year. Nevertheless, our Savior yearns to share his broken and resurrected body with each of us more often. Our Redeemer wants all of us to seek him and come to his wedding celebration in Heaven.

"**Lord Jesus,** we thank you for instituting Holy Communion. We thank you because you desire to share your broken body and shed blood with each of us. Thank you for your Love and grace that you abundantly give us. We rejoice because you invite us to your wedding supper in Heaven."

[7]"**Let us rejoice and be glad and give him glory! For the wedding of the Lamb has come, and his bride has made herself ready.** [8]**Fine**

linen, bright and clean, was given her to wear." (Fine linen stands for the righteous acts of the saints.) [9]Then the angel said to me, "Write: 'Blessed are those who are invited to the wedding supper of the Lamb!' " And he added, "These are the true words of God." [10]At this I fell at his feet to worship him. But he said to me, "Do not do it! I am a fellow servant with you and with your brothers who hold to the testimony of Jesus. Worship God! For the testimony of Jesus is the spirit of prophecy" (Rev. 19:7–10, NIV).

Weddings of the OT

The saints in Heaven continue rejoicing and praising God. The word for *rejoice* (*agalliao*) means "to jump for joy with exceeding gladness."[2] The word for *glad* (*chairo*) indicates "a person who's cheerful, calmly happy, or well-off."[3] The verses indicate that the saints of God appear happy because...*the wedding of the Lamb has come.*

The Jewish marriage consisted of three separate steps: the legal part, the bridegroom comes and takes the bride home, and the celebration of the marriage supper.

In the first step, the family sometimes sent a servant or matchmaker to find a wife for the groom (Gen. 24). They completed the legal part of the marriage and paid a dowry during the first part of the marriage process. The bride was a legal member of the groom's family. After the engagement, the bride then waited and prepared herself for the coming of the groom.

The second part came when the bridegroom took the bride to his house. Up until that time the bride had not seen the groom. The groom took his bride to his home and completed the marriage (Gen. 24:67).

The third part was the marriage supper celebration after the second part of the marriage. The Jewish marriage supper lasted seven days.

Our Marriage to Christ

In the first step, we commit our life to our Lord and Savior as his legal bride. The Bible calls people who trust in Jesus for eternal life the bride of Christ (2 Cor. 11:2, 3). Jesus Christ paid the dowry for us when he died on the cross for our sins. We wait and have not seen our Lord yet, but we have legal rights as part of our husband's family (Eph. 5:23–32). The Lord sent a matchmaker, the Holy Spirit, to bring us into the family of God.

The bride waits and...*has made herself ready.* Jesus gives us...*fine linen, bright and clean* to wear (Matt. 25:1–13). Our Savior honors us with robes of his righteousness and holiness (Matt. 22:11–14). He justifies us through our faith in him after we commit our life to him (Col. 1:22). Our husband

Jesus wants us to wait and prepare ourselves for his return. We do this by completing what he has called each of us to do (Phil. 2:12–16).

In the second step of our marriage, Jesus will take us to his home. This will happen when we die on earth, or at the end of the Age when he returns (John 14:1–3).

The third part of our marriage to Jesus or *the wedding supper of the Lamb*...will then happen in Heaven. The celebration of our resurrection and marriage to the Lamb will last forever and ever.

The angel said...*Blessed are those who are invited* to the celebration supper in Heaven with the Lamb. The word *blessed* indicates that someone's "fortunate, well off, and happy." The angel then affirms this by saying...*These are the true words of God.*

ONLY WORSHIP GOD

John fell at the feet of the angel...*to worship him.* Perhaps the splendor of Heaven influenced John. The angels probably looked like shining stars and supernatural beings. The angel told John to worship God and testify for Jesus.

The angel told John not to worship him, but to...*Worship God.* Christians should always point their worship toward God and not to men or women. We should not bow before and worship well-known men and women in the Christian Church. Leaders in the Church only have their position by the grace of God. He can raise them, and he can bring them down.

GARBAGE MEN

I once heard a minister, who taught the prosperity gospel, talk about people who work as garbage collectors. The preacher said a garbage man didn't need much intelligence to do his job. Then he said the work was OK for secular people, but a Christian was too good for this type of work. I don't think the preacher understood the teaching of Jesus.

Pride was Satan's first sin, and it's still around in God's children. We should not consider ourselves too high in our own eyes. The followers of Christ who wrote the Bible called themselves servants of Christ.

Jesus calls all people to himself where they live and where they work. It doesn't matter what we do as long as we develop a relationship with our Lord. Jesus loves the garbage men, and most work right where he wants them to work. Who would tell the other garbage collectors about Jesus Christ if all Christian garbage men changed occupations?

Yes, Jesus desires each of us to experience an intimate relationship with the Godhead. When someone does this, he will seldom walk away from his Savior. The friendship with our Lord seems awesome, precious, and wonderful. Truly, we stand blessed because Jesus invites us to his wedding supper in Heaven.

> ¹¹And I saw heaven opened, and behold a white horse; and he that sat upon him *was* called Faithful and True, and in righteousness he doth judge and make war. ¹²His eyes *were* as a flame of fire, and on his head *were* many crowns; and he had a name written, that no man knew, but he himself. ¹³And he *was* clothed with a vesture dipped in blood: and his name is called The Word of God (Rev. 19:11–13, KJV).

THE WHITE HORSE

John begins a new theme in chapter 19. He sees...*heaven opened, and behold a white horse*. These verses are one of the few places in Revelation where the different viewpoints come together in agreement. They show us a picture of our Lord as the victorious exalted Christ. The resurrected Christ rides a white horse that symbolizes victory. We view the same white horse and rider in the first seal where we witness Christ spreading the Gospel (Rev. 6:2).

The rider on the white horse has names that point to our Savior. Our Lord's eyes look...*as a flame of fire*. This reveals our Redeemer as the All-knowing God whose eyes pierce into our minds and secret thoughts. Our Savior wears crowns of victory. No one knows the...*name written* on the Faithful and True witness. Our Unlimited Sovereign God seems bigger and greater than we can imagine or comprehend.

The rider wears a robe...*dipped in blood*. Some believe that this represents the shed blood from the cross. Others believe the blood comes from the winepress of wrath (Isa. 63:1–6). John looks into Heaven for this view of the Gospel Age. I understand this view to symbolize both the Gospel Age and the judgment at the end of the Age. This indicates that the blood on Jesus symbolizes both the cross and the judgment.

> ¹⁴And the armies *which were* in heaven followed him upon white horses, clothed in fine linen, white and clean. ¹⁵And out of his mouth goeth a sharp sword, that with it he should smite the nations: and he shall rule them with a rod of iron: and he treadeth the winepress of the fierceness and wrath of Almighty God. ¹⁶And he hath on *his* vesture and on his thigh a name written, KING OF KINGS, AND LORD OF LORDS (Rev 19:14–16, KJV).

THE ARMIES OF CHRIST

Do saints or angels make up the armies that follow our King and Lord? The armies indicate more than one army. The angels will come with our Lord at the end of the Gospel Age (Matt. 25:31). The redeemed saints of God rule with their Lord and King while on earth (2 Tim. 2:12). Saints clothed with the righteousness of Christ follow the Lamb during the Gospel Age (John 10:27; Matt. 16:24).

A *sharp sword*...comes out of the mouth of the Almighty King. This symbolizes the Word of God (Heb. 4:12). The Lord...*shall rule them with a rod of iron*. The meaning of *rule* (*poimaino*) means "to tend and feed as a shepherd."[4] The phrase used here is similar to the one that Christ uses to rule the nations in Vision 4 (Rev. 12:5).

The picture shown in these verses points to both the end-time judgment and the Gospel Age. Our Lord rules the nations with his Church during the Gospel Age. He then returns with the armies of Heaven at the end of the Age.

ONE WHO HAD ESCAPED

The OT patriarchs Abram and Lot separated because the land wouldn't support their livestock (Gen. 13). Lot and his people lived near Sodom, where four kings attacked them and took Lot captive. One who "*had escaped*" from the four kings came and told Abram the bad news (Gen. 14:13). Abram took 318 trained men and went after his nephew Lot.

Abram attacked the enemy and pursued them. They brought back Lot and his people with all their goods. Abram didn't have a series of meetings to decide what to do. He just picked up and went to help the people escape from captivity.

Most of you and I stand as one who "*has escaped*" from the clutches of the Devil's kingdom. We escaped from a spiritual place of darkness without the Lord. How much are we willing to sacrifice to help another one escape?

Many of our neighbors and relatives live as captives. They don't have a way out unless someone rescues them. Do we spend time praying to rescue them? Do we reach out with the love of Christ? Abram didn't stop and count the cost: he went. Do we stop and count the cost or do we go?

WILL YOU RIDE WITH HIM

Faithful and True rides his white horse.
He wears a crown, and his eyes flash fire.
He speaks words of fire with his mouth.

The blood of salvation covers his robe.
He calls to you and me his children,
"Will you come with me and ride."
We say, "Yes my Lord and King;
We will come with you and ride."

17And I saw an angel standing in the sun; and he cried with a loud voice, saying to all the fowls that fly in the midst of heaven, Come and gather yourselves together unto the supper of the great God; 18That ye may eat the flesh of kings, and the flesh of captains, and the flesh of mighty men, and the flesh of horses, and of them that sit on them, and the flesh of all men, both free and bond, both small and great. 19And I saw the beast, and the kings of the earth, and their armies, gathered together to make war against him that sat on the horse, and against his army (Rev. 19:17–19, KJV).

THE FEAST OF GOD

John begins the third section of chapter 19. We see another short view of the Gospel Age and the end of the two beasts. John paints a gruesome picture of the end of people and nations that oppose God. They invite birds to eat the flesh of seven classes of men on the earth. The beast of the earth and the people of the earth gather...*to make war against him that sat on the horse, and against his army.*

The saints of God fight against the armies of the beast throughout the Gospel Age by the power of the Holy Spirit and prayer. The saints overcome Satan, his fallen angels, and his people on earth by the blood of the Lamb and by the word of their testimony (Rev. 12:11). We as children of God stand against the forces of darkness by our prayers, the Word, and the shed blood.

PRAYER SUMMARY

In this section, I list the types of prayer that work for me. The ultimate intercessor Jesus Christ and the Bible give us many principles of prayer. This summary shows what the Lord has revealed to me from twenty years experience in intercession.

Christ the Lord understands the kingdom of darkness better than any of us can. The Bible and the Holy Spirit has given me insight into the forces of good and evil. Yet, I don't know all that happens and all the reasons. A type of prayer that seems to work for one person may not work for others. The subject seems too large for any of us to comprehend this side of Heaven.

PRAYING FOR SELF-PROTECTION

Every Christian should ask God to station angels around their family and themselves. Each of us should walk around his or her home and property to put a spiritual line of protection with the shed blood of Jesus. Linda and I reinforce our line of spiritual protection by walking around our home at least once a year.

I pray each day against the forces of darkness in my life and my family's life. I begin by asking God to forgive me for any sin in my life. I then say the Lord's Prayer and put on the full armor of God. I then command every spirit, germ, and virus from Satan to leave Linda and me in the name of Jesus Christ. I command all these and every influence from the Devil that's not from God to leave us and go to Jesus in his name. I also stand against everything with the shed blood of Jesus Christ.

I started doing this every day sixteen years ago to keep the Devil from knocking on my door. I increased this to twice a day a year ago because spiritual warfare has increased since I started to write this book.

THE WILD ONE

The Devil's demons remind me of a wild animal that Jesus Christ holds with a choker chain. The devil and his demons run through the world seeking to mar their victims with spiritual claw and teeth marks. When they get close, they drool on the unaware to contaminate them. They then spray on their victims to mark their spiritual domain.

Jesus Christ shortens the chain when we pray self-defense prayers. The wild one may charge us in the spirit realms, but our Lord jerks him short of us. Sometimes in our spiritual walk, we can feel his hot breath against our tender skin (1 Cor. 10:13).

Every child of God needs to develop his or her own method of praying. The Holy Spirit will teach us what to do when we ask him. I use two more types of prayer that seem to have more effect. Yet, you must use them with care when praying for yourself and especially for other people.

TYPES OF PROTECTION PRAYERS

I have put a spiritual hedge around my family and myself (Job 1:10). Satan gave strong opposition when I began to build a spiritual hedge around my family and me.

In my prayers, I remind God of this hedge around us. Every few days, I ask the Lord to fill any holes the demons try to worm their way through.

One prayer keeps the kingdom of darkness at a distance. The Devil appears to resist me more when I give the Lord permission to rebuke the spirits that cross the hedge around me (Jude 1:8–10). I don't rebuke the spirits, but I give Jesus permission to rebuke them. This causes the evil forces to stand away.

Because I maintain the spiritual hedge and permit the Lord to rebuke any wayward demons, the kingdom of Satan stays at a distance from me. I use a series of self-defense prayers and increase the volume when needed. I am flexible and change types of prayers as the Holy Spirit leads. This keeps the Devil's influence away from my family and me. I pray every day with persistence because from past experience I don't want to give Satan an opening.

Some Christians may think that I spend too much time praying for God's protection. If I don't pray this way, problems happen. Every Christian has his or her separate walk with Christ. Unless you follow Christ into the heat of intercession, you probably won't need to do this.

The Devil's kingdom works in the background around many of God's children. When Christians don't stay alert, the energy from the demons of Babylon slowly increases. The change takes place over weeks, months, and years. Satan's elusive plans cause changes in what the person considers important. The child of God then begins to take his or her eyes off Jesus and fix them on the world. Our Savior of Love may then allow an incident to happen in the person's life to bring his focus back to Jesus Christ.

THE FRUIT AND GIFTS OF THE SPIRIT

I write this section for Christians who desire to imitate the actions of Jesus in their lives. This doesn't apply to self-protection, but it helps our daily walk in the world. Once or twice a week, I pray to God and put on or thank him for the fruit of the Spirit listed in Gal. 5:22, 23 and 2 Pet. 1:5–8. I also thank God for the Spiritual gifts listed in Isa. 11:1–3 and the gifts of the Spirit listed in 1 Cor. 12:7–11. I do this after saying the Lord's Prayer, putting on the Armor of God, and binding any lawless spirits (2 Thess. 2:3–10).

It takes a regular effort for a few minutes to do this. Nevertheless, I find from experience that my days finish far better when I request the fruit and the gifts from our Father who cares for each of us.

THE CALL OF INTERCESSION

Our Savior desires that all Christians pray for their family and friends. Nevertheless, the Sovereign Creator doesn't call everyone to intercede on a deeper level for others. This is not an easy call from our loving Father. Intercession appears as a special calling that the Lord gives to some of his

redeemed children. A Christian will not have effective prayers of intercession unless the Holy Spirit leads the prayers.

True intercession takes a hard spiritual and physical toil. The person
praying will experience fatigue because of the demanding nature of intercession. An intercessor commands the spirits of darkness, blindness, and
things not of God to leave the person. They speak in the name of Jesus
Christ and by his blood over and over until the resistance stops. It's not
amusing to dance with the Devil's demons.

Most called to pray for others do it out of obedience to the Savior.
Although intercession seems a high calling to God, people of prayer don't
receive much recognition on earth. The abundant love of Jesus helps intercessors to endure hard times.

The types of prayers that we pray for ourselves can also apply to others. The resistance from Satan varies when we bind the powers of darkness
over other people. Everyone that we pray for is responsible for his or her
own actions and salvation. Prayers only open the gates of hell so that the
Light from the Holy Spirit can penetrate the darkness. Then the Lord can
work in the person's life and begin to draw them into salvation.

The Bible gives several levels of prayer. Every intercessor should ask
the Holy Spirit to lead his or her prayers. The call to pray comes from the
Holy Spirit, and the Lord has to lead the task. Our Father gives us plenti-
ful grace when we pray for others. Sometimes during a time of prayer, it
seems as if we stand in the presence of Jesus Christ.

Sensitive to the Spirit

The Holy Spirit gives me sensitivity to spiritual forces. I can feel the
resistance from the kingdom of darkness when I use the name of Jesus. An
intercessor has to be pure and spotless before his prayers will prevail. When
we confess our sins, our faithful God forgives us for our sins and purifies us
from all guilt (1 John 1:9).

God uses intercessors cleansed by the blood of Christ to pray for others. If any of us have unconfessed sin in our life, the power won't flow
through us. When we carry baggage from the world, our words will float on
the wind and waste away.

I stop and ask forgiveness for any sin when I don't sense spiritual
resistance. I ask God to purify me with his blood and reveal what needs
to change. After I ask forgiveness, I then continue. From my experience, a person should feel some form of resistance when he intercedes
for others.

People of prayer cling to Christ for guidance and energy. Intercessors press against the gates of hell to remove strongholds of darkness and oppression (Rev. 11:5). We can ask for anything in the name of Jesus Christ, and he will do it when we remain in his love and his Words remain in us (John 15:5–10).

Many intercessors use some form of fasting for effective prayers. Each needs to seek the Lord's leading in this area. Fasting takes many forms. There are no set formulas in this ministry. Each called intercessor should seek the leading of the Holy Spirit on his or her own level. Effective intercession for others stirs up the kingdom of darkness.

RELATIONSHIP WITH YOUR SAVIOR

Men and women of faith, whom the Lord calls to pray, need to know who they are in Christ. They should understand that the shed blood washed away their sins and God sees them as perfect vessels (Rev. 5:6). They need to recognize the boundaries the Lord wants them to live by. God gives faith as we study the Bible, pray, and learn our authority in the name of Jesus Christ.

Intercessors should seek other people of prayer to pray with on a regular schedule. This can happen in your local church if other people of prayer attend there. Many intercessors will need to go outside their local church to find prayer fellowship. Many isolated intercessors live in the big wide world. It's okay if you cross denomination lines to pray with people. Our Lord doesn't recognize church labels when people come together for prayer.

THE SPIRITUAL HEDGE

I wrote earlier about building a hedge around our families. The Bible speaks of building hedges around other people and areas and countries. God looked for a man to build a hedge, but he found none (Isa 59:16).

Not many are called to stand in the gap and build hedges around other people (Ezek. 22:30). God only calls committed saints who are willing to stand and build walls for Jesus Christ. God has to know the heart of his man or woman before he calls them to stand in the gap and build hedges.

PROTECT YOURSELF

Effective intercession has to come from the Lord. A person of prayer needs to keep his or her own house in order. A praying Christian has a tight road to walk with Jesus Christ. They need to listen to the Holy Spirit and know when to pray and when to rest in the Lord.

I know of people who started praying with the Lord's power and an anointment from Jesus Christ (1 John 2:20, 27). They continued to pray when they should have stopped. The powers of darkness used this as an opening to attack them.

If an intercessor does not have strong defenses, he opens himself up for attack. The spirits may leave the person you pray for and come to you. It is always important to send the spirits to Jesus Christ. The Lord will then dispose of them in a proper way.

Our God of compassion knows our hearts and abilities. He knows what we endure each day. After a season of prayer, intercessors just need to stop praying for a time and rest in the Lord. We need to build up our hedge and defenses before praying for others. When a country prepares for war, they use many weapons of defense.

We also need to use our weapons of defense to protect our families and ourselves. If we don't, the spiritual attacks may spill over into our physical lives. We need to close the back door of our house, or the thief may come in to rob and destroy (John 10:10; Luke 11:21).

BE CAREFUL—COUNT THE COST

The first time I tried to build a hedge I encountered firm resistance that didn't lessen. After about ten minutes, I stopped without breaking through. I went back to the Scriptures and did a study on standing in the gap. I then prayed and asked the Lord what he wanted me to do. I felt a strong presence and assurance from the Holy Spirit. I believed that the Almighty would stand beside me. I proceeded with caution, and now I regularly use this form of praying when I feel the Holy Spirit leads me.

We can also give the Lord permission to rebuke the spirits that cross the spiritual hedge of others (Zech. 3:2). From my perspective, this takes a tremendous amount of endurance to do. I don't practice it unless the Holy Spirit leads me in a given situation. It appears that the principalities, powers, and demons hate it when I do this. It stirs them up, and then I need to spend more effort in defense against them.

I am not interested in forcing power plays with the Devil's kingdom. I don't want to stir them up. I only want to command Satan to remove from individual people: his darkness, his denial of God, his bondage, and his oppression. Then the Holy Spirit can increase his work in drawing individuals to salvation in Jesus Christ.

I say again unless you know your exact relationship and authority with Jesus, don't try to build a hedge around another person, or you may find that sly old serpent knocking at your door. The Devil forces intercessors to use protection from God. If you don't protect yourself, you may feel the wild one's hot breath and notice him drooling on you.

> [20]**But the beast was captured, and with him the false prophet who had performed the miraculous signs on his behalf. With these signs he had deluded those who had received the mark of the beast and worshiped his image. The two of them were thrown alive into the fiery lake of burning sulfur. [21]The rest of them were killed with the sword that came out of the mouth of the rider on the horse, and all the birds gorged themselves on their flesh (Rev. 19:20, 21, NIV).**

END OF THE BEAST AND FALSE PROPHET

The beast of the sea and the beast of the earth, or false prophet, meet their end. They come on the scene in chapter 13 after the Dragon arrives in chapter 12. The Dragon, or Satan, will meet his end in chapter 20 of the next vision.

These verses show us the end of vision 6. The King of Glory kills the earth's armies...*with the sword that came out of the mouth of the rider*. The birds of pray then eat their fill. Jesus shows us graphic pictures of the end of the Gospel Age.

THE WORD OF POWER

The Word of God has immense power. When the time arrives for the defeat of our enemies, God won't need help. The Creator speaks and the heavens are. The Creator speaks and the earth and everything on it is. With the Word, he speaks creation. With the Word, he speaks you and me. He can speak destruction to our enemies with the Word. Praise the Word of the Lord. Praise his Majesty of Supreme Authority. Amen!

NOTES

1. U. S. Catholic Conference, *Catechism of the Catholic Church* (Liguori: Liguori Publications, 1994) Index # 1350.
2. Rejoice, *agalliao*, G21. To jump for joy, exult, joy.
3. Glad, *chairo*, G5463. Cheerful, calmly happy, or well-off.
4. Rule, *poimaino*, G4165. To tend as a shepherd. To feed and nourish.

CHAPTER 20

One Thousand Years

DEBATE OVER CHAPTER 20

One of my antagonists who waits for failure said to me, "I don't understand the reason that you are taking several years to write a book on Revelation. You could go to a bookstore and buy one like it for less than twenty dollars."

As I stand on the threshold of chapter 20, I tend to agree with him. Chapter 20 stands as a monument to the different interpretations of Revelation. Many brothers and sisters in Christ quibble over what it means until their faces turn blue. God must sit on his Throne and chuckle.

I understand that the Creator uses the many different viewpoints to give people hope. Many dear brothers and sisters in Christ have a different understanding of the 1,000 years than I do. This should not lessen our love for each other.

Jesus Christ is Lord, and what each of us believes about Revelation does not change this truth. He created the universe, and he created each of the different viewpoints for his own purpose. An interpretation about the end times, called the "pan out theory," makes sense to me. People say, "In the end it will all pan out." Only our Lord knows the beginning and the end.

I view the Revelation of Jesus Christ as apocalyptic writing best understood in light other Scripture. Because the Bible interprets itself, I shall continue with a symbolic understanding. Chapter 20 begins the last of the seven visions in Revelation. This vision, as part of the composite picture in Revelation, gives us another concept of the Gospel Age.

As an apocalyptic book, the Revelation of Jesus Christ contains numerous pictures and symbolism. Chapter 20 follows John's pattern of images and illustrations.

> ¹And I saw an angel come down from heaven, having the key of
> the bottomless pit and a great chain in his hand. ²And he laid hold
> on the dragon, that old serpent, which is the Devil, and Satan, and
> bound him a thousand years, ³And cast him into the bottomless
> pit, and shut him up, and set a seal upon him, that he should
> deceive the nations no more, till the thousand years should be ful-
> filled: and after that he must be loosed a little season (Rev. 20:1–3
> KJV).

WHO CONTROLS THE ABYSS

John saw...*an angel come down from heaven, having the key of the bot-
tomless pit.* Is this an angel, or is this the Lord? Jesus holds the keys of death and Hades, and he holds the key of David (Rev. 1:18; 3:7). The Bible reveals Jesus as the only one who controls the key to the bottomless pit, even though; someone gave Satan a key in Revelation 9:1.

Jesus came to bind the strong man who represents Satan (Matt. 12:29; Luke 11:20, 21). By the cross, our Savior disarmed the power of the Devil, the authorities, and the demons (Col. 2:13–15; Heb. 2:14). Therefore, the angel who...*laid hold on the dragon* must represent Christ, the Power of God.

Christ the angel held a spiritual chain in his hand. The power of the long chain came from our Savior's Resurrection and his shed blood on the cross (John 12:31–33). The great chain of large size and space indicated that Satan had a limited freedom to move about on earth. He could roam and harass until our prayers encourage the Power of God to jerk his chain.

The spiritual chain keeps the Devil from deceiving...*the nations* until the 1,000 years near fulfillment. The nations indicate the gentile or Christian nations and people of the world. These verses point to the fifth trumpet where God permitted the Devil to let hordes of demons roam the earth.

The risen Savior uses his mighty strength to seize...*the dragon, that old
serpent, which is the Devil, and Satan* and throw him into the Abyss. John uses four separate names in the Greek to describe the prince of evil. The names indicate: a fabulous kind of serpent, a cunning malicious snake or

Satan, a false slanderer the Devil, and the accuser—Satan. Our Savior wants us to understand the cunning evil that he holds in the Abyss.

THE 1,000 YEARS

In the seventh vision, the 1,000 years covers the Gospel Age of the Christian Church. This lasts until just before the return of Christ when Satan leads a short brutal persecution. The number ten in the Bible points to completeness. Ten times ten times ten equals 1,000. Therefore, complete times complete times complete gives us the full and complete time of the Gospel Age.

> Rev. 20 is not difficult to understand. All one needs to do is remember the sequence: Christ's first coming is followed by a long period during which Satan is bound; this in turn, is followed by Satan's little season; and that is followed by Christ's second coming, that is, his coming unto judgment.[1]

[4a]And I saw thrones, and they sat upon them, and judgment was given unto them: and I saw the souls of them that were beheaded for the witness of Jesus, and for the word of God, and which had not worshipped the beast, neither his image, neither had received his mark upon their foreheads, or in their hands; (Rev. 20:4a, KJV).

BEHEADED FOR JESUS

John saw *souls* (*psuche*), indicating "living people, the breath of life, and our souls."[2] The word indicated "the vital force of life, the breath of our spirit," and points to the Spirit of God. The Creator breathed life into Adam when he created new life in Adam. Jesus breathed the Holy Spirit into his disciples after his Resurrection (John 20:22). God created new life in his disciples.

John saw the...*souls of them that were beheaded for the witness of Jesus.* What does this mean? John saw our spiritual souls or spirits. He didn't see physical bodies. Jesus permitted John to view the spiritual part of his Church made up of redeemed people.

Because John saw the spirits of people and did not see their physical bodies, this then symbolizes a living picture of the spiritual Church of Jesus Christ. I understand that Revelation and the 1,000 years show us God's view of the spiritual part of his Church on earth.

OUR SPIRITS LIVE

The Bible said that Jesus died for us, and we died and became new creatures in him. Because he died for us, we should no longer live for ourselves, but live for him who died for us. When we follow Christ, he makes us a new creation. Our old self has passed away; the new has come (2 Cor. 5:14–17).

We make Jesus Lord of our life when we commit our lives to the Savior. The Bible says our old self was crucified with Jesus. We died with Christ, and we live with him. We should consider ourselves dead to sin but alive in God (Rom. 6:4–11).

Our Redeemer raises our spirits to new life, and yet our body is dead because of sin. The Holy Spirit lives in us and creates new life with God out of the old dead life (Rom. 8:10, 11). The souls beheaded for the witness of Jesus gives us a spiritual picture of saints living on earth. They die to the world and themselves, and yet they live their new Christian lives in the Lord. God sees each of his children as living resurrected saints (Eph. 2:10–13).

They didn't worship the beast nor take…*his mark upon their foreheads, or in their hands.* Throughout the Gospel Age, followers of Christ have refused the influence from the beast. These children of God, whom God sealed, belonged to the Lord.

> [4b]They came to life and reigned with Christ a thousand years. [5](The rest of the dead did not come to life until the thousand years were ended.) This is the first resurrection. [6]Blessed and holy are those who have part in the first resurrection. The second death has no power over them, but they will be priests of God and of Christ and will reign with him for a thousand years (Rev. 20:4b–6, NIV).

DEAD IN CHRIST RISE

Our Lord understood today's mystery that surrounds the end times. He knew that his children would have many different views of the rapture and the 1,000 years. Paul wrote about the dead in Christ who rise to life (1 Thess. 4:13–17). He said that he didn't want us to be ignorant about those saints who have fallen asleep with the Lord.

Jesus will come down from Heaven with the shout of an archangel. The Christians on earth will rise to meet the Lord and all the rest of the risen saints who have fallen asleep. The saints of God, who have already died or fallen asleep, will rise with Christ before he catches up his Church (1 Thess. 4:15). Our Lord teaches that we will rise with him from our graves to life eternal.

> [28]"Do not be amazed at this, for a time is coming when all who are in their graves will hear his voice [29]and come out—those

who have done good will rise to live, and those who have done evil will rise to be condemned" (John 5:28, 29, NIV)

Matthew's Gospel told us that the saints who had fallen asleep rose from the grave at our Lord's death. This real event indicates that Christians go directly to his or her Savior at their physical death on earth.

> [50]And when Jesus had cried out again in a loud voice, he gave up his spirit. [51]At that moment the curtain of the temple was torn in two from top to bottom. The earth shook and the rocks split. [52]The tombs broke open and the bodies of many holy people who had died were raised to life. [53]They came out of the tombs, and after Jesus' resurrection they went into the holy city and appeared to many people (Matt. 27:50–53, NIV)

The crucifixion of the Lamb opened the way for the resurrection of God's chosen people. The people came out of the tombs to indicate that by his Resurrection God also raises the dead holy people of God. This happens from the time of Christ until the end of the Age. God put this in the Bible to help us understand that he raises us to life and we never die. Jesus told Martha that he was the Resurrection and the Life. If anyone believed in him, he or she would live and never die (John 11:25, 26).

SIN BROUGHT DEATH

A true statement says that in order to have resurrection, someone dead needs to rise to life. What does this mean? When do our souls come to life?

The Bible says that we were dead in our sins and our sinful nature, but God raised us to life with Christ (Col. 2:13). God gave the Law to Moses in the OT. The Law raised sin to life, which brought death to all men. God did not take sin into account before the Law (Rom. 5:12, 13).

> [9]Once I was alive apart from law; but when the commandment came, sin sprang to life and I died. [10]I found that the very commandment that was intended to bring life actually brought death. [11]For sin, seizing the opportunity afforded by the commandment, deceived me, and through the commandment put me to death (Rom. 7:9–11, NIV)

The Holy Scriptures say we were dead in our sins and the ways of the world. We followed our cravings and sinful desires. This made us objects of wrath, but because of God's vast love and mercy for us, he made us alive in Christ (Eph. 2:1–5).

RESURRECTION IN JESUS

Jesus told Nicodemus that if he wanted to enter the Kingdom of God, than he must be born again (John 3:3–21). When God brings us through the born-again experience, he makes us alive (1 Pet. 1:3). He resurrects us into a living spiritual child of the Father. We live forever and do not die.

> [24]"I tell you the truth, whoever hears my word and believes him who sent me has eternal life and will not be condemned; he has crossed over from death to life. [25]I tell you the truth, a time is coming and has now come when the dead will hear the voice of the Son of God and those who hear will live" (John 5:24, 25, NIV)

Jesus spoke words of life to all of us. We crossed from death to life after we heard the teaching of Jesus and believed. This then...*is the first resurrection*. The children of God who remain faithful will never experience the second death because the...*second death has no power over them*. Their Father will bless them for infinity.

People of the world who reject the gift of salvation make up the...*rest of the dead*. People without Christ living in them are dead and never experience new life in Christ. They miss the first resurrection. They will not rise from spiritual death until the Second Coming of Christ. Then they will understand the spiritual truths of God's Word (John 5:28–30).

RULE WITH CHRIST

The Almighty Creator raises us up to new life and seats us with him in the heavenly realms (Eph. 2:6). People of the Creator become...*priests of God and of Christ and will reign with him for a thousand years*. The children of God live and rule with Christ here on this earth. He makes us kings and priests to serve God, and we reign on earth (Rev. 1:6; 5:10).

God chooses us as living stones that he builds into a spiritual house. He calls us a holy priesthood that offers spiritual sacrifices to God. As royal priests, we give God praises and do his work on earth (1 Pet. 2:4–9).

We reign with Christ and rule with him through our prayers and actions on earth. Even if we can't see it in the physical world, we reign with Christ in the spiritual world. Jesus said that he had all authority in Heaven and on earth. He told the Church to go and make disciples of all nations. He promised that he would help each Christian until the end of the Age (Matt. 28:18–20).

LITERAL OR SYMBOLIC

Since the Lord already has all authority, he would need to decrease his rank if he came back to earth and set up a literal 1,000-year reign. The Bible declares him the King of Kings and the Lord of Lords.

The 1000-year reign belittles the power of the Holy Spirit and the Church. Jesus Christ instituted the Christian Church before his ascension. The Lord said that the Holy Spirit would give the Church power to witness for him. They would spread the Gospel in Jerusalem, Judea, Samaria, and to the ends of the earth (Acts 1:7, 8).

The Bible does not mention the 1,000 years anywhere except in this chapter. I understand that our Church doctrine and beliefs need to come from the complete Bible and not center on Revelation alone. The 1000 years appears as a symbolic term pointing to the Gospel Age.

The Revelation of Jesus Christ confirms many truths about the Kingdom of God. Christians who try to put the spiritual truths in literal terms encounter many problems. To explain the book, they bounce from verse to verse. They say this verse has a literal meaning: then this one has a symbolic meaning. Who than decides which verse is symbolic and which verse is literal when opinions conflict?

Our Lord gave the truth of God's Word to John in one way. He gave it either as a literal meaning or as a symbolic meaning. Christians must choose one or the other and not keep changing it to fit pre-planned ideas.

CHURCH REIGNS WITH CHRIST

We reign with Jesus in the spiritual realms while we live on earth. Our prayers activate the power of the Holy Spirit. Prayers appear as a catalyst: they seem small, but they do much. The individual prayers of the saints endure over many years.

The Holy Spirit lives in each of us who follows Christ. If we listen to the Spirit, we will pray the prayers that God wants us to pray. When we pray, Almighty God hears our requests. The Sovereign Lord then uses our intercession to fulfill his plans.

> [12]Verily, verily, I say unto you, He that believeth on me, the works that I do shall he do also; and greater works than these shall he do; because I go unto my Father. [13]And whatsoever ye shall ask in my name, that will I do, that the Father may be glorified in the Son. [14]If ye shall ask any thing in my name, I will do it (John 14:12–14, KJV).

Our prayers in the name of Jesus activate the Lord's work in people and nations. When we help direct God's actions, we help him reign on earth.

We reign with Christ by doing the works that he has called us to do. God leads each of us to individual activities. Every man, woman, and child fits into the mystical body of Christ in a unique way (1 Cor. 12–27). God uses our natural abilities to help proclaim the Gospel.

> [7]When the thousand years are over, Satan will be released from his prison [8]and will go out to deceive the nations in the four corners of the earth—Gog and Magog—to gather them for battle. In number they are like the sand on the seashore. [9]They marched across the breadth of the earth and surrounded the camp of God's people, the city he loves. But fire came down from heaven and devoured them. [10]And the devil, who deceived them, was thrown into the lake of burning sulfur, where the beast and the false prophet had been thrown. They will be tormented day and night for ever and ever (Rev. 20:7–10, NIV).

The Coming Harvest

The world approaches 2,000 years since the birth of Jesus Christ. The changing of the millennium causes Christians around the world to pause and think. The Church sees most of the prophecies that Jesus gave fulfilled. The time before the second return of Christ grows shorter.

Christian Leaders around the world speak of the coming revival or harvest. In the remaining years before the end of the Age, God will draw billions of people into his kingdom. The Almighty will shower his grace, blessings, and power upon his chosen ones. I sense good times ahead for the Church; however, another power will also expand.

We will see spiritual activity increase in the coming years. The Light of Revelation will increase among God's children. The darkness of unbelief will increase among the children of the world. As God's grace increases, Satan's deception will increase. The two forces will work side by side in opposition to each other.

Our Lord said that the days of affliction would appear worse than at any other time since creation. No person would survive unless the days stopped. Because of the chosen elect, the days will be shortened (Matt. 24:22; Mark 13:19, 20).

Revelation reveals a brief time before the end of the Age in chapters 11, 16, 19, and 20. This final battle between the saints of light and the forces of darkness takes place in the last years before the Second Coming of Christ. This severe persecution against the saints of God only lasts a short time.

THE UNCHAINED DEVIL

Satan will be released from his prison,...and then he will begin his self-appointed job. That old snake wants to *deceive the nations in the four corners of the earth.* He wants to deceive you and me. He demands the opportunity to lure and destroy all that don't have a strong bond with Jesus Christ. He even welcomes the opportunity to seduce God's children. Jesus speaks of this time in the Gospels.

The Lord declared that great tribulation would cover the earth. He stated that the distress would prove more than at any other time in the history of the earth. The Lord explained how terrible the conditions would be. He confirmed that unless the Almighty shortened the time for the elect's sake, no one would live (Matt. 24:21, 22).

The Greek word (*eklektos*) used for elect and chosen refers to the followers of Christ.[3] The NT writers didn't use the word to refer to Jews. Jesus also settled the time of the rapture when he stated that immediately after the tribulation the angels would gather his elect from all parts of the earth (Matt. 24:29–31). This indicates the rapture comes at the end of the Age when Christ returns for judgment.

We saw a preview of the great tribulation in World War 2. Hitler and his people murdered six million Jews and Christians. What Hitler did to the Jews, the Antichrist will do to followers of the Savior around the world. Most of us have not imagined how difficult the afflictions will get. The Lord informed us about the end days in Matthew 24, Luke 21, and Mark 13.

NO LOVE FOR OTHERS

The Lord spoke of love growing cold because of wickedness (Matt. 24:12; Mark 13:12). Family members will even betray each other. Children will turn in their parents. I cannot imagine someone turning in a parent or siblings. Because families live without God, many of them grow dysfunctional and bitter.

Children of light and children of darkness will live side by side. Children of the Devil will seek passing gain by the death of their family members. Authorities will turn right and wrong values upside down. Nevertheless, the Lord promises us that if we endure to the end, the Savior will set us free (Mark 13:13).

THE FINAL BATTLE

In the last few years of this Age, Satan will bring...*Gog and Magog* together, which represent the nations of the earth. Satan will deceive all the nations and encourage them to attack...*the camp of God's people.* They march across the earth surrounding the camp of God's holy saints. This reveals a picture of Satan and the nations of the world seeking out all the followers of Jesus Christ.

These verses point to the spiritual prophecy of Ezekiel 38 and 39. The Hebrew words *Gog* and *Magog* signify the enemies of Israel. The word *Gog* (*gog*) symbolizes "the name of a future Antichrist."[4] The word *Magog* (*magog*) indicates "an antichristian party."[5] The prophecy of Ezekiel indicates that Gog and Magog represent the forces of evil that stand against God's chosen people.

This battle parallels the Battle of Armageddon and the battle with the beast (Rev. 16:16; 19:17–21). The three separate visions portray the end of the Gospel Age from different perspectives. Yet, the three visions cover the same final battle. The Almighty God wants us to recognize that the sly serpent uses many different methods to attack God's holy saints.

EVIL OVERWHELMS GOOD

The...*number, they are like the sand,* indicated that the evil people on earth will outnumber the saints of God. Daniel confirmed this. He wrote that when the evil forces break the power of the holy people, then the end comes (Dan. 12:7). Our Lord said that many would fall away from the faith. He wondered if he would he would find faith left on earth when he returned (Matt. 24:10; Luke 18:8).

The Antichrist will use the government authorities to persecute and oppress the remaining Christians. They will use high-tech weapons to hunt down what they consider those inferior people who trust and obey Jesus Christ. I understand that the great tribulation will end the physical life of most Christians on earth.

The encircled camp of the saints as they...*marched across the breadth of the earth.* This does not mean some local battlefield across the width of the earth. It points to God's people throughout the world. *The city he loves*...represents the Kingdom of God or True Church of Jesus Christ (Heb. 11:16; 12:22).

The kingdom of darkness wanted to destroy all truth and righteousness on the earth. Then the Almighty sent fire from...*heaven and devoured them. Devour,* meaning "to eat," could have pointed to the last battle in chapter

19 where God invites the birds to eat the flesh of kings, generals, and mighty men. The Supreme Judge has promised to give judgment to the people of the world who attacked his children.

THE PRE-TRIBULATION RAPTURE

I hope that the pre-tribulation rapture people are right. No one wants to go through what Satan has planed for the Church. Nevertheless, because of the words of Jesus and the Bible, I know in my heart that they are wrong. I believe that Satan will cause a short time of intense persecution before the Second Coming of Christ. The last Antichrist will control the world powers.

The rapture before the great tribulation seams to indicate that Christ will take away Christians before persecution, suffering, and death. This sounds wonderful: many desire to believe it.

Nevertheless, if we study Matthew 24, Luke 21, and Mark 13, we find that Jesus did not say this. He said that if God did not shorten the time no one would live and faith would disappear. After the Antichrist begins to kill Christians on a large scale, I wonder where the pre-tribulation rapture Christians will go? Will they stand up for Jesus, or will they fall away as Jesus predicted (Matt. 24:10)?

LAST RITES FOR SATAN

Throughout Revelation, Satan persecutes the Church in various ways. Now comes his fall into the...*lake of burning sulfur*. As a spiritual being, the Devil has the ability to fly. I wonder why he can't fly away from the fire. Perhaps the Lord clips his wings and ties him to an anchor.

The Devil joins the...*beast and the false prophet* in the hot place. Satan first appears in chapters 6, 12, and 16 as the red horseman and the dragon. The beast, the false prophet, appear in chapters 13 and 16. Then the Lord reverses the order and destroys the beast and false prophet in chapter 19. The Lord then destroys Satan in chapter 20.

THE DEVIL'S DESIRES

I wanted to advance above God.
I enticed one-third of his angels.
We fought and we lost our place.
The Creator confined us to earth.
We attacked his holy children.
The Father said, "That's a no no."
I sank into the flaming brimstone.
"Woe—Woe—Woe—major error!"

¹¹Then I saw a great white throne and him who was seated on it. Earth and sky fled from his presence, and there was no place for them. ¹²And I saw the dead, great and small, standing before the throne, and books were opened. Another book was opened, which is the book of life. The dead were judged according to what they had done as recorded in the books. ¹³The sea gave up the dead that were in it, and death and Hades gave up the dead that were in them, and each person was judged according to what he had done. ¹⁴Then death and Hades were thrown into the lake of fire. The lake of fire is the second death. ¹⁵If anyone's name was not found written in the book of life, he was thrown into the lake of fire. (Rev. 20:11–15, NIV)

THE JUDGMENTS IN REVELATION

John sees a...*great white throne* with the Supreme Judge sitting on it. People call this the Great White Throne Judgment. This happens when Christ returns in glory at the end of the Age. The earth and sky that flee from his presence depict the end of the world.

The last six visions of Revelation shows us views of seven judgments. Each of these pictures of the end of the Gospel Age point to the same final verdict of the King of Kings.

TYPES OF JUDGMENT AND HELL

Death and Hades...plus the sea gave us their dead. This passage didn't mention the earth giving up its dead. We wonder where the people went that died on the land of the earth because most die and remain buried on land? This again points to the sea as representing the sea of humanity that covers the whole earth.

The Bible contains several viewpoints about the judgment of unbelievers. It's difficult to bring them together and show harmony in the death, the holding, and the resurrection of the dead without Christ. Scriptures that indicate different types of hell cause confusion in how the Lord handles the people who die without accepting the Savior.

Jesus told the parable of the rich man and Lazarus. They both died, and Lazarus went to live with Abraham. The rich man went to live in hell. The tormented rich man begged Abraham to send Lazarus to his family and warn them so God would not also send them to hell (Luke 16:19–31). This story indicates that judgment comes upon the physical death of people on earth.

Chapter and Verse	Description of Judgments in Revelation
6:16, 17	The great day of the Lamb's wrath has come.
11:18	Time has comes to judge the dead and to reward the servants of God.
14:17–20	The vine of earth cast into the winepress of wrath.
16:17–20	Armageddon, Earthquake destroys islands and mountains, 100 # hail.
18:10, 21	Judgment and end of Babylon.
19:17–21	Beast and false prophet cast into the lake of fire.
20:10–15	Devil cast into the lake of fire. Great white Throne judgment.

The story of the separation of the sheep and the goats indicates that judgment comes after Jesus returns in Glory (Matt. 25:31–46). The lake of fire shows us the imagery of a place of torment. Scripture also refers to hell as outer darkness where they weep and gash their teeth (Matt. 25: 30; 2 Pet. 2:17). The Bible also pictures a place of destruction and separation from the presence of God (2 Thess. 1:9; Matt. 7:23).

JUDGMENT AND GRACE

The Bible indicates distinct types of hell and different times of activation. The Lord did not clearly tell us all he knows about the last judgment of people. I sense that he doesn't want us to know all the details. As the Everlasting Sovereign God, he will do what he desires with the unbelievers. It's not our place to decide what the Lord of Love should do with a person. Only the Lord knows their heart.

I think of Shadrach, Meshach, and Abednego in OT Babylon. King Nebuchadnezzar ordered them to bow down and worship the golden image (Dan. 3). The king told them that he would throw them into the blazing furnace if they did not worship him. The three Hebrew men didn't bow and didn't bend, and yet they didn't burn.

By faith the fourth man kept them safe from the fire of destruction. Our Savior says that if we seek a relationship with him, we need not worry about the final verdict of the Creator.

I'M DONE

The love of the Father flows over each of us as he draws us to himself. The Father offers us his goodness and mercy here on earth to prepare us for eternity. Each Christian begins his or her life as a spiritual baby.

When a baby begins physical life, they depend on other people to take care of them. The new child seems helpless and needs constant care. The new person lives and grows through the years until old age. Some people spend the last years of their life in a nursing home and depend on other people to care for them.

The child faces potty training as one of his first challenges. The mother or father puts the child on the potty and makes him sit until something happens. As the child learns the process, he or she will begin to say, "I'm done."

People in nursing homes sometimes loose their ability to use the bathroom without help. When they finish, they may say, "I'm done."

How a person begins or ends life does not matter from the eternal sense. The most important learning experience of life comes from learning that Jesus Christ gives us the gift of eternal life without judgment. Then when we enter the eternal presence of Jesus Christ after physical death we can truly say, "I'm done."

NOTES

1. Hendriksen, *MoreThan Conquerors*, p. 222.
2. Souls, *psuche*, G5590. Breath, life, or soul.
3. Elect, *eklektos*, G1588. Chosen, elect, or favorite.
4. Gog, *gog*, G1136. From Hebrew, symbolic name for a future Antichrist.
5. Magog, *magog*, G3098. From Hebrew, nation, symbolic of an antichristian party.

CHAPTER 21

Holy City—New Jerusalem

THE BUTTERFLY MIRACLE

When I was a child, I had a butterfly collection. Each butterfly was beautiful in its own way. I had many favorites among the twenty-eight different species in my collection. Butterflies have long symbolized the Christian life.

Butterflies reveal the miracle of successive life forms. The butterfly starts as a sluggish caterpillar. The larva spins a cocoon around itself; then it goes through metamorphosis. After the proper time, the humble caterpillar larva emerges as a beautiful butterfly.

The transformation represents the life change for a person living without God into a person living for God. People in the world start out as caterpillars. They seem alive but have a limited outlook on life. They only live for what they can consume today.

Paul states that we need to die to have life (Rom. 6:7, 8). When the larva enters the cocoon and cuts off the world around him, the transformation begins. The creature then breaks out and appears as new life. This symbolizes our passage from spiritual death to new freedom in Christ.

THE HOLY CHURCH

The Creator knows how each butterfly will look before they leave the cocoon. The Father knows his butterflies, and he knows the people in his

Church. The Creator looks at his universal Church from a spiritual view-point in this vision.

Jesus gave us chapter 21 in pictures and symbols just as he gave the rest of Revelation. This indicated a symbolic meaning for the bride of Christ. The pictures pointed to both his holy Church on earth and his holy Church in Heaven. Most of the verses symbolized both the present Gospel Age and the future time after his Second Coming. Saints of God have written volumes about what the future New Jerusalem will mean in Heaven.

I will not focus on our destined life in Heaven. I will focus on the spiritual meaning of New Jerusalem on earth during the Gospel Age. We will look at what the wife of the Lamb means today. Earth is our home until we go to Heaven with the Lord. Our Savior wants us to use our stay on earth to expand his body, the New Jerusalem (Heb. 12:22; Isa. 60:11–14).

The Father views his Church on earth as the beginning of his Kingdom of Heaven (Matt. 4:17; Luke 21:31). Christ considers the Christian Church as the spiritual beginning of his body, which he will fulfill in Heaven. We live in Christ's body in part on earth. God will complete every promise in Heaven that he doesn't carry out here on earth.

Chapter 21 reveals the Lord's tender compassion. He extends his love, grace, and peace toward you and me. Our Redeemer offers mercy and forgiveness to all. Because of the Father's love, he yearns for a relationship with his children. He wants all the people in the world to go through the gate into that bright city. "Thank you, Father, for your tender affection."

> [1]And I saw a new heaven and a new earth: for the first heaven and the first earth were passed away; and there was no more sea. [2]And I John saw the holy city, new Jerusalem, coming down from God out of heaven, prepared as a bride adorned for her husband (Rev. 21:1, 2, KJV).

ISAIAH SAW THE GOSPEL AGE

Isaiah painted many spiritual word pictures of the coming Gospel Age (Isa. 59:15–21; 60:1–22; 66:18–24). In Isaiah, the Lord was disappointed with his people, so he worked out salvation with his own arm. He created a new covenant by giving them salvation, righteousness, and a Spirit that lived in them. The Redeemer came to Zion and stated that he would give to his children his Spirit and his Words forever. He promised that the Spirit and the Word would never leave them, or their children, or their descendants (Isa. 59:15–21).

The Lord came: he set a sign, Jesus Christ, among us. He sent his redeemed children to proclaim his glory to the Gentile nations. Isaiah wrote that the saints would bring people from all Gentile nations to God's holy mountain in Jerusalem.

The people coming from other nations appeared as a holy offering and as priests to God. The Lord then spoke in the same context of the new heavens and the new earth that he had made. This indicated that God spiritually created new heavens and a new earth for his new covenant of grace with Jesus Christ (Isa. 66:18–24).

Many of the images in chapter 21 come from Isaiah 60–66. Isaiah spoke of God's new covenant with man, which Jesus Christ gave to us. Isaiah wrote in pictures and symbols to foretell the future. Then John, in Revelation, used similar pictures and images to tell us about the present spiritual Church.

THE NEW BEGINNING

When Jesus died on the cross, he began a new order of creation. He created a new spiritual Heaven and a new spiritual earth (Isa. 65:17–19). The cross put in effect the beginning of a new creation (2 Cor. 5:17). Because the Creator has viewed all time in a glance, he saw as completed...*a new heaven and a new earth.*

We live in a limited environment. We believe in God and his spiritual principles by faith. The Almighty doesn't take us to his Throne and show us his view of the earth, the Church, and Heaven. Yet, he gives us glimpses of these things through the Bible and by the witness of the Holy Spirit. Although we haven't seen our Lord, we love him, and we know that he loves us (1 Pet. 1:8, 9).

Our Father gives us faith and encourages each of us to trust him. Because of the restrictions on earth, our best efforts seem less than sufficient. Yet, God gives us a living hope that all ends well.

Jesus spoke from the cross, "It is finished." From that moment, God verified the beginning of a new heaven and a new earth in the spiritual realms. Man couldn't see it or feel it, but God spoke it and made it true. We have walked by faith not by sight.

The Eternal Creator saw that...*there was no more sea.* The cross of redemption eliminated the barrier between man and God. When Jesus sacrificed himself, the power of the Holy Spirit ripped the heavy veil in the old covenant Temple. This revealed that the barrier of sin between man and his Creator was gone. The shed blood of the Savior opened the way into the Holy of Holies for each of his children (Heb. 10:19–23).

"**Holy Lord,** we thank you for giving each of us a way to reach salvation. You give each of us blessing because of your sacrifice. Thank you for reaching down and drawing us to yourself. All blessing and honor and glory to you. Amen!"

DESIRES OF HEAVEN AND EARTH

New Jerusalem comes…*down from God out of heaven*. This contrasts with Satan and the two beasts coming up from the Abyss and the earth. The Devil centers his work on earthly desires of the flesh, while God centers his work on spiritual desires from Heaven.

The Holy City originates from God in Heaven. Holy indicates "something pure, blameless, and set apart for God." New Jerusalem doesn't belong to the saints in the city. The saints making up the city belong to God. The Almighty keeps the Holy City or the body of Christ alive today for his own uses and pleasure.

The metaphor for *New Jerusalem* (*Hierousalem*) means "the City of God founded by Christ." The city wears the form of the church today, but after Christ's Second Coming, it will turn into the perfected city in Heaven.[1]

> [22]But you have come to Mount Zion, to the heavenly Jerusalem, the city of the living God. You have come to thousands upon thousands of angels in joyful assembly, [23]to the church of the firstborn, whose names are written in heaven. You have come to God, the judge of all men, to the spirits of righteous men made perfect, [24a]to Jesus the mediator of a new covenant, (Heb. 12:22–24a, NIV)

The Holy City was…*prepared as a bride adorned for her husband*. Jesus Christ prepared or clothed his bride with the garments of salvation. He adorned her with his robes of righteousness as with jewels (Isa. 61:10). Our Lord has made the Church holy today by washing away our sins.

> [3]And I heard a loud voice from the throne saying, "Now the dwelling of God is with men, and he will live with them. They will be his people, and God himself will be with them and be their God. [4]He will wipe every tear from their eyes. There will be no more death or mourning or crying or pain, for the old order of things has passed away." [5]He who was seated on the throne said, "I am making everything new!" Then he said, "Write this down, for these words are trustworthy and true" (Rev. 21:3–5, NIV).

GOD LIVES IN US

These words gave us a spiritual picture of the NT covenant. Jesus Christ sent the Holy Spirit to live in each of us after his Resurrection (1 Cor. 3:16). God took away spiritual death, crying, and pain because...*the old order of things has passed away.* The *death* (*thanatos*) pointed to "the miserable state of the dead in hell."[2]

Our Savior began a new order when the Creator glorified him after the cross. The One...*seated on the throne* spoke of new things. This appeared to point to the new covenant of grace instead of the old covenant of Law. Our Father promised that we could...*be his people,* and he would be our God.

Jesus gives hope as he speaks on a spiritual level in this vision. He proclaims freedom to the captives and comforts us by taking away our tears of spiritual death. He releases us from darkness and gives us eternal life. The Lord gives joy and peace to replace the pain of knowing that we are destined for hell (Isa. 61:1–3).

Now the dwelling of God is with men...gives us one of the keys for understanding New Jerusalem. In his new covenant after the cross, God came to live in his people. By...*making everything new,* God instituted a new order for this Gospel Age (Eph. 4:22–24; 2 Cor. 5:17). Jesus affirmed this by declaring that his Words...*are trustworthy and true.*

THE TRUE WORD OF GOD

The Word's flawless and True.
God's Word lives and endures.
Taste the good Word of God.
It pierces souls and spirits.
The Holy Word brings life.
Blessed are they who hear.
The Word lives in us richly.
The Holy Word stands forever.

This seams like a miracle when I consider the ways of man. The Almighty God, who doesn't need us, comes and offers to live in each of us. We all stand at the foot of the cross and face the risen Christ. The thought of this sometimes overwhelms me.

It's a mystery as to why our Creator could love us so much that he suffered and died for our salvation. The Father, the Son, and the Holy Spirit desired to commune with their children. Jesus did what was demanded to bury our sins. Then out of love, mercy, and grace, our God called us to himself (Col. 3:1–4).

[6]He said to me: "It is done. I am the Alpha and the Omega, the Beginning and the End. To him who is thirsty I will give to drink without cost from the spring of the water of life. [7]He who overcomes will inherit all this, and I will be his God and he will be my son. [8]But the cowardly, the unbelieving, the vile, the murderers, the sexually immoral, those who practice magic arts, the idolaters and all liars—their place will be in the fiery lake of burning sulfur. This is the second death" (Rev. 21:6–8, NIV).

DRINK THE WATER OF LIFE

Jesus points back to the beginning of the Age and the cross. He said, "*It is done,*" (*ginoma*), meaning "to cause to be, or come to pass."[3] The Lord refers to his new covenant and gift of salvation. Our Savior gives a long-lasting description of himself as the first and the last of all.

Our Redeemer offers us rivers of living water. The...*spring of water of life* helps us overcome and stay true to Jesus. Our Lord desires that all in the world come to him and drink from his living water of peace, freedom, and salvation.

Our Father promises that we who...*overcomes will inherit all this*. He will be our God, and we will be his sons and daughters. In each of the letters to the seven churches, our God promises that if we overcome, he would give his certificate of salvation to us. We overcome by seeking Jesus in our life, pressing toward the goal, and striving to win the prize that the Lamb of God offers (Phil. 3:14).

THE FATHER'S BELOVED

God offers a free inheritance to each of his children on earth. He gives us the awesome opportunity to have a new spiritual Daddy, and to have him call us his son or daughter. Our Father loves each of us more than we can comprehend.

This may surprise some of you. "Did you know that I am the Father's favorite person on earth?"

Our Infinite Creator has much room in his heart to love each of us. He has a vast love that allows him to love each of his children as his favored one. You are the Creator's favorite child and so am I.

This seems difficult to understand for some. We can only ask our Lord to show us his abundant love. I know that God loves each Christian and each future Christian on earth as his preferred one. It's as if you are the only person on earth.

⁹One of the seven angels who had the seven bowls full of the seven last plagues came and said to me, "Come, I will show you the bride, the wife of the Lamb." ¹⁰And he carried me away in the Spirit to a mountain great and high, and showed me the Holy City, Jerusalem, coming down out of heaven from God. ¹¹It shone with the glory of God, and its brilliance was like that of a very precious jewel, like a jasper, clear as crystal (Rev. 21:9–11, NIV).

TWO KINGDOMS CONTRASTED

The angel carries John…*away in the Spirit* to reveal the bride of the Lamb. To understand the spiritual meaning of Revelation, we need to ask the Holy Spirit to give us revelation. The Holy Spirit gives life and revelation about God and the Bible. Because Jesus shows John his Revelation in the Spirit, we should explain it by the wisdom of the Spirit.

The Book of Revelation shows the people of God as…*the bride, the wife of the Lamb.* Revelation contrasts the bride of the Lamb with the woman Babylon. The bride of the Lamb lives for and serves the Holy God. The woman Babylon lives for and serves the fallen angel Satan.

The angel carried John…*away in the Spirit to a mountain great and high.* On the mountain, he saw life, goodness, and the bride of Christ. The angel carried John away in the Spirit into a wilderness (Rev. 17:3). In the wasteland, he saw death, evil, and the woman from the dragon.

John sees the people of God as a bride given in marriage and waiting for the return of Christ (Rev. 19:9). John sees the woman using the people of the world through prostitution. Revelation shows us two cities. The Holy City glorifies Christ, and the unholy Babylon glorifies the Devil.

THE BRIDE OF THE LAMB

The bride or the people of God shined…*with the glory of God.* Jesus called himself the Light of the World. He said that if we followed him, we would not walk in darkness but would have the Light of Life (John 8:12). The light that our Lord has given us causes the bride to shine with God's glory for the entire world to see.

The bride looks like…*a very precious jewel.* This indicates our Father's love and favor for his children. Our Savior considers each of us precious and chosen by him (1 Pet. 2:4). The symbolism of these verses indicates our Father's joy and love for his children.

"Help us, Lord, to understand your intense Love for each of us. Help us not to take your Love and compassion for granted. You are the Holy Creator. You do not need us, but we need you. We depend on your abundant grace, mercy, and Love. Help us always to cling to your grace, and yet view you as the awesome Holy Creator. Amen!"

¹²It had a great, high wall with twelve gates, and with twelve angels at the gates. On the gates were written the names of the twelve tribes of Israel. ¹³There were three gates on the east, three on the north, three on the south and three on the west. ¹⁴The wall of the city had twelve foundations, and on them were the names of the twelve apostles of the Lamb (Rev. 21:12–14, NIV).

WALLS TO PROTECT US

*A great, high wall...*surrounded New Jerusalem. This symbolized protection for the occupants. People in the cities of Biblical times built walls around themselves for safety from their enemies. A city with high walls withstood attack better than one with low walls. In a similar way, our King of Glory has protected his children from spiritual defeat when attacked.

The Holy City has...*three gates on* each side facing toward each direction of the compass. This indicates that a child of God can enter from any point on earth. The three gates in each direction may refer to the Trinity. God's holy children enter the Kingdom of God by the Father's Love, the power of the Holy Spirit, and the redemption of Jesus Christ.

*The twelve tribes of Israel...*had their names written on each of the twelve gates of the Holy City. *The names of the twelve apostles of the Lamb...*appeared on the twelve foundations supporting the walls. This indicated that the universal Christian Church rests on the teaching of Jesus Christ through Israel and the twelve apostles. The Church came from the OT and NT fathers of the faith. They gave us the Bible and the foundation of the Christian Church.

DIFFICULT AREAS OF THE BIBLE

As I study the testimony and Words of Jesus in the Bible, I do not find a critical spirit that condemns how parts of the body of Christ worship God. When I talk to church members, I sometimes hear a spirit of judgment that says, "I am right and other churches are wrong."

Every Christian church in the body of Christ believes in these things: the Trinity, the death and Resurrection of Jesus, and in the God-man Christ sacrificed for our salvation. All the differences in practices and beliefs cover less than 10 percent of Bible teaching. The contested areas of the Bible seem open to different explanations by the Scriptures.

Christian churches teach the message of salvation by grace through Jesus Christ. If they don't teach this, than they do not belong to the body of Christ. When we criticize other parts of the body, we do injury to Jesus and his body the Church.

MARY—WHAT SHOULD WE BELIEVE?

Some of our brothers and sisters in Christ believe that Mary, the mother of Jesus, lived a sinless life. Roman Catholic men and women accept the teaching of the Roman Catholic Church. Most Protestants believe in the authority and the completeness of the Bible. Most Roman Catholics believe in the authority of the Bible and in the teachings of their Church fathers. As I understand it, The Council of Trent in A.D. 1573 accepted Mary as free from sin.

> Furthermore many Fathers and Doctors of the Church have seen the woman announced in the *Protoevangelium* as Mary, the mother of Christ, the "new Eve." Mary benefited first of all and uniquely from Christ's victory over sin: she was pre-served from all stain of original sin and by a special grace of God committed no sin of any kind during her whole earthly life.[4]

> Through the centuries the Church has become ever more aware that Mary, "full of grace" through God, was redeemed from the moment of her conception (Luke 1:28). That is what the dogma of the Immaculate Conception confesses, as Pope Pius ((proclaimed in 1854: "The most Blessed Virgin Mary was, from the first moment of her conception, by a singular grace and privilege of almighty God and by virtue of the mer-its of Jesus Christ, Savior of the human race, preserved immune from all stain of original sin."[5]

> *"All generations will call me blessed"*: The Church's devotion to the Blessed Virgin is intrinsic to Christian worship (Luke 1:48). The Church rightly honors the Blessed Virgin with spe-cial devotion. From the most ancient times the Blessed Virgin has been honored with the title of "Mother of God," to whose protection the faithful fly in all their dangers and needs…. The liturgical feasts dedicated to the Mother of God and Marian prayer, such as the rosary, an "epitome of the whole Gospel," express this devotion to the Virgin Mary.[6]

These three quotes, from the Catechism of the Catholic Church, reveal why most Roman Catholic Christians hold Mary in a higher place than Protestant Christians view her. Because the church fathers declare Mary as free from the stain of original sin, faithful Roman Catholics accept this.

The Holy Spirit works in many wondrous and mysterious ways to draw people to Jesus. The Father operates in spiritual terms to fulfill his plans. Who has known the wisdom and knowledge of God? Who knows the Lord's mind, or how he chooses to show his Glory (Rom. 11:33–36)?

There is much evidence that Mary has revealed herself in visions to Catholic saints throughout the Gospel Age. As I understand it, the words of Mary always point toward her Son Jesus. If our Savior and Creator choose to use his mother to help bring his children to salvation, who are we to say that he is not leading them?

RESPECT CHRIST'S BODY

I do not accept the Roman Catholic view of Mary living without sin because I accept the full teaching of Scripture and no more. Nevertheless, I believe that Protestant Christians should respect the beliefs of our Roman Catholic brothers and sisters in Christ. On the other side, Catholic Christians should respect the beliefs of Protestants. Christians should not worry about or quibble with other Christians. Our Lord commanded us to go forth and spread the Gospel to all nations.

Many of us have unsaved relatives, friends, and neighbors. We should use our energy to help build the Kingdom of God by proclaiming the Gospel rather than finding fault with other parts of the Lord's Church.

> **15The angel who talked with me had a measuring rod of gold to measure the city, its gates and its walls. 16The city was laid out like a square, as long as it was wide. He measured the city with the rod and found it to be 12,000 stadia in length, and as wide and high as it is long. 17He measured its wall and it was 144 cubits thick, by man's measurement, which the angel was using (Rev. 21:15–17, NIV).**

A LARGE PLACE

The city was laid out like a square...cube. There's only one other cube in the Bible. The Holy of Holies in the OT Temple, which was 20x20x20 cubits (1 Kings 6:20). In the OT covenant, God dwelt in the cube of the Temple. In the NT covenant, God began to dwell in the NT Church, pointing to the bride of Christ, pointing to the New Jerusalem, and pointing to the city as a perfect cube.

The full cube, measuring…*12,000 stadia* on each side, represents the old and the New Testament kingdom of God. Three, representing the Trinity, times four, representing all points of the world, equals twelve. Ten cubed times twelve equals 12,000 or the perfect and complete Church covering the whole wide world.

If we looked at this foursquare cube in the natural, it would give us a cube 1,500 miles on each side, an immense size. The first level has 2,250,000 square miles. Twenty levels per mile at 264 feet per level equals 30,000 levels. This gives us 67.5 billion square miles of area. The total land area on earth equals 57 million square miles. The useable area of Heaven or the cube would give 1,184 times the land area on earth. An extremely large place!

At only one level per mile or 1,500 levels, the cube would have an area sixty times the land area on earth. The first level of the cube of Heaven would sit over the western United States and overlap into Mexico and Canada. There would be so much space in this cube that saints might not find each other for a long time. No, like the rest of Revelation the cube of Heaven has a deeper spiritual meaning.

> [18]**And the building of the wall of it was of jasper: and the city *was* pure gold, like unto clear glass.** [19]**And the foundations of the wall of the city *were* garnished with all manner of precious stones. The first foundation *was* jasper; the second, sapphire; the third, a chalcedony; the fourth, an emerald;** [20]**The fifth, sardonyx; the sixth, sardius; the seventh, chrysolyte; the eighth, beryl; the ninth, a topaz; the tenth, a chrysoprasus; the eleventh, a jacinth; the twelfth, an amethyst.** [21]**And the twelve gates *were* twelve pearls: every several gate was of one pearl: and the street of the city *was* pure gold, as it were transparent glass (Rev. 21:18–21, KJV).**

HEAVEN OF PLEASURE

Jesus gives us a beautiful description of the Holy City. He speaks of twelve types of precious stones on the foundations. Single pearls make up each of the twelve gates. The Creator must raise large oysters in Heaven. Pure gold covers the street of God's city.

This description touches on the things people desire in their lives. Many people desire gold, jewels, and precious stones. Our Father wants his children to dream of going to the city and experience what he has prepared for us.

We don't know what Heaven looks or feels like. We don't know if we will walk through pearl doors onto gold streets. I suspect that God described it this way to entice people. Most people seek after the desires of their hearts. Even Christians would like riches of gold, precious gems, and mansions.

Some Christians experience physical death. Physicians and the Lord help them recover so they can live on. People with near-death experiences tell similar stories. They speak of intense love, peace, joy, and well-being. They see vivid colors that do not exist on earth. After approaching Heaven, our beautiful earth seems drab and dirty.

Others smell and taste savory offerings that words cannot describe. Some see plants and flowers beyond description. Most who approach the blissful city do not want to come back. It appears from the stories, that we should desire to spend the next few million years in Heaven.

WHERE'S OUR HEAVEN

The Bible doesn't give any specific location for Heaven. Some saints believe that we will see the Heavenly City suspended in space like a space platform. Some believe Heaven will take the place of earth in the form of a new earthly city. Others see Heaven as the bride of Christ on earth (Rev. 21:2, 9). They understand the city as a symbol of the universal Christian Church.

As I understand the teachings of Christ, Heaven is a spiritual place. Where the final Heaven will exist, I don't know. I see Scriptural passages for all three locations. Because Heaven exists in a different dimension than we have on earth, no one can comprehend it.

Perhaps Heaven exists among us. We can't see it: we can't feel it. Children of the Father sometimes can sense the glory during praise and worship and the Lord's Supper. God lives in each of us, and we make up part of his Temple. We can't see him or the angels, but they can see us. They watch our actions even in the dark places. They must have heavy-duty stomachs to watch some events on earth.

The Bible says God is Spirit (John 4:24). It says that when he comes, we shall be like him (1 John 3:2). When we see Jesus face-to-face and enter that final resting place, then we will know all the answers. I do not need to know everything about Heaven. I would prefer giving Jesus the opportunity to amaze me. I look forward to letting him show me the perfection and beauty as I wait in faith for my last sunset on earth.

²²And I saw no temple therein: for the Lord God Almighty and the Lamb are the temple of it. ²³And the city had no need of the sun,

neither of the moon, to shine in it: for the glory of God did lighten it, and the Lamb *is* the light thereof. ²⁴And the nations of them which are saved shall walk in the light of it: and the kings of the earth do bring their glory and honour into it. ²⁵And the gates of it shall not be shut at all by day: for there shall be no night there. ²⁶And they shall bring the glory and honour of the nations into it. ²⁷And there shall in no wise enter into it any thing that defileth, neither *whatsoever* worketh abomination, or *maketh* a lie: but they which are written in the Lamb's book of life (Rev. 21:22–27, KJV).

THE CITY'S LIGHT AND GLORY

John didn't see a temple in the holy city. God moved out of the OT Temple when he began the new covenant with Jesus Christ. The Holy Spirit began living in the body of his Church and in his redeemed saints after the Resurrection and Pentecost. God has lived in us to give a spiritual picture of the Temple of God (1 John 4:13–16).

Isaiah says that we wouldn't need the sun or the moon…*to shine in it* because the Lord would be our everlasting light and our glory (Isa. 60:19–21). The nations of the earth,…*which are saved shall walk in the light of it.* The saved people in each nation use the Light and revelation of Jesus Christ to guide them in their walk on earth. The Almighty God will bring the…*glory and honour of the nations* into New Jerusalem. This again points to the City of God as the Church on earth today.

The Lamb is the light…for the Holy City. This points to the Son of Man walking in the midst of the seven churches (Rev. 1:12–20). Jesus says that he is the Light of the world. If we follow him, we will not walk in darkness but will have the Light of Life (John 8:12). Our Savior gives us a spiritual picture of the Light of revelation and the leading by the Spirit of God. The Creator gives his Glory to illuminate our ways on this earth, which the powers of Satan have darkened.

Our Savior opened the gates of salvation for us and he will never shut them. The Kingdom of God stands ready to receive more people who recognize Jesus as Lord and Savior. Our Father desires that all people repent and come to him for eternal life. He offers everyone his grace of salvation to enter the Holy City.

In order to enter New Jerusalem, we must have our name…*written in the Lamb's book of life.* The book of life lists all the saints of God that have lived or will live on earth. The Supreme Judge will only let in the holy ones who carry the righteousness of Christ. Only Jesus Christ can give us the proper wedding clothes so each of us can take our place as part his holy bride (Matt. 22:1–14).

THE LAMB LOVES THE BUTTERFLY

A child of God living on earth sees the Lord only from a limited viewpoint. The symbol of the butterfly, symbolizing an individual's passage from death to life and freedom in Christ, seems relevant here. A person without Christ lives in a cocoon; he cannot see or feel the truth of God.

A Christian begins to come out of the cocoon after he commits his life to Jesus Christ. He has a limited ability to see and feel the presence of God. Disciples of Christ increase their perception and freedom in the Lord as time goes by. Yet, God's children still have parts of the old cocoon, or earthy ways, holding them back.

Like the butterfly coming out of a cocoon, a child of the Father will not have full freedom of flight until he experiences the last sunset. Our Father draws us into his arms after we pass over the barrier of physical death. Then we will have full fellowship with our Father, Jesus Christ, and the Holy Spirit. We shall behold him in his Holiness. That will be a grand and glorious day. Amen!

NOTES

1. New Jerusalem, *Hierousalem*, G2419. Metaphor, The City of God founded by Christ. The Church today and also the home of Saints in Heaven.
2. Death, *thanatos*, G2288. Future misery in hell. Misery of a soul in sin.
3. It is done, *ginoma*, G1096. To cause to be. Come into being.
4. United States Catholic Conference, Inc., *Catechism of the Catholic Church* (Liguori: Liguori Publications, 1994), Index # 411.
5. U.S. Catholic Conference, *Catechism of the Catholic Church*, Index # 491.
6. U.S. Catholic Conference, *Catechism of the Catholic Church*, Index # 971.

CHAPTER 22

River of Life—I Come Soon

LIFE-GIVING WATER

I spent the first twenty-one years of my life on the thirsty prairie of western South Dakota. In that community, people only live in about one-half the homes today that were occupied when I lived there. The owners abandoned almost every place that didn't have a good well. People and animals needed water to live. In semiarid areas, water has always had more importance than in areas of abundance.

Our Savior offers his living water to people in the thirsty world. Nevertheless, many reject the living water and don't want the Lord living around them or in them. Their places appear abandoned in the spiritual realms. Yet our Lord continues to send living water toward them in the hope that they will someday invite him in.

In this last vision, chapter 22 continues the theme of chapter 21. Our Lord finishes the picture of his holy Church. He then sums up his Revelation and gives us hope from his promises. Jesus guarantees us that if we follow him, he will bless us and give us the grace of his salvation. "Lord, we thank you for your mercy that flows over each of us. We thank you for the hope of eternal life that we will enjoy in a better place. Amen!"

> ¹**Then the angel showed me the river of the water of life, as clear as crystal, flowing from the throne of God and of the Lamb ²down**

the middle of the great street of the city. On each side of the river stood the tree of life, bearing twelve crops of fruit, yielding its fruit every month. And the leaves of the tree are for the healing of the nations. ³No longer will there be any curse. The throne of God and of the Lamb will be in the city, and his servants will serve him (Rev. 22:1–3, NIV).

RIVER OF LIFE

Our Lord resumes his description of his Holy City, the New Jerusalem. The angel shows John...*the river of the water of life*. The river flows...*from the throne of God and of the Lamb* through the streets of the city. The trees of life stand on both sides of the river. The many trees of life in the forest bear a crop of...*fruit every month*.

Jesus describes a place with abundant food and water, which gives physical life and spiritual life. The natural food and water supports our life on earth. The spiritual food and water from Jesus helps us complete our spiritual destiny on earth. These verses give us a picture of God's provision and care for his children of faith. Our Father provides for us today, and he will provide for us in our future home. (Matt. 6:25–33)

THE GARDEN IN EDEN

This scene in the last chapter of the Bible takes us back to the beginning at the Garden of Eden. What the Creator gave mankind in the Garden of Eden helps describe another special place that our Father prepares for his chosen children.

When Adam disobeyed God, he lost intimate fellowship with his Creator because of the curse of sin. Man lost the hope of eternal life and having a union with his Creator. The Almighty drove Adam and Eve out of the Garden of Eden and separated them from the tree of life (Gen. 3:22–24).

The curse of the lost relationship affected people on earth until Jesus restored it by the cross. God began a new covenant with man, which gave us new life in Christ. Therefore,...*No longer will there be any curse* (Gal. 3:10–14). The shed blood from the Crucifixion restored man's intimate union with his Creator.

THE LIVING WATER OF LIFE

Our Savior offers us living water as a gift. He promises us that if we drink from the river we will never thirst. The water will spring up into everlasting life for each of us (John 4:10–13). Our Lord says that if we thirst, we should come and drink from him.

Rivers of living water flow to us when we believe in Jesus Christ. Jesus calls his living water the Holy Spirit, which he gives to us (John 7:38, 39). The living water points to the fruit and the gifts of the Holy Spirit along with all the blessings that the Lamb of God gives us.

A river flows out of the Garden of Eden and separates into the headwaters of four different rivers. This seems backward from the way rivers flow on the earth, where small streams flow into larger streams and rivers until the river enters a sea. But then, Eden's a special place God created for Adam and Eve. The river from Eden gives us a picture of the living water from Jesus. The river coming from Eden splits into four large streams, which describes living water that flows in four directions over all parts of the earth.

The Bible showed us a similar picture of the water of life that flows...*from the throne of God and of the Lamb* (Ezek. 47:1–12). A spiritual being led the prophet Ezekiel to the OT Temple. Ezekiel saw water flowing from under the Temple of God. The water started as a small stream that increased in size the farther it traveled. The stream began ankle-deep, then knee-deep, then waist-deep, and then he couldn't cross the river.

The river from Ezekiel, representing the Holy Spirit, flowed to the dry and barren places of the world. When it flowed into the sea, the sea became fresh, and swarms of living creatures lived every where the water went. A large number of fruit trees grew on both banks of the river; they bore fruit every month. People used the leaves for healing.

THE FRUIT OF GOD

The Bible calls people of God firstfruits (James 1:18). The Holy Spirit flows as living water through the sea made up of people in the world. The river of life brings...*twelve crops of fruit* or redeemed saints into the Kingdom of God.

The word fruit (*karpos*) means "to pluck or take." The word indicates fruit from trees and vines and our works for the Lord.[1] Fruit can symbolize gathering people for eternal life (John 15:1–8, 16; Mark 4:1–20; Matt. 7:15–20). The flowing water from the Holy Spirit reaches down into the world. The life giving water plucks people away from the Devil's kingdom into the arms of Jesus.

The...*twelve crops of fruit* could symbolize the variety of people, churches, and ethnic groups throughout the world. The power of the Holy Spirit brings forth fruit for the Father in all places. Our Lord's...*servants will serve him* and help produce fruit by their actions and witness.

THE HEALING LEAVES

The tree of life from the Branch of Righteousness grows leaves for...*the healing of the nations*. The *nations* (*ethnos*) point to people in all parts of the world for today. The word indicates "non-Jewish and gentile people."[2] The healing leaves sprout in everyplace that Jesus lives in his Church. Jesus brings healing to the nations by the prayers of his Church.

Jesus comes to give freedom to the captives and release them from bondage and darkness. Our Lord desires to give us a crown of beauty for ashes and the oil of joy instead of mourning. The Lord calls us oaks of righteousness, and the leaves bring healing for our minds, bodies, and spirits (Isa. 61:1–3).

Redeemed saints drink the pure living water from Christ. Streams of life-giving water flow through us by the power of the Holy Spirit (John 7:37–39). Each child of God lives in the body of Christ. When we minister in the name of Jesus and walk in his footsteps, we will see healing for individuals and the nations.

The doors for salvation open by prayer and witness. Healing of the natural bodies and spirits comes by the Power of God from prayer and the Word of testimony. Our Lord gives us healing leaves covered with the Balm of Gilead (Jer. 8:22). He wants us to take the leaves of salvation, healing, and bondage-breaking to others around us.

THE LIVING FOUNTAIN

> There is a fountain of living water.
> Holy life flows from our risen Lord.
> Come and drink from the holy stream.
> Establish your roots deep in the river.
> Grow tall and worthy before the Lord.
> Yield fruit that gives glory our Father.
> Let your living water flow on and on.
> Flow on—flow on all over the world.

[4]And they shall see his face; and his name *shall be* in their foreheads. [5]And there shall be no night there; and they need no candle, neither light of the sun; for the Lord God giveth them light: and they shall reign for ever and ever. [6]And he said unto me, These sayings *are* faithful and true: and the Lord God of the holy prophets sent his angel to show unto his servants the things which must shortly be done (Rev. 22:4–6, KJV).

UNION WITH GOD

The saints of God...*shall see his face*. These verses give us a picture of our future Heaven, but they also reveal our new union with the Creator for this Gospel Age. To see his face symbolizes a closeness of communion with our Lord (Job 42:5). Moses spoke with the Lord face-to-face (Num. 12:6–8). The term to see his face indicates that the Holy Spirit gives Christians an awareness of him. Christians in the new covenant perceive much more about God than people of the OT covenant.

Seeing the Lord's face gives us a picture of our Redeemer holding us close to him. It describes our regained union that Adam gave up in the Garden of Eden. God gives us the goal of drawing close to Jesus for the remaining part of our life on earth (Matt. 11:25–30). The Creator stamps his name on his children...*in their foreheads*. This again gives us a flashback of the Almighty sealing his people with the precious Holy Spirit (Rev. 7:3).

Saints serious about their Creator grow in their relationship with him during their lives. People who continually ask the Lord to fill them with the Holy Spirit take on many of the characters of God. Jesus gives peace and grace that's beyond the world's understanding.

Jesus prayed, for his oneness and glory, for the Church and us (John 17:20–24). He wanted his children to experience his unity and his glory. Christians immersed in the Holy Spirit can approach the oneness with Jesus Christ here on earth. The Father gives this gift to his children who seek his face. The Lord offers an intimacy that is beyond what most people can imagine or comprehend.

LIVING IN THE LIGHT

Jesus says that he is the Light of the World. If we follow him, we will never walk in spiritual darkness, but we will have the Light of Life (John 8:12). The Gospel of John says we won't have spiritual darkness because Jesus gives light. Many words that Jesus speaks in John point to spiritual principles. We should explain his writing the Revelation of Jesus Christ with the same standards. The verse says they don't need...*light of the sun; for the Lord God giveth them light*. This points to spiritual light and darkness on earth.

We reign with the Lord today and continue to reign for eternity (Rev. 20:6). Jesus guaranteed us that his...*sayings are faithful and true*. We live by faith not by sight. He gives us confidence that when we walk through the fires of life, he will quench them with his living water. Our God who cannot lie speaks to each of us in his Word. He tells us of his intense Love, his grace, and his mercy. He tells us that we matter to him, and he desires to see us face-to-face in this world and in the next. Praise his holy name.

1900 years ago, Our Lord said that the events in Revelation...*must shortly be done.* Christians that lived in the following generations, after John wrote Revelation, experienced all the events in the Book. People on earth that live today have continued to experience the events in the Revelation of Jesus Christ.

> [7]Behold, I come quickly: blessed *is* he that keepeth the sayings of the prophecy of this book. [8]And I John saw these things, and heard *them.* And when I had heard and seen, I fell down to worship before the feet of the angel which showed me these things. [9]Then saith he unto me, See *thou do it* not: for I am thy fellowservant, and of thy brethren the prophets, and of them which keep the sayings of this book: worship God. [10]And he saith unto me, Seal not the sayings of the prophecy of this book: for the time is at hand. [11]He that is unjust, let him be unjust still: and he which is filthy, let him be filthy still: and he that is righteous, let him be righteous still: and he that is holy, let him be holy still (Rev. 22:7–11, KJV).

BLESSINGS AND WORSHIP OF MEN

Our Lord will soon return at the end of the Age. The words, "I come quickly," could also symbolize Jesus coming to each of us by the Power of the Holy Spirit. Our Faithful and True God promises us blessings when we keep...*the sayings of the prophecy of this book.* Jesus ends Revelation as he began it by saying that we are blessed when we read and follow his Revelation (Rev. 1:3).

John...*fell down to worship before the feet of the angel.* Jesus again shows us a picture of John prostrating himself before an angel after his first rebuke (Rev. 19:10). Whether John did this on his own, or whether he did it because God wanted to emphasize proper worship, we don't know? The angel says...*worship God.* This makes it clear that our hope lies in God and no other man or being.

Only the Rock of Salvation, Jesus Christ, gives us new life after this one. It doesn't help to hope in our church, our church doctrine, or in any man on earth. All a church or any person can do is point us toward the Savior and his teachings. It's always easier to worship angels and the outward manifestations of God than the True God. When we worship God, he expects us to follow him and obey him.

The Coming Harvest

Interest in angels has increased in recent years. Attraction to the Bible and angels has always happened in the past before true revivals of God started. The Savior of the World has set the stage for a major harvest of people in his Kingdom. On the other side, Satan has always used angels and other events to take people's eyes away from the Savior.

Jesus says...*behold, I come quickly.* I believe that the end of the Gospel Age is drawing near. In this last great harvest of souls, the Holy Spirit shall sweep billions into the arms of Jesus. This harvest of Christian saints shall cover the entire world. The immense growth of forgiven sinners will overwhelm many of our local churches. The increase of our local churches will seem small when compared to the gathering of souls over the world.

The river of life will flow in large streams through the eastern countries of the world. The Gospel of Jesus Christ will affect every nation, even the strong Muslim countries. I believe the Lord is ready to open the floodgates of life-giving water for the worldwide harvest.

Powers of darkness will increase to draw some away from the Lamb. Spiritual manifestations of both light and darkness will increase. Everyone will need to decide whom to follow as the signs of holiness and evil multiply. Some will follow the Lamb, and some will follow the anti-Christ. There will be good times and terrible times for Christians on earth.

Spiritual Displays

During the harvest, the power of God will increase and perform many signs and wonders. God will supernaturally heal people to show his glory. The Lord will arrange exciting events around the world. Because the Holy Spirit will activate many miracles, some Christians may take their eyes off Jesus and seek supernatural thrills and ecstasy.

We should keep a balance in our faith. I enjoy seeing the Holy Spirit operate in people's lives. I love to see the Father's children healed of physical, spiritual, and mental problems. I love to see the Lord break the bondage of darkness and unbelief through our prayers. When I see the Holy Spirit give people freedom, I just want to praise God for his grace, mercy, and Love. I also understand that it's only from the power of the cross that the Spirit flows through us.

Don't Seal the Revelation

The angel told John not to seal the Words of the prophecy of Jesus Christ...*for the time is at hand.* This showed a contrast with the vision of

Daniel about the Gospel Age. The angel told Daniel to seal up the vision, for it concerned the distant future (Dan. 8:26).

Daniel's visions about the distant future happened about 500 years before the beginning of its fulfillment. The words of John, for the time is at hand, happened 1,900 years ago and pointed to an impending time. This indicated that Revelation has seen fulfillment through the Gospel Age.

> ¹²**And, behold, I come quickly; and my reward *is* with me, to give every man according as his work shall be. ¹³I am Alpha and Omega, the beginning and the end, the first and the last. ¹⁴Blessed *are* they that do his commandments, that they may have right to the tree of life, and may enter in through the gates into the city. ¹⁵For without *are* dogs, and sorcerers, and whoremongers, and murderers, and idolaters, and whosoever loveth and maketh a lie. (Rev. 22:12–15, KJV).**

LOVE, DEEDS, AND THE GOSPEL

Our Savior brings his reward with him when he comes for us. He will give to each of us…*according as his work shall be*. God will hand out rewards in Heaven for the words we speak, the good we do, and the negative we do. Our Lord forgives our sins because of his shed blood as we repent. Nevertheless, when we call ourselves Christians, we stand accountable for our active and passive actions that hurt others. Our Lord speaks of judging even our thoughts (Matt. 5:27–30).

Jesus teaches that we are the salt of the earth (Matt. 5:13). He says that if we loose our saltiness, then we seem worthless to flavor those around us. The Lord places us where we live to give his light and principles to those around us. Our salt goes stale when we stand in silence while others abuse the less fortunate. This can apply to people with mental and physical handicaps, to people with less money and influence, and to people of different ethnic backgrounds or skin colors.

LOVE OTHERS

Jesus says that we should love others as he loved us (John 13:34). When we love, we seek the highest good for another person. By giving only good to other people, we honor the Father. It takes a conscious awareness and effort by each of us to love others with the love of Christ. Our Savior desires that we would obey him so that he can spread his love and mercy through us.

Jesus taught a difficult Gospel. It seems hard at times to follow Christ, and yet God gives endless grace. He understands our wrong thoughts and actions. We stand in the light of his undeserved mercy. As a child grows in the Lord, the Lord gives him more responsibility. When God gives much, he requires much in return (Luke 12:48).

Our Father loves his children, and he yearns to give them many rewards. The rewards will come when we walk in obedience to him (Matt. 9:13). We follow the Lamb when we stand against people who take advantage of others who can't defend themselves.

THE UNENDING GOD

John writes…*I am Alpha and Omega, the beginning and the end, the first and the last.* Again, Jesus Christ makes it clear to us that he is the Almighty God, Everlasting Creator, and Savior. The Word of Life, Jesus Christ, gives us all we need to live out our lives and follow him. He sent his Spirit to live in us and lead us. By the power of his Spirit, God holds us near his heart and will not let us stray away. By faith, we know that his promises are true because he is Faithful.

Much of this wonderful vision lies beyond our wisdom and intellect. Some of us think of ourselves as smart, and yet when compared with the Word of Truth, we seem dense. I stand in awe of the Holy God. His grace and mercy appears higher than I can grasp. I don't understand all the ways he works with the people around me. Nevertheless, I believe that God only does good.

Again our Lord says…*Blessed are they that do his commandments.* He promises that we enter the Holy City and have a part in the…*tree of life.* By faith, we recognize our Creator in the Scriptures. By faith, we recognize our Savior and Redeemer. By faith, we understand that without Jesus, we don't have a chance for eternal life.

Each of us stands in the grace of the shed blood, and we seek the undeserved love and mercy from our Father. We look at the blood-stained face of Jesus and view his pierced hands and feet. We know that the Lord did more than we can comprehend because of his Love. Jesus loves me: Jesus loves you. This statement sums up why we read the Bible and why we live.

[16]"I, Jesus, have sent my angel to give you this testimony for the churches. I am the Root and the Offspring of David, and the bright Morning Star." [17]The Spirit and the bride say, "Come!" And let him who hears say, "Come!" Whoever is thirsty, let him

come; and whoever wishes, let him take the free gift of the water of life (Rev. 22:16, 17, NIV).

WORK WITH GOD

Our Lord and Savior sends his angel to give us...*this testimony for the churches*. Jesus identifies himself as the promised Messiah from the line of King David and as...*the bright Morning Star*. Our Faithful Witness sends his testimony to each of us by the Bible and the witness of the Holy Spirit.

Our Lord desires that the saints in his Church come into a common union with each other. He desires that the churches work with God and not for God. We work with the Savior when we come into unity with his purpose. We work for God when we continue doing the things of the past and of man.

The Church can only work with God by seeking Revelation from the Word of Truth. Our Lord offers his fresh manna to feed and teach us in these last days. Jesus stands ready to speak and lead each of his children with the voice of the Spirit and his Word.

Our Lord Jesus offers...*the free gift of the water of life* to people in all the churches. He holds out his nail pierced hands and speaks, "Come if you are thirsty. Come and I will give you the free water of salvation."

LIVING WATER OF LIFE

Living Water flows from Creation.
Jesus sends the Living Water of Life.
The Holy Spirit brings Living Water
Living Water surrounds the Temple.
The Spirit says come and drink.
The Bride says come and drink.
The Savior says come and drink.
I Say—let us come and drink.

FOLLOW THE LAMB

We each, as children of the Father, stand at the foot of the cross. It is only by the grace of God that we can walk after the Lamb. Our Father gives each of us a road to walk on while on this earth. If we fall off a crooked road with deep ditches, the Holy Spirit then gently leads his children back to the center of our road.

Children of the Father encounter hard times in their walk after the Lord. Some have unsolved hurts in their background, which keep them from full loyalty to Jesus. Our Father desires to clean them and sanctify them on their walk. However, he can't do this unless they stop, repent, and cling to him. Our Father then works through all the past wounds and frustrations. He then showers his child with love, peace, and mercy.

The Lord helps us each to understand that without him we have no hope. Without God, life doesn't seem worth living. With God, we have the hope of eternal life. We have his love, his peace, and his mercy. Our Creator designs each of us for his pleasure. We give him pleasure when we follow him, and he gives us pleasure in return. Jesus calls each of us to come into his Kingdom and fulfill his desires and our desires. This brings a unity between the Everlasting Father and each of us.

> **[18]I warn everyone who hears the words of the prophecy of this book: If anyone adds anything to them, God will add to him the plagues described in this book. [19]And if anyone takes words away from this book of prophecy, God will take away from him his share in the tree of life and in the holy city, which are described in this book. [20]He who testifies to these things says, "Yes, I am coming soon." Amen. Come, Lord Jesus. [21]The grace of the Lord Jesus be with God's people. Amen (Rev. 22:18–21, NIV).**

THE KING'S KID

You are a child of the King. Royal blood flows through your veins. The King blesses you because he loves you. He alone makes you worthy to call you his son or daughter. He calls you by name and desires to become one with you, to merge with you. The King yearns for you to trust him and surrender yourself to him.

As you go through life, always remember that you are a child of the King. You belong to the Royal priesthood. The King of Glory loves you with an abounding love that will never end. You are the King's delight and he loves to spend time with you. It doesn't matter what happens in your life when you know that he loves you. Always focus on the fact that you are his unique and special child whom he loves.

Our Redeemer says…*Yes, I am coming soon.* Jesus promises that he will not leave us or give us up to evil. The King of Glory remains faithful to each of us in our lives. We can trust our Creator because he cannot and will not lie to us. The Living Water of Life offers himself to us and encourages us to…*share in the tree of life.*

THANK YOU, LORD

The God of Wisdom led me to write the words of *Walking through Revelation: With a Common Man.* I wrote the explanation from a spiritual perspective as the Spirit led me.

All credit for this book has to go to Jesus Christ. I am just a child of God whom he used to write these words. "Thank you, Father, for your...*words of the prophecy* in the Book of Revelation. Thank you, Holy Spirit, for guiding my thoughts on your Revelation."

I pray for each person who reads this book. I ask you,Father, Son, and Holy Spirit, to guide their thoughts. Give to each man, woman, and child what you want them to receive from these words.

"Thank you, Lord, for your grace, your mercy, and your compassion. Thank you for your abundant Love that you so freely give. Praise and glory to your Holy name! Hallelujah! Amen!"

NOTES

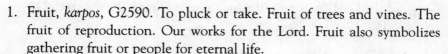

1. Fruit, *karpos*, G2590. To pluck or take. Fruit of trees and vines. The fruit of reproduction. Our works for the Lord. Fruit also symbolizes gathering fruit or people for eternal life.
2. Nations, *ethnos*, G1484 Nation, a race or tribe, non-Jewish, and Gentile.

Index

⌐

The citations in this index refer to the verse in Revelation. Simply go to that appropriate section in this book to find the subject indexed.

Bibliography

I used the books listed below to help write and gather information for Walking through Revelation. I have read other books and articles not listed in this Bibliography. I remembered the ideas but do not have the information on the unknown sources.

I use a computer program called Online Bible 6.3 for Windows to research the Bible and its words. Online Bible uses Thayer's Greek Lexicon and Brown, Driver, Briggs, Gesenius Hebrew Aramaic Lexicon. The Greek and Hebrew Lexicons give us understanding of the meaning of the original Bible words.

The Online Bible applies Strong's numbers to reference Greek and Hebrew words. The endnotes list the Greek word in italics and Strong's number as Gxxx. The endnotes list the Strong Hebrew word number as Hxxx.

Coffman, James B. *Revelation*. Abilene: A.C.U. Press, 1979.

Hendriksen, William. *More Than Conquerors*. Grand Rapids: Baker Book House, 1939, 1967.

Kretzmann, Paul E. Popular *Commentary of the Bible*. The New Testament, 4 Vols. St. Louis: Concordia Publishing House, 1923.

Lenski, R. C. H. *St. John's Revelation: The Interpretation of*. Minneapolis: Augsburg Publishing House, 1943, 1963.

McGuiggan, Jim. *The Book of Revelation*. Lubbock: Montex PC, 1976.

Strong, James. *The Comprehensive Concordance of the Bible*. Reprint.

Summers, Ray. *Worthy Is the Lamb*. Nashville: Broadman Press, 1951.

U. S. Catholic Conference, *Catechism of the Catholic Church*. Liguori: Liguori Publications, 1994.

Order Form

Postal orders:
LaVere Ray Beug, 8316 N. Lombard, Suite 319, Portland, OR 97203

Credit Card orders:
(503) 240-8723

Please send *Walking Through Revelation* to:

Name:_____

Address:_____

City:_____ State:_____

Zip:_____

Telephone: (_____) _____

Book Price: $15.00 in U.S. dollars.

Shipping: $3.00 for the first book and $1.00 for each additional book to cover shipping and handling within US, Canada, and Mexico. International orders add $6.00 for the first book and $2.00 for each additional book.